Interlochen

A Home for the Arts

Dean Boal

Foreword by Allen P. Britton

Ann Arbor

THE UNIVERSITY OF MICHIGAN PRESS

Copyright © by the University of Michigan 1998
All rights reserved
Published in the United States of America by
The University of Michigan Press
Manufactured in the United States of America
⊗ Printed on acid-free paper

2001   2000   1999   1998   4   3   2   1

A CIP catalog record for this book is available from the British Library.

Library of Congress Cataloging-in-Publication Data

Boal, Dean
      Interlochen : a home for the arts / Dean Boal ; foreword by
   Allen P. Britton.
         p.   cm.
      Includes bibliographical references (p.   ) and index.
      ISBN 0-472-10882-4 (cloth : acid-free paper)
      1. Interlochen Center for the Arts. I. Title.
   ML33.I57   I5743   1998
   780'.79'77464—dc21   98-9014
                                                            CIP

Foreword

Here is the history of Interlochen that all who love it have longed to see. The author, Dean Boal, is a distinguished American pianist, scholar, and administrator. He possesses the special insight of a past president of the institution as a whole, which was founded in 1928 by Joseph E. Maddy and T. P. Giddings as the National High School Orchestra Camp.

The original camp still exists and is now called the Interlochen Arts Camp, but it forms only part of a larger complex that includes a distinguished arts academy and a prizewinning FM radio station; it also annually presents one of the largest concert seasons in the world. The institution of today, greatly expanded and now world famous, has come to be designated officially as the Interlochen Center for the Arts. Boal's history of this fabulous institution is at once scholarly and elegant, doing full justice to one of the finest achievements of American music education, including its leading players, students, teachers, parents, and supporters, and indeed to the American people as a whole, whose love of music provided the cultural base that made everything possible.

I have often wondered about the charm that Interlochen exerts over all of us. Certainly the name itself has a magical sound. This name was the free gift of the little village located between two of Michigan's clear, sand-bottomed lakes. Certainly the personalities of Maddy and Giddings, together with those of hundreds of other conductors, teachers, and administrators, contributed their own magic to that of the natural setting.

Most of all, it has always seemed to me that the art practiced there accounts for most of the rapture we all feel when the name is mentioned. For most of us, Interlochen is the one place on earth where art, pure art, is everything. At Interlochen no one has ever had any doubts about the validity of art. There you can practice your art all day and half the night. You can draw bow, blow horn, beat drum, paint, write, dance, act, imagine. You can do what you most love to do, and you can do it in the comforting company of people who feel the same as you. It's heaven for real.

Americans are usually not thought of as being particularly modest about American accomplishments in the world. However, for reasons that historians have yet to explain, Americans are almost always quite modest with regard to our artistic accomplishments. There is really no reason to be. Our art is as great as everything else. Let us speak now, for simplicity's sake, only of music.

Consider our classical music (operas, symphony orchestras, composers, chamber music, etc.). It is superb. Consider our jazz. This indigenous art form has captured the world's admiration and respect. Consider our music education (school music, conservatories, and music schools). Consider Interlochen and similar institutions now located all over the country. All of it has come about without governmental prompting or assistance. We can well be proud of ourselves for spontaneously generating such a marvelous educational establishment.

But being proud of our music and our music education seems to be against our nature. Perhaps we should retain our humility and keep our pride to ourselves—except when we sing "Sound the Call to Dear Old Interlochen" or when we listen to the "Interlochen Theme," which Howard Hanson gave us.

Allen P. Britton

Acknowledgments

The list of those who helped me with Interlochen's story is long and includes Interlochen trustees, faculty, staff, students, and alumni. I hope this book is an accurate expression of their contributions, but where it falls short, the fault is clearly mine. Though I cannot list everyone who helped me, I owe special appreciation to the persons acknowledged here.

For my perspective on Interlochen's mission, I was assisted by former Interlochen board chairs Donald Currie and James Tolley; former presidents Karl Haas and Roger Jacobi; former interim president George Wilson; former chair of the 1966 administrative committee John Merrill; and current president Richard Odell.

For understanding of the evolution of Interlochen's academic and artistic programs, I credit Paul C. Boylan, former head of the Interlochen University Division and present vice provost for the arts and dean of the University of Michigan School of Music; Interlochen vice presidents Timothy Ambrose, Edward Downing, Thom Paulson, and David Stave; music director Byron Hanson; camp conductors Frederick Fennell and Clyde Roller; former academy directors Charles Eilber, John Hood, Bruce Galbraith, and Raymond Rideout; teachers Howard Hintze, Robert Murphy, and Jean Parsons; and former staff member Edward Banghart.

To comprehend the beginnings of the National High School Orchestra, I spoke with 1928 campers Frederick Huber and Harriet Payne before their recent deaths. Former camper Paul Hockstad gave me programs and publications dating from 1928 until 1936. Camp alumnus Kenneth Fischer, President of Ann Arbor's University Musical Society, provided documents and comments on the early relationships of Interlochen, the University of Michigan School of Music, and the University Musical Society. I thank Juilliard School president Joseph Polisi and Juilliard archivist Stephen Novak for invaluable information about John Erskine from the Juilliard School Archives. Camp alumnus Joseph Rezits provided critical material on the

1941 film *There's Magic in Music.* My conversations with trustees Helen Osterlin (deceased), Clement Stone, and Van Cliburn clarified my understanding of Joseph Maddy's actions in the 1960s.

At Interlochen, presidential assistants Geraldine Greenspan and LaVon Mattson helped to gather raw materials for the book from the Interlochen Archives. Librarian Evelyn Welliver lent critical books. Past alumni director Gayle Shaw and current alumni director Kate Murdoch provided important documents and pictures.

In Ann Arbor, the staff at the Bentley Historical Library of the University of Michigan was very supportive. The accumulation of the extensive Interlochen Center for the Arts collection is attributable to the care and diligence of Interlochen's presidents and their assistants Margaret Stace (deceased), Melba Bram, Margaret Henthorne, and Geraldine Greenspan. I am grateful to Kenneth Scheffel, Field Representative and Curator of the Interlochen Center for the Arts Collection at the Bentley Historical Library, who brought his phenomenal memory of detail and his passion for Interlochen to my work. Besides guiding me to essential information, he reviewed a final draft of the manuscript and verified my notes.

In Boulder, my general research was aided by the staff at the Norlin Library of the University of Colorado and by dean Daniel Sher of that university's College of Music. Leslie Durgin, Executive Director of the Colorado Chautauqua Association, contributed crucial information on the U.S. summer camp movement.

Special appreciation goes to Mary Erwin, Assistant Director of the University of Michigan Press, her colleagues, and the readers who provided superb underpinning and editorial guidance for production of this book.

I particularly thank Allen Britton, Dean Emeritus of the University of Michigan School of Music and an Interlochen associate for forty years. Besides writing the foreword, he contributed many Interlochen stories and reviewed drafts of the text to correct content and technical errors.

Special gratitude goes to my sons, Brett and Jed, for reading early portions of the text. But my greatest appreciation is to my wife, Ellen TeSelle Boal, who has shared this book's editing from its earliest formulation to the last proofreading.

Contents

Part 1

The Essence of Interlochen

Joseph Maddy . . . dreamed of bringing the most talented of the young musicians of the country together to study under real artists.
—Howard Hanson

The Interlochen Vision

In 1928, in a wooded section of northern Michigan, between two lakes in a vast stand of pine and oak trees, a summer program for talented high school students opened as the National High School Orchestra Camp. The trees grew to form a protective canopy over the camp, and the camp emerged as a sanctuary for the performances of young people. The camp was a success, and after many seasons, in the fall of 1962, Interlochen developed into a year-round institution by incorporating the Interlochen Arts Academy, the nation's first independent high school for the arts. To amplify its activities, Interlochen went on the air with a public radio station that same year. Interlochen is celebrated worldwide for educating young musicians, dancers, actors, visual artists, and writers.

From the outset Interlochen gloried in being the largest youth center for the arts in the United States. The inaugural class of approximately 115 musicians lived in tents and small cabins the first year. Now more than twenty-five hundred arts students attend Interlochen every year, where they live in cabins during the summer and in dormitories during the winter. Alumni, now an astonishing fifty thousand, recall fiddling in the orchestra or painting the woodland scenes of the Interlochen campus. Many of them, as professional musicians and artists, exert an influence on our culture that resonates from their days in the Interlochen woods. Some are teachers. Many others, as members of various professions, guide the artistic lives of their communities through service on symphony, museum, library, and school boards.

More than 10 percent of the musicians in the nation's major symphony orchestras performed beneath the trees at Interlochen. Among the alumni who practiced under the pines are actors Meredith Baxter, Richard Brooks, Tom Hulce, and Linda Hunt; dancers Peter Sparling and Janet Eilber; musicians William Preucil, Peter Yarrow, Jessye Norman, Peter Erskine, Gerard Schwarz, and Lorin Maazel; educators Philip Jameson, Melvin Larimer, Ann Schein, and Larry Livingston; writer Cathy Guisewite; and broadcaster Mike Wallace. Alumni David Klein and Charles McWhorter, neither one a professional artist, have long been influential in national arts advocacy, Klein through Chamber Music America and McWhorter through the National Council on the Arts and numerous other organizations.

Three venturesome men founded Interlochen and charted its direction. The daring visionary and leader was Joseph Maddy, a headstrong professor of music education at the University of Michigan and chairman of music in the Ann Arbor public schools. The guardian of the educational programs was T. P. Giddings, a dictatorial supervisor of music in the Minneapolis schools. The third man, who was to save Maddy from many financial catastrophes, was Charles Tremaine, a New York businessperson who came from a family of piano manufacturers.

The establishment of Interlochen was not their first collaboration. Prior to 1928, Maddy, Giddings, and Tremaine had labored together on significant musical and instructional projects for the Music Supervisors National Conference (MSNC), the primary organization advancing public school music in the United States. Giddings was a veteran of MSNC, having taken part in the very first meeting at Keokuk, Iowa, in 1907. Tremaine directed an organization called the National Bureau for the Advancement of Music, which published MSNC documents and distributed them to music educators. Maddy, two decades younger than the other men, had met Giddings in the summer of 1920, while studying choral conducting with him at Chautauqua, New York. The three men associated often to write new teaching books and magazine articles, with the goal of improving band and orchestra performance in America's public schools.

Following World War I, classical music was widely heard and valued in the United States. The recording and radio industries topped their bills with opera singers and symphonies. Public schools added classes in music. Performing musicians, for the first time in American history, earned a living wage for full-time work in bands and orchestras. Their good fortune occurred, largely, because of the ascendancy of a musicians' union called the American Federation of Musicians. Many professional musicians no longer needed to augment their incomes through teaching or working in jobs other than music.

Music education throbbed with idealism and high expectations. Maddy took advantage of this optimism when, in 1926, Edgar Gordon, president of MSNC, asked him to organize and conduct a student orchestra concert at the national convention in Detroit. Maddy seized this opportunity to gain supporters for the student orchestra movement in the public schools. Assisted by Giddings, Tremaine, and other music teachers, he scoured the United States for gifted students to form his orchestra. For added appeal, Gordon persuaded Ossip Gabrilowitsch, renowned director of the Detroit Symphony Orchestra, to join Maddy in conducting the concert. As anticipated, the orchestra, dubbed the National High School Orchestra (NHSO), performed brilliantly. Conventioneers and the press enthusiastically praised both Maddy and his orchestra. Maddy was so exhilarated that he promptly prepared similar programs for educators' conventions in Dallas in 1927 and in Chicago in 1928.

Maddy, excited with the triumph of his NHSO programs, considered convening a similar orchestra at a place where students could live, practice, and perform together for several continuous weeks at a time, not just for one convention performance. He shared his thinking with Giddings, who emboldened him to create such a place, a paradise for student performers. Other colleagues in MSNC also encouraged him. Thus heartened, Maddy plunged on with his plan.

Maddy remembered his own stimulating and profitable summers as Giddings's student at Chautauqua, isolated from the distractions of urban clamor. With Chautauqua in mind, the two men searched lakes and forests for the perfect location for their music camp, a search soon narrowed to the woods of either Maine or Michigan.

By chance, Willis Pennington, a Detroit businessperson, read a newspaper story about Maddy's embryonic camp. Without delay, he telephoned Maddy to proffer some of his holdings near Traverse City, Michigan, where the Pennington family's summer camp had been struggling for several years. Since Pennington was at the time wrestling with debt, he hoped to sell part of his real estate for payments toward his financial obligations. He was encouraged as Maddy and Giddings warmed to his glowing picture of northern Michigan forests. The two men drove north to the camp, where they fell in love with the terrain, a sylvan stretch of land on an isthmus between two placid lakes. This was the land they wanted for their music camp.

At first, organizing the new summer camp seemed simple. Maddy and Giddings would pattern their camp after other eminent summer camps. But Maddy soon conceded that his organizational abilities were limited. He had directed school bands, orchestras, and choral programs in Rochester, New York, and Richmond, Indiana, but creating those ensembles differed from systematizing a summer camp. He was an amateur at incorporating a nonprofit company.

So, together, Maddy and Giddings solicited their business partner, Pennington, to draw up the appropriate governing documents for the new National High School Orchestra Camp. Pennington agreed, and he drafted a contract and authored incorporation papers that the three partners signed and deposited with the state of Michigan.

Before long, Maddy grew uncomfortable with Pennington's contract. So he asked New York businessperson Charles Tremaine to review the documents. Tremaine was horrified that the contract substantially favored Pennington over both Giddings and Maddy. Sensing trouble ahead, Tremaine forced Pennington to renegotiate several terms, changes that saved the camp from financial disaster.[1] With his forceful intervention, Tremaine initiated an alliance of trust between himself and both Maddy and Giddings. Particularly in the beginning years, Maddy regularly repressed his expansive plans for the camp at Tremaine's insistence. Tremaine eventually ascended in power and, when the initial mortgage was refinanced, displaced Pennington as treasurer of the camp.

After securing the land and setting up the administration of the camp, Maddy and Giddings began admitting students for the first season. By recruiting students for the educators' conventions in 1926, 1927, and 1928, Maddy and Giddings had amassed a solid list of potential campers for the first session. In response to extensive, effective advertising, an impressive class of 115 students enrolled, and the National High School Orchestra Camp finally opened in June 1928.

Maddy and Giddings professed the highest goals for the new camp. They and their new staff members introduced what they considered to be the most successful teaching methods of the time. The camp was launched with a core faculty and staff gathered from high schools and colleges throughout the nation. Experienced educators and good musicians, they were excited about an opportunity to participate in this new venture. Faculty members received very small salaries, but they were thankful for summer employment in a period of severe economic difficulties. In a brilliant move, Maddy hired many of his teachers from the ranks of professional organizations, such as symphony orchestras, bands, theaters, art museums, and the radio networks. The idea of uniting music educators and guest artists as a team at his camp was unique on the high school level. Professional artists validated the camp program, not only for the students, but also for their parents and for the public who attended the camp's weekly concerts.

Schedules were arranged so that members of the Detroit, Minneapolis, and Cincinnati orchestras could teach the extremely gifted students for short periods, and famous music directors arrived on the campus to conduct the camp orchestra and band as guest artists. Ossip Gabrilowitsch, director of the Detroit Symphony Orchestra, Frederick Stock, director of the Chicago Symphony Orchestra, and noted band director John Philip Sousa conducted special student performances in the very first years. These stars added zest to the camp, and they were prominently featured in camp publicity. The experience was so thrilling that attending Interlochen became a compelling dream for a growing number of aspiring young musicians.

Maddy was also captivated by radio. His interest dated from 1928, when the performance of NHSO in Chicago was broadcast over the new National Broadcasting Company (NBC) network. From the first, Maddy was intrigued by radio's potential to reach the general public. Radio could advertise and promote music programs. Radio could entertain audiences with what Maddy considered good music. In 1930 the University of Michigan relieved Maddy of all his responsibilities in the School of Music so that he could teach music over radio. Convinced that radio could provide a powerful classroom for teachers, Maddy originated programs of instruction on the violin, clarinet, and other instruments over the NBC network. But his extensive work in radio convinced him that commercial radio would not support the educational aims of the schools. Over the years, he pleaded the cause for noncommercial and educational radio, paving the way for the public radio system of today.

Notwithstanding his interest in school music and radio, Maddy never wavered in his devotion to Interlochen. Government actions, lawsuits, and even a Supreme Court ruling punctuate the story of Interlochen's first forty years, but Maddy's determined faith in his vision helped him surmount many difficulties. Interlochen survived artistic stresses, financial woes, and internecine struggles among its leaders. During the 1940s, the camp outlasted the deprivations caused by World War II and its aftermath. At this time and through the 1940s and 1950s, the camp endured a twenty-year fight with the musicians' union. Because of the crisis with the union and its president, James Petrillo, no professional musicians could teach or perform at Interlochen between 1945 and 1960.

Interlochen was never officially governed by the University of Michigan, but the university saved the camp from closure during the 1940s, 1950s, and 1960s. To help the camp fill its cabins during the lean war years, the university sponsored a program for college-age students at the camp and established the All-State Program for talented Michigan high school students. The university also allotted funds to Interlochen, both in grants and in loans. In the 1940s, Maddy, emboldened by the support of the university, expanded the camp program by creating elementary and intermediate programs for campers as young as eight years old.

Giddings became less forceful in the administration of the camp after 1940, though he taught classes every summer until he died in 1954. Tremaine retired in 1958, and Maddy recruited new aides who would spur Interlochen on to imaginative ventures. In 1961, upon his retirement from the radio teaching position at the University of Michigan, Maddy devoted his full time to Interlochen.

Relieved of his winter duties, Maddy could pursue his second dream— creating a winter school at Interlochen. Over the opposition of many on his staff who preferred to live in Ann Arbor, Maddy moved the camp offices and his personal residence to Interlochen. He escalated his fund-raising efforts and procured record amounts of money from the state of Michigan, foundations, and private philanthropists, making the dream appear more possible. Even with a majority of the Interlochen trustees against his plan, Maddy persisted in his objectives to create the Interlochen Arts Academy.

The dream was secured when Maddy persuaded Clement Stone, a Chicago insurance executive, to finance the beginning years of the academy, a proposal the board approved. Maddy was elated. He hired a year-round faculty and staff to create a top-quality high school. He engaged a major architect to design new dormitories and classroom buildings. Then, appealing to the most talented campers and their parents, he recruited exceptional students for the first class, which began in 1962.

For the next four years, Maddy shaped his dream at Interlochen. He put his public radio station on the air in 1962. He expanded the camp activities, taking the student orchestra and dancers to perform for President John F. Kennedy in Washington, D.C. And the academy students excelled.

Maddy's sudden death in 1966 shocked the staff and students. Interlochen's board members and officers split into factions with differing views for the future, some backing and some opposing the academy and a proposed college for the arts. Roscoe Bonisteel, chair of the board, and Clement Stone, Interlochen's principal benefactor, reconciled the factions and provided stability through a yearlong search for a new president. At last they supported the appointment of celebrated radio broadcaster Karl Haas as Maddy's successor. Haas brought his own energy to Interlochen. Among his plans, Haas promoted Maddy's scheme to start a college for the arts. But Haas's plans were expensive, and he encountered enormous resistance from the board and the staff. Although he brought new ideas, Haas's vision for Interlochen did not prevail. After three years, he resigned abruptly. George Wilson, director of the camp, was appointed interim president while the board and staff debated Interlochen's new course.[2]

Roger Jacobi, succeeding as president in the 1970s and 1980s, calmed the conflicts within the board and the staff. Though part of the camp community still resented spending funds on the academy, Jacobi preserved and strengthened the school. The academy became an outstanding success because of its distinguished graduates. Under Jacobi, Interlochen for the first time attained long-term financial stability. Unfortunately, in the 1980s, the University of Michigan, by cutting budgets and realigning priorities, reduced its financial commitment to Interlochen and ceased over time to support the camp's college programs.

Interlochen now educates its students in much the same manner as it did in earlier years, but certain programs and procedures continue to evolve to meet current needs. Today's students mature in an environment of television and computers. They enjoy a wider variety of participation in the arts, academics, and life experiences than did students in earlier generations. Some investigate many art forms rather than one. They explore a greater assortment of subjects, perhaps pursuing environmental sciences, electronic music composition, or multimedia performances. They often engage in artistic and intellectual activities available only on college campuses a few years ago.[3]

Performance is still primary at Interlochen. During a camp season, students and guest artists present as many as eleven performances every day. Interlochen's major ensembles tour to cities throughout the country, in the tradition of the first NHSO performances in the late 1920s. An academy orchestra performed at the Kennedy Center in Washington in 1986, and the academy orchestra and chorus performed at Lincoln Center in New

York in 1992. The camp orchestra appeared at the Olympic Games in Atlanta in 1996.

Maddy's legacy in public radio continues, too. Radio station WIAA broadcasts to audiences in northern Michigan from a new, state-of-the-art broadcasting facility completed in 1995. WIAA's schedule still emphasizes concert music.

Joe Maddy envisioned a unified and grand idea. Since Interlochen's opening, many generations have shared their love of the arts and the Interlochen experience, and each generation has contributed to the institution's vision and spirit. The vision crystallizes for today's students in much the way Maddy's original vision did for his first campers. In 1928 the high school orchestra performed under conductor Ossip Gabrilowitsch of the Detroit Symphony Orchestra; in 1997 the orchestra performed under conductor Neeme Järvi of that symphony. In 1929 John Erskine, head of the Juilliard School, visited Interlochen to speak with the students; in 1993 Joseph Polisi, head of the Juilliard School, visited Interlochen to do the same. In 1928 NBC broadcast NHSO; in 1997 WIAA broadcast the World Youth Symphony Orchestra.

Interlochen is now one of the magical names among arts organizations. It achieved this high status, in part, because it survived and flourished during times when other camps and arts schools failed. The Interlochen story is a colorful unfolding of that vision, tenaciously held for most of this century.

The Interlochen Spirit

The spirit of Interlochen is that ephemeral, but definable, thing that first brings students to the camp and academy, brings them back, and brings back scores of staff, teachers, alumni, and concertgoers each year. Characterizing that spirit are early names of the lakes bordering Interlochen: Wahbekaness (Water Lingers) and Wahbekanetta (Water Lingers Again). The spirit is so infectious that the students, like the waters of these lakes, linger and come to linger again.

In many respects, the lives of campers or academy students are similar to those at other camps or boarding schools. Most Interlochen students are living away from their homes for the first time. When they arrive, students encounter limited access to telephones and few opportunities to watch television, and they can go to shopping malls just once a week. Academy students work on computers and correspond by electronic mail, but their associations with the world beyond Interlochen are restricted.

Nevertheless, the students feel stimulated, not deprived. The most common expression heard from camp alumni is, "That was the most wonderful summer of my life." An academy parent commented, "This is my daughter's home now." The isolation the students find here breaks restrictive ties to home, habits, and lifestyles, enabling Interlochen to establish a wholesome environment for growth. The Interlochen spirit links the entire community with feelings of sharing, caring, fairness, dedication, commitment to excellence, and competition. The faculty and students work and rehearse together as a family. In the artistic shelter of Interlochen, students and their new colleagues share their earnest passions for making music, dancing, or writing poems. Many activities have been initiated by students. The students find their place—a place that is nurturing but exacting, a place where talents other than athletic ability are prized, a place where talented students feel understood. Acclaimed and inspiring visitors from all over the world stimulate them in seminars, master classes, and rehearsals.

Interlochen's remote setting instills a sense of calm and detachment from unwanted distractions. Though they live in the close quarters of dormitories or cabins, students soon find secluded spots in the woods where they can be alone to paint a sunset or practice the violin at the edge of a lake. When stress from demanding class work overtakes them, they resort to the clear air and the open spaces of the campus to revitalize themselves.

Since most Interlochen students were high achievers artistically and academically at their home schools, they usually enjoy working with dedication and energy. They relish the opportunities at Interlochen to play in orchestras that perform extensive and demanding repertoires, to rehearse difficult theatrical productions, or to spend all afternoon in dance class. For the most part, they welcome the strong work ethic at Interlochen: Joseph Maddy always claimed that high school students did not tire easily, thus they should be occupied in work of some sort at all times. He and Giddings favored instructing the students with such aphorisms as "Learn more in less time."

However, students do suffer stress and find little time for activities other than those scheduled by the faculty and staff. Though their schedules approximate collegiate schedules, the students nevertheless are still quite young. So the counselors supervise their charges carefully, both socially and academically, and encourage sufficient sleep and recreation. Campers have dubbed a scheduled afternoon time for games and sports "forced fun," because they must take time from their studies to relax.

"Performance is the measure of success," said Maddy. Both Giddings and Maddy believed the students would master their studies more effectively through competition. From his earliest days in Minneapolis, Giddings initiated musical contests in the schools, and he lauded the benefits of competitive events through his writings in books and professional journals. The young Maddy, before he knew Giddings, had formed a similar view when the Minneapolis Symphony Orchestra denied him advancement because of a seniority system.[4] His anger with that arrangement compelled him to fight for merit systems when he became a teacher. He found in Giddings a person equally committed to music competition. Together, over the next three decades, they judged many music festivals and wrote several influential music instruction books advocating competition in the classroom.

With Giddings's encouragement, Maddy installed a system of promotion by contest for the first performers in NHSO. A camper who thought he or she played better than another would challenge the colleague. With Maddy supervising, the two students, in turn, played the same passage of music for other orchestra members, who voted for a winner. The victor earned the right to perform in the challenged position for the following concert, and the loser performed in the lesser position. This challenging process for determining orchestral chairs is now a tradition at Interlochen.

Competition rewards hard work. Despite some educators' negative opinions about contests, competition at Interlochen contributes effectively to the educational process. The constant competitiveness strengthens most of the students and helps them adapt to Interlochen's artistic and academic pressure.

Winning performances, of course, evoke positive responses. Celebrated in triumph, winners gain confidence to perform still better in the future. However, losers face a difficult experience, and the rivalry can be devastating to them.

Fortunately, at Interlochen the losers are not left alone to deal with their disappointments. In recent years, a strong support system was established to make competition a productive experience, even for those who fail to win. Faculty and staff console the losers and encourage them to challenge for their former positions at a later time. Often a camper forfeits a position one day but, with hard work, regains the position on another day. Many talented students lose to equally talented students for the first time in their lives, but they learn that losing is not the end of their ambitions, that they will probably win and lose competitions many times, and that learning to lose gracefully will serve them well in the future. The students preserve this caring environment as much as the faculty and staff: The loudest cheers for a winner come from his or her peers, as do the most sympathetic hugs for the loser.

Challenging continues in the camp once a week on Bloody Friday and in the academy as well, where conductors and faculty determine the chair holders. Teachers now guide the decision-making process more carefully to avoid any appearance of improper judging. Other rules have been modified through the years, but the concept remains. The competition and challenges are positive forces in the excellence found here. Today's students expect challenges in all endeavors of their lives, and they assume that the competition at Interlochen will prepare them to compete for future jobs, in whatever field.

Competitive conditions demand impartial treatment. Interlochen has historically maintained ideals of equality, embracing coeducational classes from the beginning and accepting students of all religions. A meaningful symbol of this equality is the camp uniform. Instructors, conductors, administrators, and students dress alike at the camp, wearing traditional blue shirts with navy blue corduroy pants for men and boys, knickers for women and girls (shorts have been allowed for certain occasions since the late 1980s). The academy students take part in setting their dress codes. All academy students, whether on scholarship or not, engage in a required number of hours of community service, including helping in the cafeteria.[5]

A major tradition is the playing of the "Interlochen Theme," some thirty seconds of music from Howard Hanson's *Romantic* Symphony. This theme has been performed at the end of each camp concert for years, forging a lasting bond among the campers. When a recording of the symphony is played over the air, radio announcers from all over the United States report receiving telephone calls from nostalgic Interlochen alumni who want to thank the station for reawakening their memories of the camp. The icons remain the same—the uniforms for leveling the playing field, the theme to remind students of their obligation to perform, the lakes and woods to give them space to ponder.[6]

Most Interlochen students become exceedingly loyal alumni, maintaining their childhood friendships for years. Interlochen is sometimes lovingly called a Brigadoon, because the camp cabins and outdoor performance venues come alive with all their traditions intact each summer, after slumbering during the winter months.[7] Distinguished alumni often return to share stories of their careers with the campers and academy students, and scores of alumni return again and again to the place where the waters linger.

Part 2

Les Preludes: The National Music Camp

You made the Camp, as I have repeatedly said, even though I think I saved it.

—Charles Tremaine

T. P. Giddings

Though it was the first music camp of its kind, Interlochen sprouted from the soil laid down by musical organizations early in U.S. history. Some of the first tune and instruction books in the United States were intended for teaching congregations to sing properly in worship services. Then, in the late eighteenth century, the prominent American composer Francis Hopkinson, a signer of the Declaration of Independence, taught music reading in a singing school. At first, singing schools were organized in either churches or private homes, for family members of all ages. But after the Revolutionary War, many of these singing schools evolved into advanced singing societies among adults. The singing schools were often supported by the wealthy families of Boston and Philadelphia.

But by the time of Andrew Jackson's presidency, the mood of the country had become more egalitarian. Jackson had won the presidency in 1828 over Boston's John Quincy Adams by stressing the needs of the common people rather than those of the wealthy. Learning to read music, no longer an activity restricted to wealthy families, became a goal for the common person. Ironically, the first teaching of music in the schools burst forth in Adams's Boston within the next decade.

The Boston Academy of Music, a private school, opened on January 8, 1833, and was the first school in the United States dedicated solely to music. The director of this academy was Lowell Mason, a prominent and highly regarded composer of hymns and choral music. Mason was drawn to the teaching methods of Johann Heinrich Pestalozzi (1746–1827), who held a conviction that anyone, not just the gifted, could learn most skills. The

Reverend William Woodbridge, a friend of Mason, had introduced the Pestalozzian teaching methods to Boston after observing Pestalozzi on a European visit. Woodbridge and Mason adapted these methods to teach singing and reading music. Mason was immediately successful, as evidenced·by the enrollment of five hundred students in the first season of his academy.

Skillfully, Mason allied himself with those who advocated strong public education in Boston. After Sam Eliot, president of Mason's academy, was elected mayor of Boston, Eliot used his political power to persuade the administrators in the public schools to add music classes based on Mason's principles. To show his abilities, Mason taught in the Hawes Public School without salary during the 1837–38 school year. His work was so impressive that he was appointed the first superintendent of public school music in Boston on August 28, 1838, which made him the first head of music in any public school in the United States.

Mason gradually gathered followers. In 1834 he urged a small group of prospective teachers to join him in a two-week musical convention. He proselytized heavily, his disciples multiplied, and by 1838 his musical convention for teacher training enrolled ninety-six men and forty-two women.

Mason's methods did arouse opponents. Many musicians and educators of his day believed that he degraded and cheapened great music by teaching it to the masses. He fought back, stating that his methods significantly raised the standards for singing the popular choral works of the time. Critics praised the performances of Mason's students, and his distinguished reputation as a composer allayed most fears that his methods lowered standards.[1]

Mason's reputation grew, and his publications, compositions, and teaching methods became widely emulated. Followers of Mason sustained the teaching of music in schools across the country. One young teacher, Luther Whiting Mason (not related to Lowell), began teaching music in 1857 and later moved to Boston to lead the generation that succeeded Lowell Mason.

Although most classes inspired by Lowell Mason stressed singing, some educators taught instrumental music classes prior to the Civil War. Inspired by the influx of new immigrant musicians from Europe and propelled by the patriotism of the war, wind bands became popular with the public. When peace came, conductor Patrick Gilmore of New York organized peace jubilees that highlighted bands for the first time. The band movement accelerated into the twentieth century, culminating with the professional bands of John Philip Sousa and Edwin Franko Goldman, conductors who were crucial to Interlochen's beginnings. However, though popular for fifty years, bands were not notable in the public school curriculum until after World War I.

Following the Civil War, a continuous wave of anti-elite sentiment rippled across the United States. Civil War general Ulysses S. Grant successfully ascended to the presidency by portraying Horace Greeley, his opponent of 1872, as an eccentric intellectual of high birth. A sign of the times, school officials undertook efforts to make European music available to the poorer people through the public schools. In 1869 Boston had introduced music singing classes into the high school curriculum, which completed the teaching of music from elementary through high school. In 1870 Luther Whiting Mason, in charge of the Boston programs, wrote the first nationally known, complete course for music, called *The National Music Course,* which included seven books and a special set of charts to aid music reading. Through the wide use of this course, Luther Whiting Mason became known as the founder of school music methodology.[2]

By 1900 public school music, taught in the tradition of Lowell Mason, had spread to many towns and cities throughout the United States, with exceptions in the poorer sections of the South. In the elementary schools, students learned to sing melodies and chant rhythms. In high school, students explored music along with new vocational, recreational, and athletic subjects that reflected the demand for practical subject matter. With the arrival of recorded music, classes stressing music appreciation and theory appeared in the high schools just before World War I.

T. P. Giddings was more than fifty years old in 1920, when Joseph Maddy first met and began studying with him at Chautauqua. Maddy was not yet thirty, but Giddings had already established himself as a distinguished public school music teacher who was a follower of Luther Whiting Mason.

Thaddeus P. Giddings was born on February 19, 1868, in Anoka, Minnesota. He studied music for two years at the University of Minnesota, then transferred to Western Normal Music School at Lake Geneva, Wisconsin, in 1890. He finished his collegiate studies at Highland Park, Illinois, where he received a diploma in 1892. For a short time following graduation, he taught music at his home in Anoka, but soon he accepted a position as a music teacher in the public schools of Moline, Illinois.

From the beginning of his career, Giddings was ambitious for his students. In 1893 he enlisted the complete student body of his high school, a chorus of 150, to present *The Creation* by Franz Joseph Haydn. Giddings himself sang the tenor solo, but he and the organist were the only adults in the production. High school students performed all the other parts.

After his successful tenure in Moline, he moved to his second teaching position in music in the public schools of Oak Park, Illinois. In 1910 he became supervisor of music in the Minneapolis schools, where he remained until his retirement thirty years later. Giddings was revered by his students and his colleagues. On his seventieth birthday, shortly before his retirement, a committee of Minnesotans raised money to construct an Interlochen building dedicated in his honor.[3]

In 1907, while teaching at Oak Park, Giddings attended a conference in Keokuk, Iowa, that led to the formation of the Music Supervisors National Conference (MSNC) three years later. At its first meeting, Giddings quickly recognized the strength that this group could bring to public school music. He urged them to hold similar gatherings yearly. To spread his ideas, Giddings wrote articles on his teaching systems for their newsletters. The conference leadership rewarded Giddings with an appointment to MSNC's executive committee. Through MSNC, Giddings became a pivotal spokesman for higher teaching standards. He believed that music was essential to general education and that it should take a favored place "at the head of a list of educational subjects in the curriculum."[4]

In his own teaching, Giddings insisted that the students sing and sight-read great quantities of music. He mimicked the methods of Luther Whiting Mason, whose students first sang by rote, next carefully copied a teacher who conducted them as in a chorus, then, after singing by imitation, sang do-re-mi syllables and eventually learned to read music.

In the period after the Civil War, a dispute had erupted between classroom teachers and music specialists in the schools. Classroom teachers usually taught music theory and music history classes rather than singing classes, because they preferred not to sing themselves. These classroom teachers and the school administrators dictated the content of music classes and thus did not favor singing classes under music specialists. Understandably, this situation troubled music teachers, because its result was that students often learned about music but did not learn to sing or read music.

In the 1890s, the situation began to change, as advocates of singing for its own sake gained supporters. The public was beginning to demand more practical subject matter in the school curriculum, and schools regarded the singing of music as more practical than reading about music history or theory. Several city systems installed music specialists as teachers of singing classes, and teachers in these school systems graded the students on their abilities to read music and entered the grades on high school transcripts.

Giddings approved of these practices. His motto was, "Hands off—let the children do their own learning." Giddings believed a pupil gained more musicality through playing ten pieces once than through playing one piece ten times, so he encouraged reading a great amount of music as opposed to polishing the performance of a few selections. He felt that fluent sight-reading provided the students a necessary framework for improved musical knowledge, and he asserted that sight-reading was the "password through the magic door of musical understanding."[5]

Giddings inspired his students to sing and read musical scores from a wide assortment of sources. All Minneapolis students in elementary grades sang through twenty-one books of music, most written by Giddings. Often his instructors chose music from eight more books, and many teachers taught their students to sing every song in every one of Giddings's books. In the high school grades, classes sang from twenty-six additional sets of more difficult music texts. By studying quantities of music, pupils learned not only to read and understand music but also to perform and enjoy it. Using Giddings's methods, the Minneapolis schools attained a remarkably good reputation.[6]

Giddings championed class teaching over private instruction. He himself was a product of class teaching and had always taught singing in classes from his earliest days in Anoka. He believed that the success of general education had been in class teaching, a condition he thought more efficient and economical than private instruction. For him, classes developed spirit and drive that drummed up student rivalry. Giddings was convinced that this competition among students prodded them toward greater accomplishments.

Before World War I, in the public schools, singing was taught through classes, but instrumental music was largely taught through private lessons. Giddings did not approve. He championed the instruction of musical instruments through classes and pressed to add student bands and orchestras to the curriculum. By 1919 many public schools began to organize instrumental classes. Giddings had been probing the introduction of such classes in Minneapolis, and these experiments convinced him that teachers would grasp the true efficiency of class teaching, that public school systems would draft workable class plans, and that colleges would begin to equip teachers for class instruction on instruments. He predicted that private teaching would become the exception rather than the rule.

Giddings concluded that class teaching was applicable to all branches of music. He insisted that piano should be taught in classes, and he pioneered in this field by introducing class piano into the Minneapolis schools before World War I. His opinion was that anyone who wished to understand music thoroughly should play the piano, which he considered the most important musical instrument. He wrote a text on teaching class piano, a method that included the reformation and stabilization of musical terminology.[7] But despite Giddings's experiments, school systems did not widely incorporate class piano.

Thus, by the time he met Joseph Maddy, Giddings had established himself as a foremost music educator and was an authority on class teaching. Many methods for which Interlochen became famous were Giddings's contributions. Competition in the classroom was Giddings's mode. Performance of a broad array of musical literature was at Giddings's urging. Maddy later concurred in these methods, but Giddings had formed the procedures in Minneapolis before the two men came together at Chautauqua in 1920.

As cofounder with Maddy, Giddings brought unique attributes to Interlochen. Giddings was the disciplinarian. His humor was dry and penetrating. He demanded excellence, and he could be very stern with students. Once, when a camper broke a twig from a tree, Giddings became angered at the student's insensitivity to the environment. He suggested that the student replace the twig by taping it to the branch; embarrassed, the student complied. Most students respected Giddings's serious demeanor in similar situations, and most developed a love for him. In retirement, he became revered as the "grand old man" of Interlochen.[8]

Joseph Maddy

Joseph E. Maddy was one of the most influential music educators of the twentieth century. He was a trailblazer who set up a unique music camp and a Pied Piper who inspired children to love music and other arts. His followers revered him as an inspirational leader and an innovative thinker.

Because he rose to prominence from very modest beginnings, he mirrored the Horatio Alger image of the self-made American man of the nineteenth century.[9]

Beyond orchestrating the music education of the country on a national level, Maddy sang his convictions to a wide public not ordinarily interested in young people or the arts. He was a skilled self-promoter. His colleagues heartily approved of his boldness and celebrated his audacity. When Maddy represented himself as an underdog fighting the construction of a U.S. Air Force base near Interlochen, most of the public applauded his boldness. National newspapers and magazines commended him for his unflinching stand in battles with the musicians' union. His tenacity and remarkable accomplishments sparked admiration among the populace, and boosters rushed to support him.

Though he is honored as a self-made man from a small town, Maddy's personal history reveals that his later accomplishments were the fruits of years of hard work. Joseph Maddy was born in Wellington, Kansas, on October 14, 1891. His mother was a county school superintendent who inspired her family to cherish music, visual arts, and poetry. His father, an amateur musician, was first a teacher, then a banker.

Joe mastered several instruments, concentrating on the violin, viola, and clarinet. Joe's brother, Harry, a year and a half older, was a talented violinist who eventually spent most of his life in the Minneapolis Symphony Orchestra (now the Minnesota Orchestra). Because of their versatility, both Joe and Harry were sought out to anchor Wellington's many musical productions, and they played together in the Wellington Boys Band. With their parents, the brothers formed a family quartet, often enlarged with other musicians from Wellington. Flutist Fay Pettit, later to become Joe's second wife, was among the added musicians.

When the boys reached high school, they craved new and challenging musical activities. Each young man dropped out of high school in his freshman year. After Harry enrolled at the Wichita College of Music in Wichita, Kansas, Joe attended Bethany College in Lindsborg, Kansas, for one year, then transferred to Wichita to join Harry.

In 1909 the restless Harry grasped at a chance to join the violin section of the Minneapolis Symphony Orchestra, an ensemble only five years old. A few months later, Joe followed his brother. At eighteen, Joe became the youngest member of the Minneapolis orchestra, where he played viola and clarinet for the next five years.

Joe was not happy in the Minneapolis orchestra, however. Management confined him to the last chair of the viola section, behind players he considered inferior. He languished, unable to advance because of a seniority system. The situation became intolerable, so in 1914 he moved across town to become the assistant concertmaster of a newly organized orchestra in St. Paul, Minnesota. But the move was unfortunate, since this new orchestra soon disbanded for financial reasons, leaving Joe without work. Maddy labored in several lesser positions over the next year. First, he played clarinet in a vaudeville orchestra in Peoria, Illinois. Next, he moved back to Wellington to conduct an orchestra. Then, in 1915, he moved to Wichita Falls, Texas, where he became director of a local college of music.

Over the next two years, Maddy formed his first ideas about managing music groups. He organized a volunteer orchestra for high school students, where he dealt with his students quite differently from the way he had been treated in the Minneapolis orchestra. From the start, Maddy rejected seniority as the measure for advancement. Instead, he conferred advancement on students in the orchestra as a reward for improved sight-reading and growing musicianship.

In 1917 Joe moved to Chicago, where he altered his life from teacher to performer. For over a year, he played clarinet with a jazz group called Winds. In addition, he performed as a freelance musician with symphonies, theater orchestras, jazz bands, and opera companies. He tutored only a few students at the Metropolitan School of Music, mostly for added income.[10]

In the next year, a challenging job offer finally persuaded Maddy that his career ought to be in education. Kodak founder George Eastman financed a new music supervisor's position in the school system of Rochester, New York, and Maddy was offered the position. Though Joe lacked a high school diploma, he persuaded the president of the University of Rochester to grant him a diploma through an examination. Thus certified, Maddy accepted the position and plunged into his new work.

However, not completely satisfied with Maddy's accomplishments, Eastman engaged Pittsburgh's music supervisor, Will Earhart, as a consultant to recommend musical and educational upgrades for Rochester. Earhart, a product of Midwestern music programs, had been a pioneer in public school string programs. In 1898, about twenty years after B. W. Merrill, a high school student from Aurora, Illinois, had organized the first American public school orchestra, Earhart created an acclaimed high school orchestra program in Richmond, Indiana.[11] Eastman accepted many of Earhart's suggestions, including the establishment of the Eastman School of Music at the University of Rochester.

During his visit to Rochester, Earhart befriended Maddy and recommended that he move from Rochester to take Earhart's former Richmond position. Protesting that the Richmond position required both instrumental and choral skills, Maddy said that he was not prepared to teach choirs, but Earhart proposed that Maddy take a summer course on choral teaching at Chautauqua, New York, under the noted T. P. Giddings of Minneapolis. Maddy accepted the position, studied under Giddings, then moved to Richmond and elevated the high school orchestra into still greater national prominence by winning national competitions.[12] Until his death in 1960, Earhart remained a valued supporter of Maddy's Interlochen and came to exert great influence on the camp's music programs, though he never visited the camp. In his later years, Maddy would call Earhart the grandfather of his National Music Camp.[13]

Maddy and Giddings experienced the Chautauqua environment firsthand in 1920. They returned to Chautauqua for a second year in 1921, when Maddy joined Giddings as a visiting instructor as well as a student. Although they taught elsewhere in the following summers, they found that Chautauqua provided the seminal experience for their later collaboration at Interlochen. From that time forward until Giddings's death, the two men worked together every summer.

At Chautauqua, Maddy and Giddings began drafting new books on methods of teaching in music education. Their methods came to the attention of administrators in several prominent university music schools, and as a result of these contacts, they were hired to teach summer courses in music education at the University of Southern California in 1922, 1923, and 1924. Then, during the summers of 1926 and 1927, both men taught in New York City at the Teachers College of Columbia University.[14]

During the Chautauqua summers of 1920 and 1921, Giddings taught Maddy how to organize and discipline large ensembles. Maddy found that he could apply Giddings's choral principles to high school orchestras. Discovering a common bond, the two men jointly wrote a pioneering series of textbooks on teaching musical instruments to groups. Though Giddings had previously written books on teaching groups (primarily for piano and voice study), his publishers were not interested in the new series. Then, in 1922, Maddy persuaded Carl Greenleaf, head of the C. G. Conn instrument

manufacturing company, to publish their series. Called *Universal Teacher,*
this series soon became an authoritative text for teaching orchestra and
band instruments to groups.[15] The series remained in use throughout most
of Maddy's lifetime, but it fell out of favor with teachers following World
War II.

In 1920 Maddy, now twenty-eight and emerging as an important leader,
accepted the Richmond position and also secured an instructorship at Earl-
ham College. But while his career seemed on a fast track, his national ambitions in music education were blocked because he lacked a universally
accepted high school diploma, and he could advance no further. So he
reluctantly studied academic subjects for four months, took qualifying
examinations, and finally secured a high school diploma. Maddy was forever sensitive to his lack of academic credentials. In later years, he proudly
accepted honorary doctorates, which unlocked doors previously closed to
him.

Maddy joined MSNC, where he turned to activities that propelled his
career. In 1922 the leaders of MSNC invited his Richmond High School
Orchestra to play the featured program at their meeting in Nashville. To
prepare the orchestra, Maddy initiated competition among his students to
decide who would perform at the coveted concert. To gain their
confidences, he allowed the students to vote for the best musicians to go on
the trip. The competitiveness worked. The Nashville venture was a great
success and catapulted Maddy into the national limelight among music
educators.[16]

Maddy's reputation spread in music circles, where his work caught the
attention of Earl Moore, the new head of music at the University of Michigan. Moore offered him a university position that began in 1924. Then
thirty-two, Joe Maddy accepted two positions in Ann Arbor: one as supervisor of music in the public schools and another as head of music education
at the university's School of Music. He promptly threw himself into these
new opportunities, and in the first three years of his work, Maddy organized a high school band and other instrumental ensembles. Though
Maddy's assignments changed many times at the university, and though he
taught no classes for the School of Music after 1930, he began an association with Moore that lasted thirty-five years, until Moore retired in 1959.
Maddy himself continued at the University of Michigan for two additional
years, retiring in 1961, just before his seventieth birthday.[17]

With his arrival in Ann Arbor, Maddy mounted the primary platform of his career. To promote his educational ideas, he spoke before and joined the influential music organizations in the country. He addressed civic clubs, teachers' organizations, and the National Federation of Music Clubs, and in 1925 he joined the Music Teachers National Association.

Throughout the years, Maddy's passion was conducting a symphony orchestra, where he performed his favored nineteenth-century romantic overtures. Following Giddings's example, he formed an educational theory differing from that of most leading music supervisors of his day. While others concentrated on drilling for perfection, Maddy did not. Though he demanded technical competence, he spent little time on interpretative shadings, for he was far more concerned with the mechanics of performance. In this way, he acquainted the students with as much worthwhile musical literature as they could absorb and perform.[18]

After the camp at Interlochen opened, Maddy chose the musical selections for most programs there. He often included performances of contemporary music, particularly that composed by Americans. In the 1950s, he championed new electronic music for the camp educational programs, to the dismay of many musicians reluctant to accept such experimental music at the camp.

Maddy was less experienced in choosing plays and dance productions than in selecting music. In the late 1950s, dance teacher Joe Gifford and his assistant produced a modern dance program at the camp. One selection included high school girls rolling on the stage, by which Maddy's wife, Fay, was greatly upset. She found the dance offensive and sexually explicit, and Maddy himself was troubled. Mrs. Maddy insisted that her husband call an emergency meeting to review the production and prevent a recurrence of a similar dance. The meeting was heated, and Mrs. Maddy did not change her opinion, despite pleas from the dance teachers. Roger Jacobi, then director of personnel, argued that, just as the camp always performed controversial but significant contemporary music, the camp should also promote significant contemporary dance. Maddy listened, agreed with Jacobi, and decided that the camp should not halt similar productions, even if controversial.[19]

One of Maddy's loves was inventing new methods to hurry or ease the learning processes. In an effort of 1925, he designed aluminum violins that the Conn instrument manufacturing company later built for his high

school classes. Unfortunately, the sound of the instruments was unpleas-
antly metallic, so teaching with these violins foundered. Still, the venture
typified Maddy's continual pursuits to improve instruction.

While many of his ideas were unworkable and readily discarded, his
daily insights could be stunning and effective. Maddy concocted new ways
to attract youngsters to his camp orchestras, particularly in weak sections,
such as the section of violas. Since Maddy was partial to the viola, he
insisted that violin students study the viola as well. In this way, he gained
converts to the viola and also persuaded violinists to accept the importance
of the instrument.[20] In the very first camp season, one young camper acci-
dentally broke the neck of his violin. After consoling the boy, but also without hesitation, Maddy suggested that maybe he should now "switch to the
viola." Rather than sulking, the boy took Maddy's advice and became a violist for the rest of his life.[21]

Maddy repeatedly showed a practical side. In the camp's second year, he
realized that he needed counselors and managers for the camp but could
not pay competitive salaries. His solution was to create a college division at
the camp, where the collegians could both secure academic credit and work
for the camp during their free hours.[22] Had he not conceived this idea,
Maddy would have needed to turn to the job market for help.

Maddy perfected his organizational skills in his school programs and at
MSNC conventions, education meetings, and appearances at world's fairs.
For all these events, he shouldered heavy responsibilities. He planned and
carried out the logistics, financing, promotion, and content. But because of
his personal involvement in each aspect of a project, he developed peculiar
spending habits. Maddy seemed always to be responding to emergencies or
creating crucial opportunities or needs. When he budgeted money for a
project, he depleted the account, then he focused on a new project and the
need to raise money for it. His friends report that his personal money
habits were the same; he rarely carried money for everyday needs and often
borrowed emergency funds from his colleagues.[23]

Maddy's views sometimes seemed haphazard. Impulsively, he experi-
mented and contrived many new notions every day. When his scheme to
popularize roller-skating ballet fizzled in the late 1950s, Maddy quickly
abandoned the effort. Faced with similar setbacks, he was usually resilient
and flexible. When projects did not work despite his best thought and
efforts, Maddy did not complain. He quietly dropped the matter and
passed on to other activities.[24]

Since he was not a musical perfectionist, critics often attacked his performances. Some detractors thought he was an unsuccessful conductor, perhaps short on musicianship. Among them was Earl Moore, his boss at the University of Michigan, who observed that Maddy's performances were often sloppy.[25]

Joe's conduct was generally positive and friendly. He maintained good terms with everyone, donors and custodians alike. He hunted and fished with both maintenance staff and board members. Nonetheless, when times were tough, he persisted. If he thought he was in the right, he persevered. He was self-assured and proud of his independent nature. When he believed he held the correct position, he was sometimes in conflict with others who thought he was dead wrong. Because of his strong beliefs, Maddy acquired many critics, and at times of controversy, he was not always easy to get along with.[26]

Most of the time, Maddy was approachable, even on very controversial issues. He frequently changed his mind when he saw fit or when someone convinced him to change course. While often characterized as a benevolent dictator, Maddy exhibited little hostility toward his staff, faculty, or campers. He toiled next to them and devised slogans for their guidance, firmly empowering them to act on his vision. He promoted debate among them, and he honored their suggestions. But Maddy decided the most important issues. He maintained tight control of the camp, normally surrounding himself with very conservative people who loyally fulfilled their tasks. Busy day and night, the faculty and staff achieved a mutual respect and love that fostered solid discipline. Maddy could arouse such loyalty and familial feelings that the staff sometimes accused departing workers of betrayal to the Interlochen vision.[27]

Maddy called out to and succeeded in co-opting the powerful leaders of his day. He organized coalitions of teachers, students, audiences, board members, legislators, and business leaders. Responding to Maddy's sense of urgency, these groups led his efforts for Interlochen. With them, Maddy created the essential vision for his National Music Camp. Unabashedly, he pleaded with professors, celebrities, and presidents of the United States to join his cause. He coaxed John Philip Sousa, Ossip Gabrilowitsch, Frederick Stock, Van Cliburn, and Eugene Ormandy into the Interlochen circle. More importantly, he wheedled each one into thinking each was personally responsible for Interlochen's continuance. Maddy's charm became legendary. Always upbeat, he built teams that told the Interlochen story among the most influential people of the time.

Maddy dedicated himself to Interlochen's progress, and everything else in his life was completely subordinated. When thwarted, he could rail at the trustees and revoke their policies if, in his opinion, their actions seemed detrimental to Interlochen. He was single-minded in focusing on his main concerns, such as the camp orchestra, and in creating secondary projects to support the main one. He formed the camp band primarily to attract players of wind instruments for his orchestra. As mentioned earlier, to attract camp counselors, he started a division for collegians who could also work for him. To secure a larger financial pool for music scholarships, Maddy transferred tuition funds paid by theater, art, and dance campers, whose programs received less financial support as a result.[28]

Though Joe Maddy became a legend in music education and broadcasting, his schooling in Kansas was modest and would not have foretold his fame. Both he and T. P. Giddings were essentially self-taught. While Interlochen eventually became a model for other music camps, its beginnings were difficult and could have been unfavorable. Most observers agree that Maddy's personality shaped Interlochen's success. Interlochen's appeal arose from his ability to pipe artists, teachers, and students into his dream. He tapped them through many groups, including business, philanthropic, and, most particularly, artistic organizations. Maddy worked the professional music societies because, historically, these associations promoted excellence in music education. He identified with that excellence and hoped that conferees would recognize the performances of his high school orchestras as the highlights of the conventions. He competed to be the best music educator.

Popular culture loves an individual who has climbed in society through personal merit and hard work. The average person esteems a figure who exhibits personal tenacity, as played in the movies or the political arena. Maddy was just such a pioneering figure in American history.[29]

The National High School Orchestra

Joe Maddy's lifelong love was the symphony orchestra, a love that grew out of his experiences as a young man in the Minneapolis Symphony Orchestra. He was fortunate to obtain a position in that orchestra in 1909, as it was then one of the very few professional orchestras in the country. (New York claimed two symphony orchestras, and Boston, Chicago, Philadelphia, and St. Louis each nurtured one.)

Joe relished playing magnificent music with the Minneapolis musicians. They were older and more experienced than he, but most were also foreign-born and foreign-trained. After a while, he began to resent the foreign domination of American orchestras and resolved to work for the improvement of music education in the United States.

The quality of teaching music in the United States had first become a concern for musicians during the last quarter of the nineteenth century. On December 27, 1876, Theodore Presser, later a music publisher in Philadelphia, called music teachers to a national meeting in Delaware, Ohio. The purpose of the convention was to gain "mutual improvement by interchange of ideas, to broaden the culture of music, and to cultivate fraternal feeling."[30] Eben Tourjee, founder of the New England Conservatory of Music, chaired the symposium, and prominent musicians and educators participated. Enthusiasm ran high, so the participants decided to create an ongoing affiliation. They called the new group the Music Teachers National Association (MTNA), the first national organization of music teachers in the United States. Those attending the meeting, in turn, formed state chapters of MTNA. Spreading widely and becoming influential, MTNA has continued as a primary organization of music teachers in the United States.

Also in the last quarter of the century, music magazines materialized to sound the cry for higher standards among teachers. In 1880 *Musical Courier* published its premiere issue of instructive articles. *Etude Music Magazine,* first printed in 1883, swiftly joined the chorus for substantial new requirements in music education.

The following year, the National Education Association (NEA), itself about twenty-five years old, responded to the mounting pressure for standards. NEA created the Department of Public School Music to write national standards for music teachers. In 1885 this department initiated examinations for music teachers. New textbook publishers and magazines entered the market, replete with plans to prepare teachers for music examinations. By 1892 master teachers, through their books and articles, were proposing minimum standards for public school music in the primary grades. Additional magazines, such as *Musical America,* published relevant articles by celebrated musicians and educators.

As the number of public school music educators grew, their problems parted from the concerns of private music teachers. School boards and school administrators were generally unsympathetic to requests for added rehearsal time. Often, to the alarm of music specialists, administrators asked classroom teachers to instruct music classes. While MTNA served the private music teachers well, it no longer met many concerns for the public school teacher. To address their worries, Philip Hayden convened a conference of public school music supervisors in Keokuk, Iowa, on April 10, 1907. Hayden, supervisor of music in the Keokuk schools, was also the secretary of the Department of Public School Music for NEA. Among the noted music educators at the conference was T. P. Giddings. The meeting, a popular success, became the first of yearly gatherings, and the attendees eventually organized to become the most influential affiliation for public school teachers in the United States. MTNA, the older organization, remained the principal alliance for private music teachers.[31]

At a Cincinnati meeting in 1910, Hayden's conferees called their new organization the Music Supervisors National Conference (MSNC), a name changed to Music Educators National Conference (MENC) in 1934. At the 1912 conference in Detroit, they proposed that all work in music should receive credit comparable to mathematics and English. Their superiors, the public school administrators, did not accept the proposal, but MSNC members continued to press their cause. They began publishing their views, and in 1915 Peter Dykema, then music supervisor in Indianapolis, became the forceful editor of MSNC's magazine, *Music Supervisors Journal (MSJ)*. Later, while at Teachers College and on Interlochen's advisory committee, Dykema continued the march to recognize music in the schools. Through articles in *MSJ*, he guided the music teachers to form alliances of mutual support and mounted campaigns to add better music to the curriculum. His persistence, and that of his colleagues in MSNC, finally produced results in the 1920s.

At the 1922 convention, an educational committee of MSNC submitted a highly praised report entitled *High School Credits for Applied Music Study*. Though this report echoed earlier statements, it outlined still higher standards for instrumental ensembles. Concurrently, at the same convention, Maddy burst on the national scene of MSNC. His high school orchestra from Richmond, Indiana, played a winning performance, illustrating what high school students could accomplish in an excellent public school system.

Maddy's student orchestra began to model itself after the professional orchestras of the 1920s. By the conclusion of World War I, American symphony orchestras had begun to set high performance standards. Audiences lauded both the orchestras and their members, who were primarily European-trained. These immigrant musicians had been teaching children in private music lessons, but seldom in American schools, where orchestras like Maddy's were rare. Until the Rochester, New York, convention in 1913, MSNC had never featured a high school orchestra. Violin classes were presented at a later, 1916 conference in Lincoln, Nebraska.[32]

But after World War I, music programs in the public schools blossomed. Teachers specializing in music studies were hired in greater numbers. Many high schools established bands and orchestras, which were convened outside the normal class schedules. In Detroit, Cass Technical High School inaugurated a daring new music program in 1919, and within a decade, Cass employed a faculty of seventeen music teachers and maintained a full symphony orchestra, a symphonic band, string quartets, woodwind ensembles, harp ensembles, and dance orchestras.

In 1921 a sufficient number of teachers were interested in string programs to allow Will Earhart to conduct a teachers' orchestra at MSNC in St. Joseph, Missouri. Membership at the conference ballooned with new music teachers interested in string programs and excited about varied music studies in the schools. By 1922, when Maddy's Richmond High School Orchestra stormed the Nashville convention, MSNC membership exceeded eighteen hundred music supervisors, an unprecedented number.

Following his Richmond orchestra's success, Maddy became a leader on MSNC committees, where he created competitions, promoted higher performance standards, and wrote pamphlets and books for teacher training. His influence expanded to public school systems across the country, where he became a sought-after consultant and master teacher.

In 1923 he was appointed to an MSNC committee on instrumental music headed by Victor Rebmann, future president of the Eastern Music Camp. The committee, which included T. P. Giddings, also brought Maddy and Charles Tremaine together for the first time. Tremaine, secretary of the committee, guided the agenda, and Giddings, Tremaine, and Maddy began their thirty-year collaboration. In the next year, while pursuing a pet project, Maddy helped Rebmann draft a survey of orchestra literature, which listed required and recommended music selections for music contests featuring large ensembles, soloists, and small ensembles. These lists would form the ensemble repertoire in the first season of Maddy's camp in 1928. Maddy followed Rebmann as chairman of MSNC's instrumental music committee in 1925. Taking initiative with the committee, Maddy joined Giddings to write a pamphlet entitled *Orchestral Technique,* and they drafted a booklet entitled *School Orchestras*, describing in great detail how to organize ensembles.

In 1926 the committee created a survey of band literature, called *School Bands*, which established standards for the quality and instrumentation of high school symphonic bands. Maddy secured endorsements for the standards from bandmasters John Philip Sousa and Edwin Franko Goldman and symphony orchestra conductor Walter Damrosch. At previous MSNC conventions, each of these conductors had spoken in favor of improved standards for school bands, so Maddy easily persuaded them to approve his survey. Tremaine's National Bureau for the Advancement of Music published the band and orchestra reports and donated them to all music supervisors in the name of the committee.[33] Committee members wrote articles promoting the standards and published them in *MSJ, Musical Courier, Etude*, and *Musical America.*

Maddy's committee also sponsored MSNC's first national high school band contest. Tremaine persuaded several music instrument manufacturers to fund the first contest in Chicago, and Maddy managed the event. Thirty bands enrolled the first year, and, repeated yearly, the contest rapidly became popular. In 1937 the national contest was replaced by ten regional contests, which were discontinued during World War II and not reinstituted.[34] Prodded by Interlochen's three leaders, MSNC's band contests reshaped the public perception of music programs in America's schools. The public increasingly judged the adequacy of school music programs by the quality of the performing groups rather than by other educational standards, such as theoretical knowledge or understanding.

By 1926 the conferences attracted so many registrants that MSNC administrators decided to hold future conventions biennially. They also chose to upgrade the 1926 convention in quality and in the number of performances. Clarence Birchard, a Boston publisher and member of the program committee, suggested that a concert highlighting students in an orchestra would be exciting. He knew that Joe Maddy had organized orchestras in Indiana in 1923 and 1924 that included the best students from the high schools. Approaching MSNC president Edgar Gordon, Birchard proposed that Maddy organize a similar, but national, orchestra for MSNC's convention in Detroit on April 26, 1926.

Maddy agreed to organize this all-American high school orchestra, called the National High School Orchestra (NHSO), but he insisted that its concert should be a showstopper. From the beginning, he executed his plans on a grand scale. He and his colleagues wrote letters to the music supervisors across the country, encouraging them to identify their best students for participation. Local communities were approached, and they agreed to pay students' expenses to the convention. After considerable preparation and anguish, Maddy and the supervisors chose the students for inclusion in the convention program, and some 230 players traveled from twenty-five states to play in NHSO. Following five days of strenuous and exacting rehearsals under Maddy's direction, the mammoth ensemble presented its concert in Orchestra Hall in Detroit.

To make the experience more exciting and meaningful for the students and the audience, Gordon asked Detroit Symphony Orchestra conductor Ossip Gabrilowitsch to conduct several numbers. Gabrilowitsch accepted, and as a result, he and Maddy shared the conducting. Maddy, not offended by this intrusion, grasped hold of the idea to engage celebrated conductors for student concerts.

The Detroit MSNC represented a turning point for school orchestras and student studies in music. NHSO motivated students to compete for positions in local and state orchestras. Inspired to progress by competing in contests and cooperating with one another in ensembles, they were rewarded by being selected to play under the baton of a venerated conductor of national reputation. Maddy, recognizing the sensational success of the first concert, began preparations for future NHSO programs. In all, he organized five NHSO programs or touring orchestras over the next half-dozen years, in 1926, 1927, 1928, 1930, and 1932.[35]

The second NHSO concert Joe planned was for a National Superintendence Conference in Dallas on March 3, 1927. Randall Condon, superintendent of schools in Cincinnati and the person in charge of the program, decided to concentrate on music education for this convention, and he asked Maddy and Walter Aiken, supervisor of music in the Cincinnati schools, to arrange the events. Condon, Aiken, and Maddy planned the program to show off student performances, with the hope that, after attending the conference programs, the administrators would endorse music in the curricula of the nation's high schools.

For the program, the supervisor of music in Dallas conducted a chorus of about eight hundred boys and girls from Dallas elementary schools. Their performance was followed by Maddy's NHSO. Finally, Superintendent William Webster of Minneapolis, T. P. Giddings's supervisor, spoke, extolling the virtues of music in the school curriculum.

Maddy, steeled with his previous success in Detroit, attracted even more students for the Dallas conference. Two hundred sixty-eight players, selected from a list of twelve hundred candidates, arrived from thirty-nine states to play this concert. To display the students' talents further, Maddy divided the orchestra into smaller ensembles that played for eleven meetings over six days. His extravaganza overwhelmed the superintendents, who showered Maddy with acclaim. At the conclusion of the convention, they passed a resolution recommending that every public school give credit for musical instruction,[36] a longtime objective of music lovers. Thus the performance of Maddy's NHSO became a powerful influence for establishing music in the curricula of the nation's schools.

Charles Tremaine, Willis Pennington, and the Interlochen Property

Excited by the students' performances at the first NHSO concert in Detroit, Maddy conceived the idea for an NHSO that would perform over several weeks during the summer. In December 1926, upon hearing of Maddy's success, Charles Warren of Brunswick, Maine, contacted Maddy with the offer of a joint interest in 150 acres of land in Maine for a commercial music camp.[37] Though he would not agree to Warren's moneymaking venture, Maddy took hold of the notion of an orchestra camp. He began hunting for quiet, remote spaces, withdrawn from the bustle of cities, and offering privacy, where students might perform without disturbances or dissonances. At that time, summer camps with crafts and outdoor activities had mushroomed throughout the country, but none offered high school music programs, such as Maddy's inventive mind imagined and heard. Maddy and Giddings recalled their memories of the summer programs at Chautauqua, where lectures and concerts were designed for all ages. Located on a peaceful lakeshore in western New York, Chautauqua oozed with intellectual openness and artistic vigor.

Summer music schools and camps on the college level were firmly established by 1920, when Maddy traveled to Chautauqua to study with Giddings. Several different types of camps had arisen. For instance, commercial music publishers Silver Burdett and Company, the American Book Company, and Ginn and Company had introduced one type in the last quarter of the nineteenth century to market their publications. The authors of the books served as the master teachers for these summer programs, which offered college-level credit. Religious communities started another type of camp, geared toward families, with activities to fit all ages. College students could earn credit at such camps, but at least in the early years, formal class work was not the goal of their offerings; the thrust was for personal edification, not professional advancement. By the 1920s, summer music courses were also common offerings at many universities. The University of Michigan had offered music courses during the summer session of 1902.[38] And in 1907 Cornell University became the first institution of higher education to grant credit to music teachers in a six-week summer session.[39]

The Chautauqua movement began as a religious community in the summer of 1874. Two Methodist churchmen, Bishop John Heyl Vincent and Lewis Miller, established the first assembly on the shores of Lake Chautauqua in western New York State. The setting, chosen for its natural beauty, attracted an allegiant following. In this place, Vincent and Miller proffered lectures on politics, classes in literature, and concerts of classical music. Families began to build summer homes on the grounds to ensure their admission to favorite events, and they returned year after year. Eventually, compact rows of white frame houses clustered around a wooden auditorium on the shores of the lake.

The New York Chautauqua was so popular that similar programs were started in many locations throughout the United States. As the movement expanded, the Chautauquas created an association for sharing the best events. Distinguished speakers and musicians were engaged, and they traveled throughout the summer season, performing in a circuit at various Chautauquas. In the years before the arrival of radio, movies, and the automobile, Chautauqua organizations built about twelve thousand sites throughout the United States. Students could receive collegiate credit for classes taken at the New York site. But slowly the public's vacation and study habits changed, and eventually the economic difficulties brought on by the Great Depression in the 1930s closed a number of the Chautauquas. The New York Chautauqua endures, still presenting well-attended events. Two other Chautauqua institutions also survive: the Chautauqua on Lake Erie, founded in Ohio shortly after the New York settlement, continues with venues of contemporary appeal; the Chautauqua in Boulder, Colorado, begun in 1898, seeks to preserve the spirit of Chautauqua programming in the original buildings.[40]

Music camps for high school students did not appear until early in the twentieth century. Jack Wainright started the first high school band camp, at Oliver Lake, near Lagrange, Indiana, in 1927, one year before Maddy opened his Interlochen camp. But the depression forced Wainright's camp to close within a few years of its opening.[41] At least one pioneering camp was still operating in 1997: the Perry-Mansfield Performing Arts School and Camp in Steamboat Springs, Colorado, began in 1913 and maintained a six-week program for high school and college students. But while Interlochen emphasizes orchestras, Perry-Mansfield has always featured vocal music, vocal ensembles, and musical theater, with some activities in dance, theater, and visual arts.

With thoughts of a camp devoted to music in mind, Maddy wrote an article, "Just an Idea," for *MSJ*, floating the suggestion of an orchestra camp for high school students. To gain support among music supervisors and their students, he persuaded the publisher to print the article in the March issue, scheduled for distribution just before the NHSO concert for the National Superintendence Conference in Dallas on March 3, 1927.

A week before the Dallas meeting, he spoke at a civic dinner in Detroit, where he honored the Detroit high school students chosen to play in NHSO. In his speech, Maddy broached the idea of starting a summer camp for orchestra students. Those at the dinner were very enthusiastic, and the *Detroit News* highlighted the camp proposal in an article on the following day. On the day that article appeared, Maddy also placed an ad in the *Detroit Free Press* seeking a site for his proposed camp. By the day of the Dallas conference, Maddy had already drawn considerable attention to his proposed music camp.

The Dallas performance of NHSO was a triumph that, along with Maddy's article in the *MSJ*, stimulated great interest in the orchestra camp. The concert aroused students' passions and inspired the audience. Maddy now needed to translate student emotions into attendance at the camp. After the concert, he climbed a ladder backstage and yelled, "How would you like to come to a summer camp to continue playing together?" Students responded with a boisterous chorus of support. Shrewdly, Maddy began to nurture the feelings of elation that the students experienced while playing with talented peers. In the next days, he referred to the students' enthusiasm whenever building support for the camp. The ploy was so successful that, many years later, Maddy turned the story around and ascribed the original camp idea to the students in Dallas, though Charles Warren had originated the idea several months earlier.[42]

As the camp idea matured, Maddy turned his attention to finding a site. Charles Warren's property in Maine was one possibility. Warren offered to sell his property to Maddy, and several eastern music supervisors expressed interest in working there. After the Dallas conference, Maddy traveled to Maine to spend a night on Warren's property. New York music educator Edwin Barnes and three or four other eastern supervisors joined Maddy. He was not impressed with the location: "We were eaten by mosquitos and our food was carried away by the high tide and altogether it proved to me that such a location was impossible."[43] Barnes, though disappointed, was attracted to a different site in Maine. There he banded with other eastern music supervisors to create the Eastern Music Camp in 1931. This camp rivaled the National High School Orchestra Camp for several years in the 1930s.[44]

Another possible site for Maddy's music camp materialized almost simultaneously. Just before the Dallas convention, Willis Pennington of Detroit read about Maddy's plans in the papers and called him with a proposal. Pennington, president of the Interlochen Resort Association in northern Michigan, hoped to sell some property to reduce his indebtedness. Already, Pennington had resourcefully sold land to the state for Michigan's first public state park (now Interlochen State Park) in 1917. So Maddy, after his disappointing trip to Maine, agreed to his first visit to Interlochen in the spring of 1927.

Maddy invited three music colleagues to join him in inspecting the Interlochen property. Invited were Mrs. Harry Bacher, chair of public school music programs for the National Federation of Music Clubs; Ada Bicking, Michigan director of music education; and Edith Rhetts, one of Maddy's MSNC colleagues. They found Pennington's land lying between two lakes, about fifteen miles south and west of Traverse City, Michigan. Two camps, one for boys and one for girls, were nestled in oak and pine forests.

Pennington proposed that Maddy build the orchestra camp on one of the lakes, just south of the state park. But Maddy preferred sites for separate boys' and girls' camps, oriented toward the two lakefronts, on Green Lake and Duck Lake. The site would also include a resort hotel that Pennington had built in 1909.

The Pennington property impressed Maddy so much that he asked T. P. Giddings to join him there as soon as possible. A few weeks later, Giddings and his sister drove from Boston to meet Maddy at Interlochen. Maddy and Giddings stayed in two cottages near the Pennington camp's mess hall, and they spent a day looking at that camp site and others. They found none so attractive as the Pennington properties.[45]

Maddy and Giddings savored the beauty of the north woods, the allure of the lakes, and the relative isolation from the outer world, qualities that today's residents and campers still value. The environment was unique and unforgettable. Looking at the small camp dwellings congregated along dirt tracks through the woodland, Maddy foresaw a campus with buildings, roads, and parking, one that would maintain a balance between the art venues and the natural setting. Paved roads did not exist in northern Michigan in 1927, but the site was accessible by car to summer residents, campers, and concertgoers. The Pere Marquette Railroad also offered excellent service from Chicago and Detroit.[46]

Inspired, but with no money to purchase the site, Maddy and Giddings left not knowing how to start their camp. On July 6, still with no resources, Maddy surprised participants of the Art Association at Wayne State University by announcing that he would incorporate his orchestra camp on that day. He engaged a notary public in Detroit to draw up the Articles of Association of the National High School Orchestra Camp, and the camp was chartered as an educational, nonprofit organization in the state of Michigan. Joseph E. Maddy, as president and musical director, headed the incorporating board. Thaddeus P. Giddings was vice president, and Willis Pennington was secretary-treasurer.[47]

Pennington, whose camp was in difficult straights financially, finally conceived of the plan that made the orchestra camp feasible. In September, Pennington approached Maddy with a proposition to exchange the use of his land for a food contract. Pennington would serve meals to students and faculty. Profits from selling the meals would pay toward the purchase price of the fifty acres of land that Maddy sought for the orchestra camp. After ten years, the fifty acres would belong to the camp. Maddy was not especially interested in the business arrangements, but he was ecstatic that Pennington had found a way to get started. They signed a contract. Pennington's salary would be five thousand dollars, Maddy's would be two thousand dollars, and Giddings's would be one thousand dollars.[48]

However, signing the contract was not the end of their transactions. If it had not been for Charles Tremaine, Pennington could have taken over the camp during the depression years. By his own admission, Maddy had little knowledge of or interest in the business aspects of the camp. He told his friend Tremaine that he did not want to be bothered by financial concerns. But when Maddy showed Tremaine the contract he had signed with Pennington, Tremaine was disturbed and asked Maddy to renegotiate. Maddy convinced a reluctant Pennington to travel to New York to get Tremaine's opinion, approval, and advice. They spent several days together, and Tremaine picked out many flaws in the contract.

The original contract had put the entire business management and financial control of the camp in Pennington's hands, with no restrictions or requirements on Pennington. A new agreement devised by Tremaine cut back on the benefits that Pennington had secured. In the new plan, Pennington's salary as treasurer and general manager was reduced from five thousand dollars to two thousand, matching Maddy's salary; Giddings's salary remained at one thousand dollars. Tremaine made another major change by reducing the time over which the profit from the dining operation was to go to Pennington in payment for the fifty acres of land. Tremaine proposed that after five years, not ten, the fifty acres would belong to the camp.

Tremaine's lawyer drew up a new contract, which, when signed, became the basis for starting the camp. Pennington signed under pressure from Tremaine, who pointed out that because the camp had no money, Pennington could not enforce the previously signed contract. In the years to come, and much to Maddy's irritation, Tremaine often reiterated the flaws in Maddy's original contract. Tremaine felt Maddy did not understand the important, and frequently unexpected, effect that contracts and commitments have on organizations. Tremaine never let Maddy forget his lack of business experience.[49]

Maddy and Interlochen profited greatly from Tremaine's astute help. Charles Milton Tremaine was a musician who grew up in a family engaged in music businesses. His father published music in New York from 1865 to 1868. An uncle, William Tremaine, organized companies that led to the founding of the Aeolian Company, a ten-million-dollar corporation that manufactured pianos, player pianos, and organs. Charles, born in 1870, joined the family business in 1888 and remained in it until 1916. During his last ten years with the Aeolian Company, he supervised advertising and sales as a manager and vice president. For three years, when the president was ill, Tremaine was acting chair of the Aeolian board of directors. He was proud that, during his tenure, sales increased by ten times.

In 1916 Tremaine left Aeolian to establish the National Bureau for the Advancement of Music. The National Bureau was an altruistic venture known primarily for establishing National Music Week and the Music Memory Contest for student musicians. The National Bureau also published teaching materials for music teachers.

In 1920 Tremaine, under the auspices of the National Bureau, inaugurated a celebration of classical music by establishing New York City's first Music Week. Four years later, in May 1924, he expanded that idea into the first National Music Week. Four hundred fifty-two cities and towns in the United States participated that first year, and every state was represented. Tremaine chronicled the observance of this first Music Week in a book, the *History of National Music Week.* The United States still celebrates National Music Week yearly in the first week of May.[50]

Tremaine, who remained with the National Bureau until his retirement in 1942, was very successful in business and was expert at marshaling forces for music events. Friends recall that he was a great negotiator, a shrewd tactician, and a brilliant bridge player. And he understood how organizations could advance the cause of music.[51]

Tremaine became one of Maddy's closest friends. The National Bureau published and distributed many documents that Maddy assembled for MSNC in the 1920s. Tremaine also gave the National Bureau's mailing lists to Maddy, who added them to Interlochen's student recruitment lists.

Maddy and Tremaine worked well together, productively supplementing one another. Maddy was the genius promoter and creator. Tremaine was the careful and orderly financial officer. Lacking financial experience himself, Maddy often railed at Tremaine, but in truth, Maddy was fortunate that Tremaine devoted his time and expertise to Maddy and the camp. Tremaine understood and applauded Maddy's need to expand the size of the camp for its survival. However, he also curbed many of Maddy's unproven impulses that may have threatened the survival of the camp.[52]

After rescuing Maddy from the Pennington contract, Tremaine became part of Maddy's inner circle. Tremaine joined the advisory committee for the camp, and Maddy quickly put him on the camp's first board of financial control. In 1933, at the conclusion of the Pennington contract, Tremaine replaced Pennington as treasurer of the camp. Fortunately for

Maddy, Tremaine managed the camp's financial affairs from that time until he retired in 1958.

In the fall of 1927, Maddy began preparations to open the orchestra camp the following summer. But Otto Haisley, superintendent of schools in Ann Arbor, was not pleased with the time Maddy devoted to his new venture, and he fired Maddy from his half-time job as supervisor of music in the Ann Arbor public schools. This firing was a major problem for both the university and the schools, since Maddy's appointment in the Ann Arbor schools was traditionally joined with his half-time appointment as music education head at the University of Michigan. However, according to Maddy, he had resigned the Ann Arbor school position to devote at least half of his time to the camp. Superintendent Haisley called him "a crazy damn fool for giving up a good job to undertake a fool project like the camp."[53] In any event, Maddy did not suffer financially. He received the same two-thousand-dollar salary as president of the National High School Orchestra Camp that he had received from the Ann Arbor schools.

Earl Moore, head of the university's School of Music, remained supportive of Maddy, who continued to teach at the University of Michigan with a half-time appointment. Joe continued his duties at the university with zeal, teaching the university's first course in ensemble conducting, during the fall of 1927. But at the same time, the University Musical Society (UMS), which administered the School of Music, underwent a change in leadership.

The UMS organization in Ann Arbor is one of the nation's oldest and most respected presenters of performing arts, but from its beginning in 1879, it also administered the University of Michigan's School of Music. Francis Kelsey, UMS president at the time of Joe's appointment, died and was replaced by Charles Sink, who administered the School of Music until 1940, when the school ceased to be governed by the society.[54] Maddy's preoccupation with the camp during its first years irritated Sink. To resolve his conflict with Sink, Maddy enlisted the aid of Alexander Grant Ruthven, president of the University of Michigan. Finally, in 1930, Moore, with concurrence from Ruthven and Sink, released Maddy from his teaching assignments for five years, using funds from a Carnegie Corporation radio grant to support Maddy's activities in both radio and the camp. Ruthven also agreed to serve on Maddy's new advisory committee, helping to ensure the camp's success.[55]

Maddy spread the word about his camp wherever possible—through speeches to music, arts, and civic clubs; in correspondence with students; and at music festivals. When he conducted his children's chorus at the UMS's May Festival in Ann Arbor in 1927, he tantalized prospective campers with visions of superior orchestras playing together for several weeks at a time.

Maddy heavily promoted Interlochen through newspapers, magazines, and radio. As early as September 1927, Russell McLauchlin described the new camp in an article in the *Detroit News*, announcing openings for three hundred campers of high school age. The camp orchestra, he wrote, would be financed with scholarships provided by schools, clubs, citizens, or business firms. Any high school could nominate a student for the orchestra, with the understanding that, if their student were accepted, the nominators would raise scholarship funds for the student's attendance.[56]

McLauchlin's article praised the site's position in the northern Michigan resort area, easily accessible by means of several main highways. He wrote that students were to sleep in cottages, each housing ten players and a counselor. Maddy promised future practice rooms, rehearsal buildings, assembly halls, tennis courts, boats, and swimming facilities, which took shape over the years. He even dreamed of a golf course, which never materialized.[57]

At least, through the promise of cafeteria sales, Maddy was close to owning Pennington's wonderful property for his camp. Maddy's dream was still fragile, but he was able to limit his time in other jobs and concentrate on his beloved orchestra camp.

The National High School Orchestra Camp: The First Two Years

"I have witnessed a miracle," declared Ossip Gabrilowitsch after conducting NHSO in Beethoven's Symphony no. 1, during the camp's first season.[58] But nine months earlier, Maddy's Interlochen seemed far from a fanfare. By late 1927, Maddy had secured the land for his camp, but he had no classroom buildings, no auditorium, no scholarships, and no staff. He needed to raise funds, so during the winter, Maddy spent much of his time in New York, seeking money from corporations and foundations. Many turned him down. He also received a number of positive responses and promises, some of which, according to Maddy, were not kept.

In February 1928, Maddy announced that he had received fifteen hundred dollars for scholarships from John Erskine on behalf of the Juilliard Foundation. Erskine's name and moral support were as important as the financial assistance. Erskine, besides heading the foundation, was the first president of the newly organized Juilliard School of Music (now Juilliard School), and his goodwill toward the camp would be invaluable. Maddy announced 280 scholarships in the next issue of *MSJ*. In 1929 the Juilliard Foundation gave another grant of three thousand dollars to the camp, and the foundation continued to support the camp with scholarships for over a decade, until Erskine resigned the presidency of the Juilliard School of Music.[59]

In February, Maddy announced that publisher G. Schirmer had given a grant to build a new outdoor auditorium to be called the Interlochen Bowl. The Bowl, completed in time for the first session of the camp, permitted weekly public orchestra performances. Maddy boasted that it seated fifteen thousand people, though even before nearby buildings limited the seating area, the Bowl entertained capacity audiences of approximately eight thousand. George McConkey was the architect for the Bowl, a rustic structure set in a natural depression overlooking Green Lake.[60]

In an effort to secure additional building funds, Maddy approached Carl Greenleaf, president of C. G. Conn and publisher of Maddy's instrumental music series, the *Universal Teacher*. In March 1928, Greenleaf persuaded the National Association of Band Instrument Manufacturers to lend the camp ten thousand dollars. A month later, Joe went back to Greenleaf, who promised five thousand dollars more if people in Traverse City would match the amount on the same terms. Two banks in Traverse City agreed to match the money, with the condition that the camp would repay its outstanding loans at the end of the season. With loans in hand, Maddy began to build campus structures. Besides the Bowl, he built thirty-two cabins and ten classrooms.

During the winter, the enrollment campaign had gone well. Tremaine stepped in to help with brochures. He wrote announcements about the new camp, persuaded his Aeolian Company to pay for the printing, and mailed them at the expense of the National Bureau for the Advancement of Music. *MSJ* announced that the camp had received 150 applicants by February, and Maddy was optimistic about high attendance for the first season.

But as the summer approached, Maddy realized that only eighty-nine students had enrolled. He would be unable to field a complete symphony orchestra unless he could find oboe, bassoon, horn, string bass, tuba, and harp students. Maddy sensed the need for quick action. He decided that to attract students of wind instruments, he would need to add an appealing National High School Band (NHSB). He and Giddings scoured the public schools, searching for students to fill the empty positions. Maddy offered large scholarships to students who played the needed instruments, and these awards pushed the camp into still greater debt. Finally, the official count rose to 115 campers, each paying three hundred dollars in tuition, less scholarship awards. Because of these last-minute recruiting efforts, NHSB played as often as NHSO in the first season, and the printed programs began to promote the new camp as the National High School Orchestra and Band Camp.[61]

Miraculously, the first season of the camp, eight weeks long, opened on June 24, 1928. Classes offered included band, choir, composition, conducting, ensembles, drama, and beginning instruction in all instruments. The staff included twenty-two faculty members, eighteen counselors, and Dr. F. W. Clements, the first medical director, who was aided by one nurse.[62]

Camp music ensembles gave forty concerts that first season. The band and orchestra presented a concert every Sunday, and Maddy shared the conducting of most orchestra concerts with a distinguished guest conductor. Gabrilowitsch, conductor of the Detroit Symphony Orchestra, began the tradition of guest-conductor visits, at the third concert of the season, on Sunday, July 15. Howard Hanson of the Eastman School of Music conducted on July 22, Earl Moore of the University of Michigan on July 29, and Leo Sowerby, a distinguished organist and conductor from Chicago, on August 5. Maddy also invited noted composers to conduct their works with NHSO. Carl Busch conducted two of his compositions on July 12. Edgar Stillman Kelley, a prominent composer who had studied in Stuttgart and taught in Berlin, conducted his arrangement of Schubert's *Romantic Overture.*

Lee Lockhart, conductor of high school bands in Council Bluffs, Iowa, led NHSB, which played on an equal footing with NHSO from the very first concerts. In comparison, the choir was a recreational activity. Jacob Evanson, director of high school music programs in Flint, Michigan, conducted the choir, which was made up of students from NHSO and NHSB.[63] The first season featured a drama class under the direction of Mrs. Lee Lockhart, the wife of the band director. The drama class, all musicians, presented four programs, including a native American pageant called *Fallen Leaf.*

That first camp season established the spirit that was to guide Interlochen for the rest of the century. Following that summer, Marguarite Kerns, in an article in the *Grand Rapids Sunday Herald*, wrote, "Nothing like the National High School Orchestra camp, which opened its first session [at Interlochen] in June, exists anywhere else."[64]

Maddy communicated the purpose of the camp through the program booklets, for all faculty members, campers, parents, and audiences to see.

Purpose of Camp

The purposes of the National High School Orchestra Camp are:

To provide an incentive to all musically talented school pupils to work for scholarship awards.

To reward music students of outstanding ability by giving them the advantages of the camp, including participation in the orchestra, band and other musical and camp activities.

To give prospective teachers, music supervisors, symphony players and conductors a splendid start in preparation for their life work.

To interest many of these talented students in the profession of school music.[65]

Camp discipline was strong and restrictive. Maddy asked Chester Belstrom, the camp director from 1928 until 1940, to establish the camp's uniform rules. Students wore white uniforms for the first year, but in the following year, light blue shirts and dark blue corduroy slacks or knickers became the uniform for all students, faculty, and staff. Belstrom was stern, even chastising the faculty for not always measuring up: "May we ask you to help these boys and girls conform to camp rules by complying with them yourself? We are all responsible for their well being, and by all carrying out the same rules, no hard feelings will result."[66]

Campers were instructed to memorize and carry the following regulations.

1. All players must be in their seats with instruments tuned, ready to begin the rehearsal EXACTLY on time. Smaller instrument cases must be placed under the chairs of the players. The rehearsal hall will be ready 30 minutes before each rehearsal and players may arrive early to practice and warm up their instru-

ments. Tardy players will lose their seats and be placed at the foot of their respective sections, unless previously excused. Inexcusable tardiness or absence will result in expulsion from the orchestra, and notification of parents by wire.

2. There shall be NO TALKING during rehearsals. You may do your talking before rehearsals, during intermissions, and after the close of rehearsals.

3. Tuning will be done by sections as designated by the conductor. No "tooting" or practicing will be tolerated during rehearsals.

4. Players who do not play in all of the numbers must keep their seats and remain silent unless dismissed by the conductor. There is much to learn by watching and listening and you came to learn.

5. Your friends may attend rehearsals providing they keep silent.

6. Every player must carry a red-and-blue pencil for marking music at rehearsals. Librarians have them for sale.

7. Music may be taken out for practice by arranging with librarian of your section. Announcement will be made as to how to do this.

8. At the close of each rehearsal, arrange the music in your folio and close the folio, leaving it on your chair.

9. Players must carry all equipment that may be needed at rehearsals, such as mutes, extra strings, rosin, reeds, etc.

10. Watch position of instruments while playing. Sit with both feet on the floor. Observe uniform resting position during rests; violins and violas under right arm, wind instruments across knees with mouthpieces to the left. Have instruments in position, ready to attack the next entrance THREE COUNTS BEFORE THE END OF THE REST.

11. Do not notice the mistakes of others in rehearsals or concert (Golden Rule).[67]

However, besides the rigor, the camp featured many lighthearted moments suitable to a camp environment. A Faculty Frolic was presented on July 30 of the first year. The harp teacher, Pasquale Montani, led a faculty jazz band. Cellist Hanns Pick of the University of Michigan played "El Toro" (The Bull) in a farce called *Carmen in One Act*. Giddings was credited with convulsing the audience with a heartrending performance of Pick's Open String Concerto for Cello with jazz band accompaniment.

Maddy inaugurated the challenge system for campers during the first year. He fostered competition among the campers and rewarded them with higher placement in the orchestra or solo performances with the orchestra. The camp curriculum stressed learning to read music quickly at a first sitting, and conductors established regular sight-reading periods. This practice, taken over by the public schools, greatly aided music literacy.

Interlochen's first session inspired a laudatory article in *Etude,* the national music magazine. The magazine's editors reported that, arriving at night on August 19 for the last concert of the season, they came on "hundreds of automobiles in the woods." They found no room in the hotel and so slept in a motor bus that belonged to T. P. Giddings. The article described a fine outdoor auditorium, a modern camp hotel, and numerous newly built cabins for the girls and boys. The writers heard the orchestra play Richard Wagner's overture to *Die Meistersinger* at sight in such a manner that, in their opinion, would have delighted Wagner, and they gushed that a committee of European orchestra experts would have been dumbfounded by the superb playing of these American boys and girls.

The *Etude* visitors met Allen Smith, a young timpanist from Detroit, whose work with NHSO attracted their attention. They said Smith was already drawing widespread attention from some great orchestras. They wrote: "Al needs experience and practice only. Some day he will have a fine position with one of our leading orchestras. If it were not for the camp at Interlochen, he would have to waste two long valuable months. In no other way could he get the experience at a rate his means would permit."[68]

Besides Interlochen's camp, *Etude* lauded summer music schools and camps throughout the United States, noting with pride that "for twenty years we have strongly endorsed the Summer School idea." The magazine observed that the music students progressed rapidly because summer studies and performances were intense and demanding. The students could accomplish as much in six or eight weeks of summer study as they could during a regular school year. Conductor Rudolph Ganz of the Saint Louis Symphony remarked: "The Summer Musical School in America is one of the most distinctive things about our cultural advance. It is the musical leaven of the land."[69]

The negative aspect of Interlochen's first camp season was its financial instability. After camp began, Maddy realized he might be unable to repay the camp's loans, and he called on Tremaine for help. Tremaine devised a plan to sell promissory notes to secure the debts. John Minnema, concert manager of the camp, worked hard and sold most of the notes. To spur the cause, Giddings and Maddy each bought one note for one hundred dollars. But the debt mounted, and Maddy was still unable to repay the loans.[70]

At the end of the summer, as the camp was going heavily into debt, the Traverse City bankers called their loans. With Pennington's concurrence, the bankers insisted that Maddy create a board of financial control to develop a plan for recovering their money. Howard Musselman of the First National Bank of Traverse City was chair of the board, which included other bankers, Tremaine, Pennington, Giddings, and Maddy. This financial control board continued oversight of the camp until 1942, when it was dissolved and its functions were absorbed by a new Interlochen board of trustees. Maddy was bitter toward the bankers, later complaining that, within sixty days of an agreement, they broke a promise to him by calling their loans.[71]

Maddy had been counting on campers' fees to repay his loans, and he had directed massive promotions to entice students to enroll in the first camp. Besides the musical incentives, he touted the advantages of camping near a state park. Then, seeing that great numbers of students were not enrolling, he soon downplayed his primary appeal to the most gifted students. He wanted parents to understand that, while the camp would unearth and develop a great deal of real talent, Interlochen would not cater to geniuses alone. Most students, he said, would be amateur music lovers, and a few would become concert artists.[72]

But though the first year's registration was larger than for other camps, Maddy was greatly disappointed in the final enrollment. Out of more than three hundred applicants, only 115 campers were enrolled. In the future, greater enrollments would be necessary to pay for the camp of his dreams.[73] To increase admissions and revenue for the second season in 1929, Maddy beefed up the camp's offerings. He created new programs for college-age students, adult music supervisors, and returning campers who were no longer in high school. The 1929 enrollment doubled to 232 campers.

Living conditions also improved for everyone in 1929, though most of the faculty and staff lived in tents and cooked their own food, just like tourist campers. New tennis courts were built. To placate objections from audiences, the Board of Supervisors of Grand Traverse County agreed to limit the use of powerboats on Green Lake during NHSO concerts.[74]

NHSB was officially given equal footing with NHSO in the second year. To underline his commitment to the band, Maddy appointed respected conductor Austin Harding to direct the band in 1929 and 1930. Harding's University of Illinois Concert Band was considered a superior organization. Even the eminent John Philip Sousa had expressed the opinion that the University of Illinois band was the finest college band in the world. In Maddy's view, Harding would attract excellent band students who would play in NHSO. And excellent students did enroll in the camp to play under Harding. The now internationally renowned band conductor Frederick Fennell played under Harding at Interlochen as a camper. Of the experience, he has written: "Many campers probably had their initial and emotionally-moving experience performing music by Richard Wagner with Harding, securing the sleeping Brünnhilde in her ring of magic fire, or playing the Gods up to Valhalla on their rainbow. . . . there was that unique reward of discovering how the great marches *swing* when the conductor and players ride the same wavelength. These were great gifts to us all."[75] Howard Hanson returned and starred as guest conductor for two weeks during that second season. Other NHSO conductors included Orien Dalley, Vladimir Bakaleinikoff, Leo Sowerby, William Revelli, and Guy Fraser Harrison.

The conductors had initiated student conducting among the campers in 1928, and a formal competition to conduct an ensemble began the following year. Concerto contests began in 1929, giving students an opportunity to perform with NHSO. To add prestige to the finals, Tremaine's National Bureau for the Advancement of Music awarded medals to the solo winners. Also that year, the camp demonstrated exemplary rehearsal techniques for high school music directors. Sectional rehearsals led by professional performer-teachers gained adherents in the public schools and in professional symphony orchestras after initially beginning at Interlochen. Interlochen also emphasized practicing chamber music as the best means to develop musicianship and independence in the larger ensembles. Furthermore, in that year, the camp hosted the first national clinic to select music for school ensemble competitions. In this clinic, camp groups played examples of new music for invited directors of school bands and orchestras. Following Interlochen's lead, public schools throughout the United States began to include ensemble competitions in their curricula.[76]

Some campers who would later assume great leadership roles at Interlochen attended for the first time in 1929. Future conductor Thor Johnson came to Interlochen as a camper playing viola, recruited while Maddy was visiting Asheville, North Carolina, to conduct the first All-Southern High School Orchestra.[77] George Wilson, future interim president of Interlochen, came as the music librarian in 1929, during his senior year in college.[78]

Maddy had bought many music scores for his ensembles, and he needed to organize these scores for quick usage. Austin Harding had developed a remarkable library system for handling band, orchestra, and chorus music at the University of Illinois, and Wilson, a student of Harding, set up a similar system for the camp. Following its installation at Interlochen, this Interlochen library system was widely duplicated in schools and professional music organizations throughout the United States.[79]

Programs in 1929 included a performance of Gilbert and Sullivan's *Pirates of Penzance* in the Interlochen Bowl. Sydney Morse conducted the camp choir, orchestra, and soloists in the presentation, hailed as the first performance of opera at Interlochen. Also that year, the Northern Michigan Festival Chorus, composed of students and adults, assembled and performed.[80]

On July 28, 1929, in a gesture to an early foundation benefactor, Maddy invited Juilliard president John Erskine to play the Schumann Concerto for Piano and Orchestra with NHSO, with Harding as conductor. Erskine's performance drew the biggest crowd in the Interlochen Bowl during the first two years. A news reporter counted car licenses from twenty-eight states in the parking area. Interlochen had become a reality.[81]

Part 3

Performance, the Measure of Success

The support of all art depends entirely upon those who love art for art's sake, and as music is universal, it becomes necessary to heed the wishes of the masses if one hopes to succeed.

—John Philip Sousa

The Quest for Acceptance

In 1930 John Philip Sousa arrived to shore up Maddy's band program at the camp. He was the most famous of the many celebrities Maddy brought to the camp to enrich the students' educations, attract the best student players, and give the new camp credibility. In his later years, Sousa had become increasingly devoted to the growth of high school bands and orchestras. He accepted invitations to conduct outstanding school bands, where he presented loving cups and trophies. The Sousa Band also frequently invited high school and college bands to play during intermissions of its concerts. Sousa often judged band and orchestra competitions, sympathetically encouraging student instrumentalists. He was delighted to attend the National High School Orchestra and Band Camp, where he was the star attraction in 1930 and 1931, just before his death.

Sousa's influence was extensive. He had written memorable marches for many events and organizations, such as his "University of Illinois," written for Austin Harding. The Sousa Band's excellence was equal to the country's leading symphony orchestras, partly because Sousa hired some of the best musicians from those ensembles. Sousa was a celebrity, a superstar. His name was magic. He was important in dissolving the notion that only European musicians could be competent. Sousa ridiculed those who belittled bands, saying that there was no hierarchy in art, and he was effective in winning over those who practiced what he called "artistic snobbery."[1]

Sousa was a showman, and his bandsmen were entertainers. "When the personality [of the soloist] is missing, the ear is bound to tire," he would say.[2] Concerts were fast paced: Writes Sousa's biographer, Paul E. Bierley, "The curtain went up; out came Sousa, who took one short bow, and quickly stepped up onto the podium; and immediately the band began. Sousa would permit no pauses of over twenty or thirty seconds, and he never left the conductor's stand except for intermissions."[3] Sousa played eclectic programs, in the same concert piping a variety of styles—marches, waltzes, symphonic overtures. His concerts were filled with encores. He played ragtime and jazz because his public liked it. A concert with about ten pieces listed on the printed program often finished with twenty-five to thirty-five selections, with encores announced by large display cards paraded across the stage.[4] Camp concert programs copied many Sousa ideas, and in the 1990s, Interlochen still presents an annual Sousa Band concert.

For his 1931 visit, Sousa wrote the march "The Northern Pines," which he dedicated to the camp. He conducted NHSB in the first performance over an NBC camp broadcast, where he also announced that he would donate royalties from "The Northern Pines" to a camp scholarship fund.[5] "The Northern Pines" was one of the last marches written by Sousa. When he visited Interlochen for his last summer of 1931, the camp named Sousa the honorary president of the National High School Orchestra and Band Camp.[6] The following March, Sousa died of a heart attack in Reading, Pennsylvania.[7]

In 1932, following Sousa's death, Maddy invited another celebrated bandsman, Edwin Franko Goldman, to conduct at Interlochen. Goldman, taking Sousa's lead, composed a march and dedicated it to the camp. Interlochen programs frequently include the complete version of his "Interlochen Bowl," but the version most familiar to campers is a truncated and accelerated rendition, renamed "Sound the Call" and sung to open the first assembly of each camp session.[8]

The best-known symphony conductors in the Midwest joined the celebrity parade. Following the tradition begun with the first performances of NHSO under the Detroit Symphony Orchestra's Ossip Gabrilowitsch, Maddy persuaded celebrities to travel to Interlochen, live in the cabins along the lakeshore, and perform with the students. Maddy maintained that these guest conductors donated their services to the camp, though he did provide housing and transportation.[9]

The students were thrilled by opportunities to rub shoulders with their musical heroes at camp outings or in the cafeteria. Gabrilowitsch, a camp supporter until his death in 1936, had been the camp's first guest conductor, visiting in July 1928. He was a famous pianist who had become the conductor of the three-year-old Detroit Symphony Orchestra in 1917.

Frederick Stock of the Chicago Symphony Orchestra conducted the campers in 1929, and Henri Verbrugghen of Minneapolis conducted in 1930, highlighting the visiting conductors for NHSO performances in the first years.[10] Stock had conducted NHSO for Chicago's 1928 MSNC convention. Violinist Stock had been the concertmaster of the Theodore Thomas Orchestra of Chicago, and when Thomas died in 1904, Stock become conductor of the orchestra, then renamed the Chicago Symphony Orchestra. Stock, until his death in 1942, generously wrote solicitation letters for Maddy's fund-raising campaigns.

Eugene Ormandy replaced Verbrugghen as Minneapolis Symphony Orchestra conductor and joined Maddy's music advisory committee in 1931. Ormandy remained a strong camp supporter even after moving to the Philadelphia Orchestra in 1936. Three decades later, Ormandy brought the Philadelphia Orchestra to Maddy's National Music Camp as the first professional symphony orchestra to perform on the Interlochen campus.

Besides conductors, famous guest soloists also played with the student campers. Pianist Percy Grainger was a great favorite with the campers, because he also composed music and conducted student ensembles. He gave master classes in piano, where he astonished the piano students with his complex and brilliant performances. He also conducted NHSB, the camp's A Capella Choir, and NHSO, often conducting his own compositions, such as *To a Nordic Princess* and *Spoon River*. The campers were amazed at his dazzling intellect. Somewhat eccentric, he displayed great physical energy and stamina, and, on occasion, he walked the fifteen miles back and forth to Traverse City, accompanied by his wife, striding several steps behind him.

Maddy thought his campers should also perform with famed conductors and solo musicians in the big cities, where music critics would hear NHSO and take his camp seriously. Moreover, since Maddy had isolated NHSO geographically by establishing the camp at Interlochen, he needed to arrange periodic visits to musical centers to maintain the orchestra's currency and prestige. Besides fame, these tours generated additional benefits. Above all, the campers cherished the roaring applause of the audiences in the large cities. They also enjoyed performing with the world-class artists who would not otherwise travel to Interlochen but could be engaged to perform on the road.

Unmindful of the expenses of travel, Maddy embarked on a major tour series. On February 23, 1930, Maddy launched the first of two major trips with NHSO. In Atlantic City, students made their second presentation to a national superintendence meeting. On February 27, they gave a concert at the Metropolitan Opera House in Philadelphia, and on the next day, they traveled to Carnegie Hall in New York, where the orchestra played under Walter Damrosch. At the time, neither Damrosch nor piano soloist Ernest Hutcheson had visited Interlochen, but John Erskine, their Juilliard friend, quieted their concerns and vouched for Maddy's accomplishments with his student orchestras.[11]

Sixty-eight years old in 1930, Damrosch was entering the last decade of his life. A member of a musical dynasty, he had burst on to the stage at twenty-two, when he replaced his recently deceased father as conductor of the new Metropolitan Opera Orchestra. Walter's father, Leopold, had founded the Symphony Society Orchestra of New York, and his brother, Frank, had started New York's Institute of Musical Art, one of the schools that evolved into the current Juilliard School. Walter first conducted his father's orchestra, later directed the New York Philharmonic, and in 1929 attained still greater national fame by broadcasting orchestra concerts for children over NBC.

Using Damrosch's influence, Maddy secured an NBC broadcast of the NHSO Carnegie Hall concert. NBC not only aired the concert but also relayed the broadcast to Berlin, Germany, an important first-time event for a U.S. student group. Concluding the tour in Washington, D.C., on March 1, 1930, Maddy took the orchestra to perform for President Herbert Hoover and Michigan senator Arthur Vandenberg, whose daughter, Betty, played a piano concerto with NHSO.[12]

Because the 1930 NHSO tour was so expensive, Maddy waited three years to field another one. This time, Maddy mounted the tour during the last week of camp, in August, when Chicago was hosting the Century of Progress Exposition, featuring the Chicagoland Music Festival. Festival officers had asked MSNC to arrange the music programs, and Maddy was put in charge of all music education events. Taking advantage of his MSNC position, Maddy invited every camper to perform at the exposition, where ensembles played in rotation and premiered new compositions written for the occasion by Edgar Stillman Kelley, Charles Sanford Skilton, Carl Busch, Leo Sowerby, and Edwin Franko Goldman.[13]

The 1933 tour almost brought the camp to financial ruin. Tremaine again came to the rescue, by establishing and implementing an austere financial recovery plan. Much to Maddy's displeasure, the plan precluded future touring for six years, but Tremaine prevailed, and the camp slowly recovered from the tour's debts, which had been aggravated still further by the depression.

In 1939 Maddy jumped at the next touring opportunity, which presented itself when New York City mounted a world's fair. Music critic Olin Downes, who organized the fair's music programs, invited Maddy and NHSO to perform nine concerts at the end of the camp season. This time, Tremaine supported Maddy's tour plan.

The NHSO tour featured a composition by fifteen-year-old Dika Newlin, later a noted composer and musicologist, but the sensation of the 1939 tour was nine-year-old conductor Lorin Maazel, a protégé of Vladimir Bakaleinikoff, who had first taught at the camp in 1929. By 1939, Bakaleinikoff had become an assistant conductor of Fritz Reiner's Pittsburgh Symphony Orchestra. Maazel enthralled the New York audiences by conducting NHSO in Mendelssohn's Italian Symphony. The tour was triumphant for Maddy and NHSO, and Maazel's career as a distinguished international conductor accelerated. Two years later, in November 1941, Maazel was engaged to conduct two network broadcasts with Arturo Toscanini's NBC Symphony Orchestra. In his adult years, Maazel's distinguished career included appointments as conductor of the Cleveland Orchestra, the Vienna Philharmonic, and the Pittsburgh Symphony Orchestra.[14]

In Maddy's mind, the tour to the New York World's Fair reaffirmed the importance of parading the camp ensembles, since the performances of talented youngsters attracted new students and donors to Interlochen. Though World War II intervened, Maddy continued the tours of camp ensembles whenever possible, and he added tours for the academy ensembles immediately on its opening.

Though tours established the artistic credibility of his camp, Maddy thought he should secure testimonials for his camp from prominent educational administrators, music educators, and volunteer heads of civic organizations who would serve on a camp music advisory committee. He enlisted prominent musicians, but he also sought the presidents of the

National Education Association, MTNA, MSNC, the National Federation of Music Clubs, and the General Federation of Women's Clubs. He added music industry heads, such as Clarence Birchard, a publisher and the originator of the NHSO idea. Maddy honored his advisory committee members, frequently telling them that their guidance was essential to Interlochen's success.

Maddy also sought some manner of national accreditation for his new venture. Unfortunately, no organizations yet accredited music camps, though Maddy's camp had received an endorsement from MSNC. But in 1930 a rival, the Eastern Music Camp in Waterville, Maine, was asking MSNC for an endorsement comparable to Maddy's.

Eastern claimed more varied music programs than Interlochen's orchestra and band programs. Not to be outdone by Eastern, Maddy revisited his camp's name. Maddy had, within the initial year, changed the name from National High School Orchestra Camp to National High School Orchestra and Band Camp. But in 1932, to top Eastern Music Camp's name challenge, Maddy changed his camp's name to National Music Camp (NMC), so he could appropriately advertise a wider array of music programs. The new name indicated a broader interest in music but not in other arts, though theater, dance, and visual arts had been part of Interlochen's offerings since the early 1930s. Almost sixty years passed before the name of NMC was changed, in 1991, to Interlochen Arts Camp, reflecting both the location of the camp and the inclusion of additional arts in the curriculum.[15]

Maddy was not pleased about the competition from Eastern Music Camp. In 1931 *MSJ* advertised four music camps in the United States: National High School Orchestra and Band Camp; Eastern Music Camp; the small Wainright Band and Orchestra Camp near Lagrange, Indiana; and the Winona Camp, a small camp organized in 1930 near Marion, Indiana.

Eastern, which opened on July 1, 1931, was started by music educators who had wanted Maddy to accept Charles Warren's property proposal for a camp in 1926, though the educators changed the location to a site near Waterville, Maine. Edwin Barnes, a music educator who had tried to persuade Maddy to join Charles Warren in 1927, was a sponsor of the camp, as was William Arms Fisher, an MTNA president who had served on Maddy's first advisory committee. The administration and staff of Eastern were Maddy's former allies at Interlochen, a fact that he accepted begrudgingly.

Willis Pennington at Interlochen in 1952. (Interlochen Center for the Arts Archives, Interlochen, Michigan, IA 28.)

Charles Tremaine in the 1920s. (Interlochen Center for the Arts Collection, Bentley Historical Library, University of Michigan, B 74.)

Joseph Maddy with John Erskine at Interlochen in 1929. (Interlochen Center for the Arts Archives, Interlochen, Michigan, IA 29.)

Joseph Maddy, Ossip Gabrilowitsch, Howard Hanson, and T. P. Giddings at Interlochen in 1928. (Interlochen Center for the Arts Archives, Interlochen, Michigan, IA 28.)

T. P. Giddings, Joseph Maddy, John Philip Sousa, and Austin Harding at Interlochen in 1932. (Interlochen Center for the Arts Archives, Interlochen, Michigan, IA 32.)

Earl Moore, Howard Hanson, and Burnet Tuthill, founders of the National Association of Schools of Music, reunite at Interlochen in 1977. (Interlochen Center for the Arts Archives, Interlochen, Michigan, IA 77.)

Frederick Fennell in the summer of 1992. (Interlochen Center for the Arts Archives, Interlochen, Michigan, IA 92.)

Heimo Haitto, Susanna Foster, and Allan Jones in Paramount's 1941 film *There's Magic in Music*. (Interlochen Center for the Arts Collection, Bentley Historical Library, University of Michigan, B 74.)

Paul Whiteman with Interlochen campers in 1941. (Interlochen Center for the Arts Archives, Interlochen, Michigan, IA 41.)

Herold Hunt, president of the American Association of School Administrators; Representative Carroll Kearns; Luther Richman, president of MENC; and James Petrillo, president of AFM, sign the 1947 Code of Ethics. (Special Collections in Performing Arts, University of Maryland, College Park.)

Joseph Maddy; Meg Nichols, director of junior girls; and Parker Pennington at the dedication of Pennington Hall in 1944, following the acquisition of Camp Interlochen. (Interlochen Center for the Arts Archives, Interlochen, Michigan, IA 44.)

John F. Kennedy welcomes Joseph Maddy and the National High School Orchestra to the White House in 1961. (Interlochen Center for the Arts Archives, Interlochen, Michigan, IA 61.)

Van Cliburn and George Wilson rehearse with the World Youth Symphony Orchestra on the Kresge Auditorium stage in 1968. (Interlochen Center for the Arts Archives, Interlochen, Michigan, IA 68.)

iendship
The Arts

Eugene Ormandy rehearses the World Youth Symphony Orchestra in 1964. (Interlochen Center for the Arts Archives, Interlochen, Michigan, IA 64.)

Clement Stone talks to Interlochen Arts Academy students in 1971. (Interlochen Center for the Arts Archives, Interlochen, Michigan, IA 71.)

Thor Johnson in his Interlochen studio, 1967. (Interlochen Center for the Arts Archives, Interlochen, Michigan, IA 67.)

For instance, Walter Damrosch, who conducted Maddy's triumphant Carnegie Hall concert, was Eastern's honorary president. Damrosch, crediting Maddy, said that the Eastern Music Camp would provide for students in the East the same focus that the National High School Orchestra Camp had provided for the Midwest. But Maddy was offended by Damrosch's comparisons, for he did not believe his camp served only the Midwest. He hoped to eclipse Eastern Music Camp with the more encompassing name National Music Camp.

Eastern's president was Victor Rebmann, Maddy's predecessor as head of MSNC's instrumental music committee. Vice presidents were Will Earhart, Maddy's mentor and predecessor at Richmond, Indiana, and Peter Dykema, who headed Maddy's music advisory committee. Even several Eastern conductors were Maddy's friends: Howard Hanson conducted Eastern's orchestra in its first season, the same year he presented the "Interlochen Theme" to Maddy's camp.[16]

Maddy had known Dykema since joining MSNC in 1920. Dykema had been appointed chair and professor of music education at Teachers College in 1924, the same year Maddy moved to the University of Michigan and Howard Hanson became director of the Eastman School of Music. Dykema was a national music education leader who had been the first editor of *MSJ*, MSNC's influential magazine.

Born in Grand Rapids, Michigan, in 1873, Dykema graduated from the University of Michigan with a bachelor of science degree in 1895 and a master of law degree in 1896. In 1903, after teaching for a short time in Indianapolis, he enrolled at Frank Damrosch's new Institute of Musical Art in New York City, where he studied theory and singing. In 1911 Dykema studied composition with Edgar Stillman Kelley in Berlin, Germany. He returned from Berlin in 1913 to head the University of Wisconsin's public school music department, where he remained until his appointment at Teachers College.

When Maddy's camp opened, Dykema helped him solicit prospective teachers and campers from the New York City area. But Dykema foresaw many camps like Interlochen throughout the United States, and from Maddy's point of view, Dykema had just one fault, which was to promote not only Interlochen but also other camps, such as Maine's Eastern Music Camp.

Maddy wanted parents and potential campers to comprehend that NMC was superior to the other camps, but in the early 1930s, no accrediting body separated superior from inferior music camps. Maddy, sure of his camp's excellence above other camps, had sought some sort of national approval for his camp from MSNC in 1929. At that time, MSNC responded, recognized Maddy's accomplishments, and gave his camp its unanimous endorsement. However, the following year, MSNC, agreeing with Dykema's advice, decided to consider additional camps and delayed an endorsement, which disappointed Maddy. MSNC appointed a committee on music camps and made Dykema the chair. Maddy was also placed on the committee, where he and Dykema penned the criteria for music camp accreditation, which included standards already met at Interlochen. MSNC printed these accreditation standards in its 1930 *Journal of Proceedings,* several months before Dykema and his colleagues opened the Eastern Music Camp.

The MSNC assembly delayed action and did not adopt the new standards until 1933. By then the Eastern Music Camp had been established, and Dykema made certain that MSNC accredited both Eastern and NMC. Since, under Maddy's urging, Dykema's committee approved no other camps, the less prominent and less successful music camps were excluded, and many closed. Dykema truly believed that many more strong camps like NMC and Eastern should have been established, but Maddy never wanted any camp to rival Interlochen. According to Maddy, MSNC's accreditation became a boon for NMC, since recruitment of the most talented students rose during the following years, despite the depression.

Eastern closed after the 1935 season, and though prominent music educators tried to revive and reformulate it, Eastern never competed successfully with Interlochen again. In a letter to Marie Maddy, Tremaine wrote that because of the collapse of Eastern, she should aggressively recruit campers from the East.[17]

During the initial camp years, Maddy seemed obsessed with gaining camp accreditation. Some friends believed that Maddy harbored personal insecurities that fed his anger toward the competitive camps. He was defensive about the fact that he had only a ninth-grade education, though he had finally completed his high school work by examination. He feared that his lack of collegiate degrees deprived him of opportunities to advance academically at the University of Michigan and to accomplish his ambitions for the camp. Thus his pursuit of camp accreditation included a quest for personal accreditation for himself.[18]

In 1929 Burnet Tuthill, registrar of Maddy's camp until 1935 and head of the Cincinnati Conservatory of Music, arranged to bestow on Maddy an honorary doctorate from Cincinnati. Tuthill, son of the architect of New York City's Carnegie Hall and an erudite musician, had been the principal organizer and first secretary of the National Association of Schools of Music, higher education's music accreditation organization. While a student at Columbia University, he had studied English and often played clarinet in amateur ensembles with John Erskine, Maddy's benefactor and the future president of Juilliard.

With the Cincinnati honorary doctorate in hand, Maddy was appointed professor of public school music at the University of Michigan. By 1931 he listed himself in the Interlochen promotional brochures as a professor and doctor of music.[19] Maddy enjoyed his new academic and artistic attainments. He began signing his name as Joseph (not Joe) E. Maddy, despite his mother's documented objections. In 1932 his mother was a vibrant seventy-year-old, still driving her own car and working for the county Republican Committee in Wellington, Kansas. *American Magazine* quoted her as saying: "He was baptized *Joe,* and that's his name. Besides, it fits him better."[20]

With academic recognition, Maddy gained confidence to advance his causes on the national level. MSNC was now much larger and more influential. To reflect an increased membership of music teachers and college educators, officials thought MSNC needed a new name, so they changed it from Music Supervisors National Conference to Music Educators National Conference (MENC) in 1934. Maddy captivated the rising MENC leaders and rapidly climbed through the ranks of this invigorated organization.[21] In April 1936, Maddy became the national president of MENC for a two-year term. With his influence extended in music circles, Maddy traveled widely for MENC in 1936 and 1937, always remembering to seek new campers along the way.

After his camp's first season, Maddy decided to increase enrollment by adding students older than high school age. In 1929 he started an alumni division, so that experienced students who had graduated from high school might return for a second summer. Joe was interested in these older students for additional reasons. He needed experienced help to manage the camp, and college-age students were ideal workers. They were committed to his vision, hardworking, and inexpensive. For their part, the students enjoyed their return to Interlochen, where they could renew their friendships, polish their performance skills, and earn a little money.[22]

Fifty-one college students attended Interlochen in 1929, and three insti-

tutions offered credit at the camp. One was Dykema's Teachers College at
Columbia University; another was Tuthill's Cincinnati Conservatory of
Music; and the third was Earl Moore's University of Michigan, which contributed most of the faculty for all three institutions.[23] Maddy appreciated
the credibility given his camp by associations with prestigious colleges. He
continued the college programs in 1930, and he formally named the College Division in 1931.[24]

In 1932 Interlochen's appeal to college students was blunted by competition from other institutions, as college-age summer programs prolifer-
ated across the land. Dykema was busy stimulating programs at the Eastern
Music Camp and in New York City. He even approached Juilliard's John
Erskine, who had just completed a new building near Columbia University
in New York. Erskine was proud of his new building, a sturdy structure
that, after Juilliard moved to Lincoln Center in the 1960s, became the home
of the Manhattan School of Music. Erskine, later recalling Dykema's 1932
proposal, said: "I received a letter from Professor Peter Dykema, the head
of the music department of Teachers College. I had known him for a number of years. He was famous for his audacity. Now he was making the amiable suggestion that since the Juilliard had this fine building, with complete
equipment of Steinway pianos, and since this equipment would be standing idle during the summer, Teachers College would be glad to make use of
it in order to install a summer session." Erskine thought Dykema had originated a splendid idea, but he did not wish to turn his new building over to
another school, so he telephoned George Wedge, the head of Juilliard's theory department, who quickly planned a summer session for the benefit of
Juilliard and not Teachers College.[25]

After 1932, with the coming depression, Teachers College, the Cincinnati Conservatory of Music, and the University of Michigan could not sustain their activities at Interlochen. The camp did not affiliate with a college
or university again until 1937, when Joe persuaded Illinois State Normal
College at Bloomington to organize a college division.[26] The alliance with
Illinois Normal was often troubled. Officials at the college expressed their
disappointment with NMC. Emma Knudson, who was in charge of the Illinois Normal program, wrote to Helen Hollingsworth, Maddy's secretary:
"I'm glad of your assurance that registration will be carried out in better
form. Frankly, you were so close to losing your affiliation last year [1938]
that it was hardly a hair's breadth that saved you. . . . [it is expensive for
Normal, but] our interest in the permanence of anything as fine as National
Music Camp makes that secondary."[27]

Unhappy with his relationship with Illinois Normal, Maddy approached several other universities and colleges. One he sought was Northwestern University. In a letter to John Beattie, dean of that university's School of Music, Maddy boasted that Northwestern would profit greatly from an affiliation with the camp, where approximately one hundred students were seeking college credit. Maddy asserted that NMC offered superior teaching, because Interlochen employed a different teacher for each symphonic instrument, a claim no universities could make. He boasted that NMC employed "musicians of the highest attainment, chiefly principals of major symphony orchestra sections." Making his point, he listed Boris Schwarz and Oscar Zimmerman from the NBC Symphony Orchestra; Vladimir Bakaleinikoff, conductor and former solo violist of the Cincinnati Symphony Orchestra; and Frank Miller, cellist in the Minneapolis Symphony Orchestra. Regardless, Beattie turned Maddy down, and Giddings told Maddy: "Don't depend on Beattie. I know how he stands toward us unless he has changed."[28]

Rejected by Northwestern, Maddy approached his own University of Michigan, with no success. He shared his dejection with Giddings: "The credits at the University of Michigan are definitely off. They gave no reasons,—I could get nothing except that they are 'so involved' that they could not consider any arrangement. I have heard that before. . . . Of course Marie [Maddy's first wife] has been busy—and she can be extremely vicious." Giddings replied: "Too bad about the credits at the University of Michigan. . . . Better not blame Marie wholly. I think Marie has little to do with your troubles at the University. I suspect that they will not take over credits shared by another college."[29]

So Illinois State Normal College continued to direct the college division for five years, through the summer of 1941.[30] Then, in 1942, the University of Michigan became the crediting institution, an arrangement that continued for almost forty-five years.

Lows and Highs

NMC succeeded educationally and artistically in the 1930s, but it hovered on the brink of financial ruin yearly. Maddy had been in debt ever since the camp lost forty thousand dollars in the first year. Bills went unpaid because he habitually overspent the budget for camp activities, buildings, and staff. To meet expenses, he patched together income from gifts, loans, sales, and advertising, and for one year, 1930, he enjoyed money paid by the Columbia Broadcasting System (CBS) for radio broadcasts. Since the beginning, he had collected donation money by encouraging patrons to toss coins into blankets at the conclusion of concerts, and from that first year, he had sold advertising in camp publications and program booklets.[31]

To pay for additional NHSO scholarships, Maddy reallocated funds from tuition paid by campers in the theater or dance programs.[32] In 1930, to attract campers who played wind instruments, he started classes in marching band tactics and drum majoring. To attract singers, he continued the Gilbert and Sullivan tradition with a performance of *The Mikado*. The enrollment that year was a record 286 high school and thirty college-age campers from forty-three states.[33]

The economic depression in the United States reduced the enrollment in 1931, but Maddy continued with ambitious programs, including an opera on a native American theme, called *Lalewela*. While the artistic standards of the camp climbed higher than ever, Maddy's spending seemed out of control. Despite escalating deficits, he increased emphasis on NHSB and the chorus, and he upgraded the health services, hiring Dr. Mark Osterlin as medical director. Osterlin and his wife, Helen, first hired as a stenographer, would play pivotal roles at the camp. Mark was camp treasurer in the late 1950s, and Helen, who became a trustee following Mark's death, made vital contributions to Interlochen's later development, until her death in 1996.[34]

The depression hit hard in 1932, and enrollment at the camp dropped again. But as the camp plunged into still greater debt, Maddy continued to invite top conductors, such as St. Olaf College's F. Melius Christiansen, to upgrade the camp's voice offerings. Maddy also invested heavily in publicity for the camp, in an attempt to regain better enrollments. And though he had documented the camp in pictures from its beginning, he now hired James Larson as the first staff photographer,[35] thus inaugurating the tradition of NMC's rich pictorial history. Maddy supported camp photography throughout his life, and when the academy opened in 1962, he started classes in photographic art.

Boarding bills and building expenses drained camp funds. Then, in January 1932, the camp had surprisingly enrolled only one hundred students for the following summer. This enrollment would not meet the terms of Pennington's ongoing food contract, which guaranteed two hundred boarding campers. Maddy realized that the camp would either have to buy out Pennington or pay him ten thousand dollars for students not enrolled.[36]

Both Pennington and Maddy were strained under the pressure of the depression. But though Maddy had mounting debts, Pennington labored under an even more burdensome bank mortgage on his hotel. Flush with 1930 tuition in 1931, and in defiance of Tremaine's objections, Maddy had bought a parcel of Pennington's land. So, in 1932, knowing of Pennington's need to sell more of his holdings, Maddy brazenly offered him $150,000 for four hundred acres of woodland plus the hotel. Pennington thought the offer was ridiculously low but accepted it anyway. After the deal was complete, the camp's indebtedness rose to $145,000. Maddy quickly secured from individuals promises for a total of one hundred thousand dollars to help retire his new debt, though many well-meaning donors later reneged on their pledges. Maddy pressed his friends to "help buy off Pennington,"[37] and Giddings stepped forward to make his first large investment in the camp by purchasing a thousand-dollar note. Pennington would never collect the full $145,000, and years later, he would finally realize just $103,500 for the land and hotel.

Though heavily in debt, Maddy had made a shrewd purchase. He sorely wanted this new expansion, because he had already been audacious enough to build forty small buildings on the land while Pennington still owned it. Seizing on new promotional opportunities presented by his purchase, Maddy renamed the Pennington Hotel, calling it the Interlochen Bowl Hotel. To bring attention to his augmented camp, he publicized the purchase widely in newspapers and wrote letters to donors, staff, and prospective campers.

> You will be interested . . . that we have arranged to purchase Hotel Pennington and the adjacent property on both lakes (Duck Lake and Green Lake) for the purpose of unifying the project and protecting the Camp. This will materially increase the revenues of the Camp and lower its operating costs.[38]

Unfortunately, purchasing the Pennington property did not lower the camp's operating costs. Tremaine and the other members of the board of financial control were perplexed with the new debt. Before the 1932 season began, Tremaine had lowered the debt from sixty-seven thousand dollars

to thirty-seven thousand, but by September 30, with the Pennington purchase, the camp's obligations skyrocketed. Tremaine presented the members of the board of control with two solutions, neither of which was pleas-
ant for the Traverse City bankers holding loans on the camp. One plan
asked the creditors to sell their note claims at a 50 percent discount, and the
other asked the creditors to accept a 25 percent reduction of the debt, with
reduced interest. Tremaine pointed out to the creditors that refinancing the
loans would recover part of their money, while foreclosure would close the
camp and deprive them of any return on their loans. The bankers each
grudgingly accepted one of Tremaine's plans, and the camp opened with
confidence.[39]

In 1932, with Maddy's purchase of his property, Pennington had
resigned as camp treasurer, but because he was still a major creditor, he
remained on the financial control board. Tremaine replaced Pennington as
treasurer, and Joe appointed Marie, his wife and business manager, as an
officer and secretary.[40] In 1933 Howard Hanson was elected an officer and
director, and the camp's top management remained intact until Joe and
Marie divorced in 1937.[41]

Building maintenance and Maddy's expansion plans erased all of
Tremaine's refinancing gains. Maddy continued to hire illustrious visitors
to the camp, including pianists Guy Maier and Dalies Frantz and violinist
Michael Press. Maddy stepped up his fund-raising efforts to pay for his
1933 Chicago tour, and 320 high school and college campers enrolled,
which was shy of the 1930 record enrollment but better than the previous
two years. But the 1933 tour to Chicago, though a wonderful journey for
the campers, was a crowning economic disaster for the year's budget. In
August, the camp was practically in a state of bankruptcy, with a total debt
of over $145,000 and with only $600 in the bank. Moreover, the camp
anticipated no income until the following June.

Tremaine again went into action. He had difficulty persuading the
financial control board to consider a reorganization plan, because he used
the same argument as before—that the creditors would secure some of
their funds with reorganization but none with a camp closure. Maddy publicized the camp's predicament widely in newspapers and magazines, warning, "Unless financial aid is forthcoming from some source or reorganization is possible, the National Music Camp at Interlochen will pass into
history at the close of this year."[42]

The creditors resented hearing the story again, but Tremaine sought long-term refinancing under terms NMC could manage successfully, no matter how difficult. He finally persuaded the creditors to help the camp, and their five-year notes were extended to ten years, without further payments and with reduced interest rates. The payments on the ten-year Pennington land contract were also reduced. At the conclusion of the negotiations, Maddy was jubilant and quickly returned to fulfilling his dream. Tremaine had saved the camp, and despite the depression, bright spots began to appear. Giddings donated money for construction of a chorus building, and money was donated to build practice cabins in the woods and a mess hall for the boys.

But again, in 1934, the depression deepened, and the tide turned against Maddy. Enrollment dropped precipitously, as only 127 high school and 112 college campers paid the $250 tuition costs. Not anticipating an enrollment drop, Maddy had hired a sterling and expensive schedule of teachers, and he was determined not to let the low enrollments hurt the quality and number of camp programs in either that year or 1935.

In January 1935, A. F. Rebhine, the Interlochen caretaker, discovered a fire that eventually destroyed one of the original cottages in the camp. But typical of a dedicated staff determined to keep the camp in operation, Rebhine helped to rebuild the structure before the camp season opened. To quiet their fears, Tremaine wrote the Traverse City members of the financial control board, advising them that he had reduced the indebtedness to about $133,000. Wrote Tremaine, "All of the creditors have consented to the extension of time and the reduction of rate of interest."[43]

Maddy plunged on that summer. Guy Fraser Harrison conducted sparkling orchestra concerts, and *H.M.S. Pinafore* shone as the Gilbert and Sullivan operetta. The camp offered new classes in visual arts for the campers and classes in opera for college-age students. In tune with Maddy's bold ideas, Frederick Fennell, later the director of the Eastman Wind Ensemble, introduced a course in drum majoring and twirling.[44]

Though the year started optimistically, Tremaine recoiled in July 1935 and told members of the control board that donations to the camp had decreased and that they needed to organize a new fund-raising campaign. The season's loss was more than $7,000, increasing the total liabilities to more than $140,000, about the same as three years earlier. On a brighter side, he could report that assets, including buildings, had now grown to almost $230,000.[45]

Though the camp's financial difficulties during the depression were oppressive, they were not unique. Less tenacious camps disbanded while NMC survived. Furthermore, Maddy was slowly building credibility among his national constituencies. New York's Carnegie Corporation gave one thousand recordings, scores, and books to the camp. The Sousa Foundation contributed the first royalties from John Philip Sousa's march "The Northern Pines."[46]

The year 1936 was good, and Maddy persuaded Walter Damrosch to conduct a concert at Interlochen on August 16. His appearance was warmly received by his fans among the young campers, who had grown up listening to his radio broadcasts. They were particularly moved because they knew that Damrosch would end his NBC career the following year and that this concert would likely be their last opportunity to perform for him.[47]

Maddy increased his programmatic experiments in 1936, initiating accordion instruction under the acclaimed Anthony Galla-Rini. Later, in 1940, after promoting accordion study at the camp for four years, Maddy wrote: "Efforts to introduce the accordion into the symphony orchestra have failed. . . . Its greatest claim for popularity is that it is a portable 'whole band'!" He gradually phased accordion study out of the camp's offerings.[48]

Also in 1936, the American Bandmasters Association (ABA) held its seventh annual convention at Interlochen. With the help of Austin Harding and the University of Michigan's William Revelli, the convention was a great success. At the end of the season, ABA gave NMC the funds to build a camp store. Constructed near the Interlochen Bowl, this building was refurbished many times, as an ice-cream parlor, a ticket booth, and an office building. The building was eventually removed in 1993 and replaced by the Osterlin Garden, built in memory of Mark and Helen Osterlin.[49]

The year 1937 brought Maddy personal and professional challenges. His marriage to Marie broke up, and the separation was painful. Lawyer Fred Cochran, in a letter to Joe, said: "I had rather expected that she would desire to go all over the matter for an indefinite length of time, but from your standpoint, and also from hers, I don't think that would be good. . . . When I get to Ann Arbor I would like to have a talk with you. . . . I am glad the children are not entirely heart-broken. They have my sympathy. In fact you all have. It is a delicate situation. . . . I think the agreement, as made, would stand, and be recognized by the Court as a property settlement, and I doubt if it will do any good for you to undertake much more than the agreement calls for."[50]

Marie had been the hands-on bookkeeper and business manager in the first decade of the camp. She had maintained the books, restrained many of Joe's financial excesses, and gained the confidence of Tremaine. Since Giddings, Tremaine, and Maddy had all depended on her steady oversight of the camp business, her departure strained the relationships among the three.

That summer, with Marie's departure, Joe took on the job of board secretary, aided by his personal secretary, Helen Hollingsworth. Though Tremaine was displeased with Maddy's bookkeeping, the camp survived Marie's absence. Camp enrollment, including the college division, edged above three hundred, and guided by a faculty of twenty-nine, Interlochen presented forty-two programs during the season.

But after a decade of Michigan weathering, the hotel and other living spaces needed repair. The plumbing burst on opening day in 1937. To meet the emergency, Maddy borrowed three thousand dollars on his life insurance, and Giddings lent the camp five thousand dollars. For the first time, Joe hired professional fund-raisers, but their efforts failed. Hoping to help the camp, Burnet Tuthill wrote an article for the *New York Times* in which he said that since the camp had eliminated most scholarships and reduced tuition from three hundred dollars to two hundred to attract more students, Interlochen required donations to meet bond payments. Tuthill's campaign was moderately successful, and at the end of the year, the camp paid ten thousand dollars toward the debt resolution. In a grand finale to the season, Wurlitzer Organ Company gave funds for a new building, called Apollo Hall.[51]

In April 1938, Joe married his second wife, Fay Pettit, a childhood friend. She brought a new perspective and direction to the camp and eventually to the academy. Born two years after Joe, in Monroe City, Missouri, Fay spent her adolescent years in Wellington, Kansas, where she first met Joe. Fay, with her sisters, had played flute on the Chautauqua circuit before World War I.[52]

The 1938 camp enrollment paralleled the previous year's. The legendary Maynard Klein conducted the choruses for the first time, and Maddy hired Carlos Lopez, a Michigan painter, to teach visual arts classes. Though income topped fifty-four thousand dollars, expenses expanded to fifty-five thousand. A financially frustrated Maddy was angry that, for the first time, the Juilliard Foundation did not contribute to NMC. President John Erskine had guided funds to the camp in the first decade, but following a serious automobile accident, he had resigned. The new president, pianist

Ernest Hutcheson, stopped the contributions, so Maddy wrote to him, protesting that the Juilliard, Carnegie, Eastman, and Presser Foundations had previously provided scholarships "through which we were able to obtain proper instrumental balance." He complained, "Last year was the first in which the Juilliard School of Music [sic] failed to contribute toward this fund."[53] Maddy persistently rallied his friends to help, even persuading pianist Percy Grainger to join in asking Hammond Organ Company to provide an organ for the camp, a request that, despite Grainger's fame, Hammond ultimately declined. In another fund-raising project, Maddy offered free tuition to any camper who sold $250 worth of season tickets to NMC concerts.

Grainger remained fiercely loyal to Maddy. In 1939 he lauded NHSO in an interview for *Musical Courier.*

> Again, Dr. Joseph Maddy's National Music Camp orchestra for high school boys and girls, at Interlochen, Mich., gave a most spirited and meticulous performance of Cyril Scott's *Festival Overture,* which I consider the most exquisite recent orchestral composition of the British school. When I heard it played later by one of our leading orchestras, it was hardly to be recognized.[54]

The 1939 season was exciting for the campers. Stewart Bosley and Douglas Ferguson directed a play each week and organized the first drama classes at Interlochen. Lucien Cailliet joined Howard Hanson as a composer at the camp. Students that year included later renowned pianist Seymour Lipkin and future Interlochen board member Charles McWhorter.[55]

But 1939 was a turbulent and difficult year for Giddings and Maddy. Besides settling into his new marriage, Maddy split with Giddings over the future of the camp. Their disagreement had begun in 1938, when Maddy invited Olin Downes, the music critic of the *New York Times,* to visit Interlochen. An impressed Downes invited NHSO to perform at the 1939 World's Fair in New York City. Maddy wanted to accept the invitation, but both Giddings and Howard Hanson believed the undertaking was too expensive.

Maddy was particularly angry at Giddings's opposition, and the tour issue started the first of several disagreements between the two men. They began to quarrel about other plans for the camp. Maddy suggested that they start an elementary camp division, but Giddings objected. "The kids' camp does not appeal to me," said Giddings, who added, "We really must cut somewhere and also get a lot more pupils."[56] Giddings began to insert himself into financial and programmatic planning that had previously been Maddy's domain.

Giddings sought favor with Tremaine, who observed that the business aspects of the camp were out of hand. Tremaine, in turn, raised complaints with Giddings: "Marie Maddy played a much more important part in the Camp's success than either you or Joe realized while you were concentrating on her faults."[57]

Fuel for the fire in the heating relationship was that Giddings, now seventy, retired from his Minneapolis position in 1939 and could devote more time to the camp. He was feeling good about himself because his retirement brought great fanfare and accolades from musicians and educators throughout the country. Minnesota colleagues held parties for him, and the *Minneapolis Journal* of February 19, 1939, published a full-page fake publication roasting him. His friends organized a party for eight hundred people and raised fifteen hundred dollars to build a recreation building at Interlochen.[58]

But Maddy was not pleased with Giddings's new time for Interlochen administration. He sniped at Giddings, saying to Tremaine that, until the opening in 1928, "Giddings hadn't put a nickel into the Camp, and hardly knew what it was all about, except that he was Vice President (because we had to have three officers in order to incorporate)." Maddy began to write revisionist histories of NMC and omitted Giddings's contributions. In these new publications, Maddy refuted the notion that Giddings was a cofounder of the camp. "So far as I can remember Giddings knew nothing about the camp idea until the Dallas meeting, although I might have written him about it," he wrote Tremaine. He added: "As I told you when you were here I want to make this picture book history factual, which will destroy the build-up of TP [Giddings] as *the* co-founder of the camp. One question is still in my mind. Did Giddings donate Giddings Hall [built in 1933], or is the note for $1,750 due him in repayment for it? If he didn't donate it, then we shouldn't give him credit for it."[59]

The feud posed grave challenges for the camp. Maddy soon realized that if his conflict with Giddings continued, the campers, parents, and donors, not fully aware of the issues, would grow unhappy and flee the camp. In a power play, Maddy threatened to resign if the board of financial control did not permit the orchestra to tour. Next, his professional crisis deepened when he learned that he would lose his Carnegie Corporation grant for radio teaching at the University of Michigan and that NBC would cancel his radio program, *Music and American Youth.* Fearing he would lose his University of Michigan appointment, Maddy applied for other college positions, first a teaching position at Michigan State College (now Michigan State University) and then the deanship of Indiana University's School of Music.[60]

Recognizing Maddy's centrality to the camp's success, Tremaine stepped forward to support Maddy over Giddings. Though he had always opposed tours, he said he would back the New York tour and would resign if Maddy were not in charge. Tremaine argued, "There cannot be two heads to an institution or a project." Tremaine put the authority entirely in Maddy's rather than Giddings's hands. Asserted Tremaine: "the Camp would not be half its present size, or have rendered half the service it has, if [Maddy] had followed my [and Giddings's] counsel many times—although it would have been on a more solid basis financially. [Maddy was] the pioneer and creator—I the safety man and helper."[61]

Thus confronted, Giddings was forced to relent. He reconciled with Maddy over the next few months and then reestablished an amicable relationship that lasted until Giddings's death in 1954. Though they overcame their split, Maddy emerged as the dominant figure in the Interlochen story from that time, since he would control the NMC both artistically and educationally. While Tremaine continued to restrain Maddy financially to some degree for the following twenty years, Maddy thrust ahead with new projects even more energetically, bending Tremaine and the trustees to his bidding most of the time. At about this time, Maddy persuaded a Hollywood film company to make a motion picture based on the camp, and within a decade, over Giddings's objections, he expanded the camp population by admitting elementary school children as campers. Maddy's work at the university also improved, as he focused on developing the new educational radio programs in Michigan.

While Maddy now enjoyed the allegiance of most members of the board of control, Tremaine continued to admonish Maddy for his grand schemes. Mimicking Maddy, Tremaine wrote a letter to the board of control saying he should resign as the treasurer "while finances are in a comfortable position." With a backhanded compliment, he recommended that Maddy be the treasurer "so that he may feel a keener sense of financial responsibility."

Maddy thanked Tremaine for the letter, noted that the camp was reducing the debt, and continued with his plans to expand the camp.[62]

In 1940, as the depression abated, Tremaine reduced the camp's indebtedness to $102,000. Additions to the camp faculty that year included Frank Miller, then the prominent principal cellist of Toscanini's NBC Symphony Orchestra. Miller was joined by Chicago Symphony Orchestra conductor Frederick Stock, who, in addition to directing NHSO, keynoted a funding campaign for NMC through several testimonials. Stock wrote: "I never have been at any place in the whole world where young people were so busy as I found them to be at your camp. . . . And such admirable discipline! Discipline of the kind which knows how to give and take, and thus create a desire for helpfulness and co-operation."[63]

In 1940 a department of new dance was created by Hildegarde Lewis, an exponent of Martha Graham. She began with five dancers, practicing in Grunow Hall. By 1945, Lewis would claim two hundred participants in the dance program.[64]

Also in 1940, Joe hired a new secretary, Margaret "Peg" Stace. Margaret, whose father was the editor of the *Ann Arbor News,* became Maddy's first assistant, a position she filled until his death more than twenty-five years later. Prior to 1950, Margaret Stace "did everything." Under Maddy's guidance, she hired people and answered all correspondence, and she even admitted campers until 1956, when Roger Jacobi joined the staff.[65]

The camp financial outlook improved, as Tremaine halved the debt to $47,845 in 1941, despite adding more staff members, such as resident conductor Fabian Sevitsky. With improving finances, Tremaine could say, "The fact that the Camp has made an average reduction of liabilities of nearly $7,000 annually over the past eight years, and has survived through a depression in which many hundred-million-dollar concerns succumbed, clearly demonstrates the inherent merit and vitality of the National Music Camp." Still mindful of Maddy's expensive projects and the remaining debt, Tremaine continued, "Perhaps some of the [note] holders would like to turn in their [notes] as their contribution."[66]

Maddy paused to reflect on the legacy of the camp. He wrote to Tremaine, "Before it is too late we must write the early history of the camp and include the details which have been covered up or lost track of."[67] Still smarting from his confrontation with Giddings, he pondered how to guarantee a long future for the camp. He reasoned that he would need to write articles and give more speeches to connect his earlier vision for the camp to his more recent dreams. Many of NMC's earlier accomplishments were by then recognized traditions both at the camp and in many public school systems, as the camp had evolved new rehearsal techniques used by orchestra and band directors throughout the land. A 1942 article in the *Southwestern Musician* detailed Maddy's accomplishments and lauded the camp's recordings of student performances, particularly the performances of American music.[68] As he proudly considered his personal role in founding NMC, Maddy decided that, with his recognized success, he should now devote more time and energy to promoting what he called good music to a broader public, using NMC as his national forum to democratize music in the United States. Tremaine had assured the financial stability of the camp, and now Maddy could gear up for new battles.

Maddy and Tremaine turned to recordings of symphony orchestras as the best way, besides radio, to educate the public. Tremaine had pioneered in education through recordings, and in 1916, before he knew Maddy, Tremaine had organized a national program, called the Music Memory Contest, to promote recognition of classical music. On both local and national levels, the contest required high school students to compete with one another in identifying segments of classical music on recordings. The contest proved an immediate success, prompting Tremaine to leave his family's Aeolian Company to establish the National Bureau for the Advancement of Music, a nonprofit support company for the contests.

In 1917, when the Music Memory Contest began, the recording industry was still in its infancy. The Columbia Phonograph Company was producing only condensed versions of single movements of symphonies, most recorded under Walter Damrosch, and only this type of recording was available to the contest participants.[69] In 1918 Tremaine found his Music Memory Contest venture successful, and he addressed MSNC to gain the music educators' support for his contests.[70] Within five years of its beginning, the Music Memory Contest swept the country, and by 1926 the contest was held in more than a thousand cities. The contest became so effective that Tremaine extended it to foreign countries in 1936. The Music Memory Contest became the most broad-based national project for music appreciation in the years before World War II.[71]

By the summer of 1939, building on the increasing popularity of recordings, staff at the *Washington (D.C.) Star* conceived of a new project to promote classical music. Their goal was to democratize good music and give joy, comfort, inspiration, and love of good music to every family in America, regardless of position, circumstances, color, or creed. To launch the project, several series of complete symphonic recordings, each produced on three or four double-faced twelve-inch records, were sold in stores for less than what customers would expect to pay for a single record. The inexpensive distribution of the records was made possible through the cooperation of orchestras, conductors, and recording companies.[72]

The staff of the *Star* asked MENC, under Joe Maddy's leadership, to organize the project and name it the National Committee for Music Appreciation, and Maddy headquartered the campaign at Interlochen. Only the recording musicians received payments for the project, as recording industry personnel waived their royalties and profits to support what Maddy called "America's growing taste for good music."[73] Tremaine's National Bureau for the Advancement of Music provided mailing addresses of amateur and professional musicians to help publicize the campaign. Newspapers in several cities arranged the distribution of the recordings, and according to newspaper articles, record sales increased by 50 to 300 percent in stores in Washington, D.C.[74]

In 1940, as the project grew, Maddy recruited Juilliard's John Erskine to head the National Committee for Music Appreciation. In September, Erskine spoke to more than fourteen hundred musicians, artists, and well-known business people at a dinner for the committee at the Waldorf Hotel in New York. He announced that a series of records of the opera *Carmen* would be sold without profit in department stores on the following Saturday. But soon after the dinner, several participants told Erskine they disliked Maddy's arbitrary procedures for selecting the music for future distribution. Though he thought the recordings were excellent, Erskine grew concerned that Maddy was keeping the origin of the recordings secret from the public, since the record labels omitted orchestras' and conductors' names. Record dealers also began complaining that the project spoiled their sales of records at full price. Erskine, greatly troubled, confronted Maddy with the unhappy reactions of their supporters. Following a series of conferences with Maddy, Erskine and other members of the committee resigned, and the highly publicized project ended.[75]

Thwarted on the national level, Maddy turned to international music circles. In the summer of 1940, Maddy organized an Interlochen conference to discuss the growing Pan-American movement to promote classical music. Following the conference, Maddy's old mentor Will Earhart named him to a new State Department advisory committee on inter-American music. In his acceptance speech, Maddy asserted that music, more than any other field, afforded the best means of surmounting the language barrier among nations. At these international meetings, he solicited Latin-American music leaders to visit Interlochen, shrewdly recruiting students from their countries to attend NMC.[76]

The "Mighty Monarch of the Air"

Though the first network broadcast of an NHSO concert originated at MSNC's Chicago convention on April 18, 1928, Maddy claimed that part of NHSO's concert at MSNC's 1926 convention had been broadcast locally over radio station WWJ in Detroit.[77] The Chicago broadcast, over NBC's Blue Network, headlined conductors Frederick Stock of the Chicago Symphony Orchestra, Howard Hanson of the Eastman School of Music, and Joe Maddy. Guy Maier was the featured piano soloist. Sixty-six music educators from across the country selected some three hundred outstanding high school musicians to participate in the event. At the conclusion of the broadcast, NBC permitted Maddy to read a promotional announcement for his new National High School Orchestra Camp, which would open the following July. Later, Maddy observed that the publicity from the broadcast had promoted the camp more than anything else he did.[78]

Maddy sensed that radio would become one of the most compelling forces for music in his lifetime, for the medium was already attracting audiences in the big cities of the East. By 1926, about five and one-half million homes contained radios, and listenership grew rapidly because of the reach of the first national radio networks. At that time, most stations in the country still broadcast with low power, so radio receivers needed to be located within a few miles of a transmitter. In December 1926, NBC launched the first radio network, the Red Network; it was followed a month later by the Blue Network, which took up symphony concerts in its programming. Within a year, the CBS radio network was created. A year and a half later, with the first NHSO broadcast over the Blue Network, Maddy tapped into this resource to further music education overall and the camp in particular.[79] The new networks exerted a profound and lasting influence on music and the other arts in America, programming concerts with opera stars, instrumental performers, and symphony orchestras.

Before 1926, the quality of radio sound had often been unpleasant for listeners because most radio receivers were homemade, battery-powered crystal sets, requiring earphones. Finally, in 1926, about half the newly sold sets ran on electricity and featured external speakers. These greatly improved speakers helped to popularize symphony orchestras and other ensembles that could exploit the richer sounds now attainable over the air. Producers needed to broadcast music from on-site locations, since the quality of recorded music remained unsatisfactory for a few more years. Thus the larger stations broadcast live dance orchestras, symphony orchestras, and operas from hotels and concert halls.

Maddy always planned to broadcast concerts from Interlochen. In anticipation, he had built a radio room, a small backstage booth in the newly constructed Interlochen Bowl. But he was unable to arrange broadcasts in either 1928 or 1929, so the booth went unused until CBS aired the first radio series from Interlochen on July 6, 1930.[80]

By the time of the Interlochen broadcasts, CBS was three years old and had acquired fifty-three affiliates. Its New York station had recently increased power substantially, so listeners as far away as forty miles from the transmitter could hear NHSO. Throughout the country, about six hundred radio stations then reached 40 percent of the American population.

Early in 1930, Earl Hadley, representing the maker of Majestic radios, had approached Maddy with a plan to sponsor eight weekly NMC programs over CBS. Besides production costs, Hadley's company would pay the camp sixteen thousand dollars for program broadcast rights. Maddy knew Hadley, because, as a salesperson, he had previously sold Cable pianos to the camp in 1928 and 1929.[81] Maddy hesitated at first, because broadcasting over CBS would break his three-year ties with NBC, wherein the Blue Network had broadcast all NHSO conference and tour programs. But CBS had begun to compete with NBC for prestigious educational programming, such as the 1930 National Education Association Convention. The CBS offer proved very attractive, and NBC made no counteroffer, so Maddy switched his allegiance from NBC.

Eight NMC concerts became part of an existing summer broadcast series called *Majestic Theatre of the Air,* sponsored by the Grigsby-Grunow Company, maker of Majestic radios. These CBS Interlochen concerts were among the first classical music programs broadcast from an outdoor auditorium, so the producers encountered special acoustical problems. They were familiar with CBS headquarters, where audiences were separated from the performers, who were in soundproof studios. But the Interlochen Bowl had no sound isolation. Microphones picked up audience chatter, which was sometimes pleasing, but the engineers had to place the microphones judiciously so that the outdoor noise would not overpower the musical ensembles. The radio engineers struggled to balance several microphones, but faulty feedback screamed into the radio signal. Finally, the sound engineers used just one microphone to pick up the performance of a whole ensemble. Fortunately, by 1930 focused and clear ribbon microphones had replaced both the carbon and the condenser microphones of the 1928 NHSO Chicago broadcast. Though the quality of broadcast sound was still poor by modern standards, the engineers in 1930 resolved many microphone placement problems in ways that remain unchanged to this day.

A logistical dilemma also surfaced at the first Interlochen broadcast. Since the camp programs included several large ensembles, crews were pressed to move these groups on and off the stage throughout the program. The Bowl's stage was large, about one hundred feet wide and forty-five feet deep, and moving ensembles on and off involved actions that stage crews had to accomplish swiftly, silently, and efficiently. In addition, something had to occur over the air while the stage crew made changes. Maddy suggested solo performances by individual students broadcast from the radio room he had built on the Bowl's stage in 1928. The CBS producer, saying that the room was not soundproof, preferred a musical interlude originating from the CBS studios in New York. Maddy compromised and accepted both solutions, and he eventually built a new, soundproof room for his student soloists.

The program on July 6, 1930, began at 7:00 P.M. From the CBS studios in New York, an announcer declared that NHSO was "the world's largest orchestra." From Interlochen, Ray Erlandson, CBS announcer and director of *The Majestic Hour,* continued:

> In the Majesty of motion
> From the boundless Everywhere
> Comes the magic name Majestic
> Mighty Monarch of the Air!
> Ladies and Gentleman;—The Majestic Hour.[82]

NHSO played first. Then the program switched to the New York studios, where radio personality Redfern Hollingshead sang an operetta aria, accompanied by a studio orchestra. After the stage crew had quickly changed the setup, the signal returned to Interlochen for an NHSB performance. Next, according to Maddy's wishes, camper Reinhardt Elster played a xylophone solo in the cubicle at the back of the stage. Because that radio room was still not completely soundproof, the stage crews had to concentrate and move the chairs and stands quickly and quietly. The live broadcasts prodded the stage crews to be nimble and precise, and today Interlochen's stage crews are still models of efficiency at musical performances.[83]

The successful transmission of the program took the cooperation of the American Telephone and Telegraph Company and the CBS technicians. Technicians at Interlochen listened to the New York inserts and beamed the distant program to the audience in the Bowl. The producer then cued the Interlochen orchestra conductors and announcers by voice announcements heard by everyone over the air. The music signal was picked up by microphones in the Bowl and relayed by telephone to Cadillac, Michigan, where it was amplified and sent to Grand Rapids, from there to South Bend, Indiana, and ultimately to a main telephone circuit for the fifty-three stations in the CBS network. Understandably, the quality of the broadcast sound diminished considerably by the time it reached the ears of the listeners, but loyal camp fans responded with letters of appreciation and marveled that they could hear the student performers broadcasting from the remote forest of northern Michigan. Little more than a decade after the nation's first radio station was licensed in 1920, Interlochen had begun a twelve-year tradition of weekly radio concerts transmitted from the camp.

Maddy also reaped some extra money from his first broadcasts. Using some of William Grunow's sixteen thousand dollars, Maddy remodeled an assembly hall built by Willis Pennington in 1926 and renamed it Lois Grunow Memorial Hall.[84] In 1939 a portion of Grunow Hall was fashioned into a studio and control room for a radio workshop. Refurbished several times over the years, Grunow Hall has been used continuously for music, visual arts, radio workshops, dramatic presentations, and various other classes, so students of all disciplines fondly recall Grunow Hall. CBS's Mike Wallace, once a radio workshop participant, has said that he and his friends referred to a weathering Grunow Hall as "Grungy" in 1939, but the hall remained in use until it was condemned in 1997.[85]

In the second season of the camp broadcasts, in 1931, CBS and Majestic radios dropped the camp programs, and NBC took up the broadcasts, which were now noncommercial. Maddy persuaded NBC to broadcast the concerts for eleven years. This was a coup for Maddy, because more stations had affiliated with NBC than CBS and, further, because NBC was wealthier than CBS. Maddy was grateful to NBC, and he later attributed good camp enrollments during the depression years to camp promotion on the broadcasts.[86]

The NBC programs preserved the same format as the CBS programs of 1930, when large ensembles were interspersed with small ensembles. Maddy did secure one change, however, in that all performances emanated from Interlochen rather than sharing the broadcast with a singer and ensemble in New York City. Maddy's original glassed-in radio room at the back of the Bowl was replaced by a control room built four feet behind the back of the stage, thus allowing better isolation and performing conditions for the small ensembles. Oliver Reihl, program director from Chicago's NBC station, wrote the following description after the opening broadcast in July 1931.

> This is the point where Mr. Eichorst and assistants and equipment step in to make some adjustments. Let's step back to the control room. Briefly, he reproduces and reduces in size faithfully and accurately, the tonal picture we have just heard in front of the bandstand to conform to the size tonal picture which would nicely fit into your living room at home.[87]

To conclude the opening 1931 broadcast, conductor and composer Howard Hanson presented to the camp a musical excerpt of fourteen bars from the second movement (Andante con tenerezza) of his Symphony, no. 2, op. 30 (Romantic), for use as a broadcast theme song. At twenty-four, Hanson had become the first American to win the prestigious Prix de Rome for music composition. Three years later, after his studies in Italy, he became the director of the Eastman School of Music, and in 1928, at age thirty-one, he had conducted NHSO at the Chicago MSNC convention. Hanson loved the camp, and with the exception of the union boycott years, he returned to Interlochen almost every season until just before his death in 1981.[88]

Hanson's haunting theme has taken on special significance for campers, because it was performed to open and close each Interlochen broadcast over the next decade. When the network broadcasts ended, the Hanson theme continued as a tradition at Interlochen, and ever since, camp ensembles have played or sung the theme to close every major orchestra, band, and choir concert. Thus it is often performed several times daily in the summer, and every performance is followed by silence in the audience, though sometimes with a "Shhhh!" to curtail clapping from the uninitiated.

The *Romantic* Symphony had been commissioned three years earlier by conductor Serge Koussevitzky for the fiftieth anniversary of the Boston Symphony Orchestra. Hanson began composing the symphony in April 1928 and finished it in July 1930, doing much of the work in an Interlochen cottage overlooking Green Lake. In those early years, the campers' cabins were inland, and the lakefront cabins housed Maddy, donors, and distinguished visitors, such as Hanson. Gazing out a wall of windows in his cabin, Hanson credited his view of beautiful, tree-lined Green Lake as inspiration for the theme of the second movement, so he was moved to present a portion of it to the camp as a heartfelt testament to his feelings.[89]

NBC executives considered the 1931 broadcasts so successful that they gave Interlochen a long-term commitment to broadcast eight concerts each season. In all subsequent camp seasons through the summer of 1941, NBC broadcast a total of 127 programs. NBC announcer William Kephart opened each concert by saying, "From the shores of the twin lakes Wahbekaness and Wahbekanetta comes the music of . . ."[90] The campers, because of the broadcasts' prestige, competed vigorously to play on these programs.

The popularity of the NMC broadcasts grew until just before the outbreak of World War II, when live broadcasts began to fade from all network radio schedules. Maddy savored his camp's inclusion in this golden age of live classical music broadcasting. Then, abruptly in 1942, live music radio programs ceased when a nationwide labor dispute erupted between the musicians' union and the networks. Because of the dispute, recorded music programs, interspersed with newscasts, replaced live concerts in all radio schedules, both locally and over the networks. The labor dispute eventually grew to such tragic proportions that Maddy was unable to schedule NMC broadcasts over NBC again until 1961, twenty seasons later.

The potential for educating children through radio had gripped Maddy, and he wanted radio to be in his personal future as well as in the future of his new camp. In 1926 he had explored radio for music instruction, experimenting over Detroit's WWJ in conjunction with his classroom teaching at the University of Michigan. Earl Moore, his university supervisor, warmed to Maddy's radio ambitions and agreed to assign him to radio instruction. When Alexander Ruthven, the university's president, released Maddy from classroom teaching duties in 1930, he and Joe agreed that part of Maddy's mandate would be teaching music over radio. The following year, Joe started the University of Michigan Broadcasting Service, and as his first project, he taught band and orchestra classes over WJR in Detroit, where he eventually expanded the classes to include vocal instruction and even a popular hymn course.

To tune his skills, Maddy appealed for help from his collaborators at the national radio networks. Knowing them well by 1935, he persuaded NBC's Franklin Dunham to join the camp's advisory committee. In the following year, Dunham engaged Maddy to teach instrumental music nationally over the Red Network. By 1937 Maddy had brought his musical desires, his radio teaching, and his MENC ambitions together into a frenzied climax. The University of Michigan appointed him professor of radio music instruction in the extension division. He had just been elected president of MENC, where he praised radio in his inaugural speech. Commencing a two-year term with MENC, he traveled widely, conducting all-state, regional, and national high school orchestra festivals. He supervised school band and orchestra contests, and whenever possible, he arranged his NBC broadcasts to highlight these events. Above all, during his travels, he recruited students and promoted NMC.[91]

Between 1938 and 1940, glowing with the success of his MENC presidency, Maddy produced an NBC noncommercial program called *Music and American Youth*. Each program originated in a different city. During the program, Maddy asked that instrumentalists join in performance with the radio orchestra. In this way, Maddy spotlighted the achievements of school bands, orchestras, and choral groups in various parts of the country.

In 1938 Maddy asked NBC producer William Dow Boutwell to establish a radio workshop at NMC. In this workshop, Boutwell taught classes in script writing, program planning, direction, and production, and for the first time, he asked students to announce the camp's NBC broadcasts.[92] Boutwell imported several professionals, such as NBC's musical director, Rudolf Schramm, to staff the new radio courses, but he also recruited less experienced radio engineers as technicians.

Among this young technical crew was twenty-three-year-old Jerome Wiesner. Wiesner was assistant director of radio at the University of Michigan, where he recorded music and sound effects for Maddy's educational broadcasts. Maddy had always encouraged the technicians in their radio experiments at both the camp and the University of Michigan, where he provided the latest and best recording equipment available. Wiesner stood out from the other technicians because of his demand for excellent productions. Later he embarked on a brilliant career, first as an acoustical engineer at the Library of Congress, then as a professor at and eventually president of the Massachusetts Institute of Technology. Quite famous at MIT, he took a leave to serve as special assistant on science and technology for President John F. Kennedy.

The camp's radio workshop was expanded in 1939 to include radio drama. Blevins Davis, supervisor of NBC's *Great Plays* series, organized the workshop schedule, and professional actors Stewart Bosley and Douglas Ferguson joined the radio faculty.[93]

At the 1938 workshop, Wiesner, foreseeing the loss of commercial network broadcasts, suggested that university radio stations band together to form an educational radio network. A concerned Maddy agreed and asked W. W. Charters, head of educational and radio research at Ohio State University, to head a conference contemplating such a network.

In the fall, Maddy persuaded Michigan's governor, Frank Murphy, to host the educational radio conference in Michigan. During the sessions, Wiesner argued that commercial networks were now offering dwindling airtime for educational programming and that to preserve instructional radio, educational stations would need to collaborate with one another. He suggested that by pooling resources, each station could produce programs that all stations could share. In his presentation, Maddy extolled government support for an educational network but warned that commercial stations would lobby against any plan for tax-supported educational radio.[94] Though the conference rallied the educational stations, the initiative for a network failed at that time because the stations could not agree on future procedures. Maddy would persevere anyway, and ten years later, educational stations finally formed a network and restored many of Maddy's instructional programs.

In 1940 NBC canceled future broadcasts of Maddy's educational radio program, *Music and American Youth.* Neither NBC nor CBS would continue to sustain the cost of instructional radio. NBC also curtailed most other noncommercial programming, and Maddy's colleague Franklin Dunham left NBC.[95]

Disappointed but undeterred, Maddy was forced to concentrate on radio instruction in the state of Michigan, where the university named him acting director of broadcasting. He still produced concerts at both the camp and the university, but his programs were now local, rather than network, broadcasts.

The Hard-Boiled Canary

Joe Maddy, always alert to positive stories about youth in America, was stirred by *Boys' Town,* a critically acclaimed motion picture of 1938, starring Spencer Tracy and Mickey Rooney. The film about a school for disturbed boys in Nebraska had earned an Academy Award for Tracy and a special citation from the Academy of Motion Picture Arts and Sciences for Rooney, who was honored for "bringing the spirit and personification of youth to the screen."[96] Maddy determined that Interlochen should be able to garner the same recognition for wholesomeness and spirit. NMC was now well established, and he reasoned that a major motion picture based on the camp program could help him recruit students and sponsors, so he wrote MGM studios in Hollywood to suggest such a film. The request came to the attention of Lester Cowan, an independent producer, who responded to Maddy with an invitation to meet and talk about going forward with the project. Maddy was planning the tour of the camp orchestra to the New York World's Fair in the summer of 1939, so Cowan arranged to see Maddy at that time. When Cowan and Maddy met in New York, the orchestra and its nine-year-old conductor, Lorin Maazel, were being feted by Mayor Fiorello La Guardia.

Maddy and Cowan rapidly came to an agreement to make the picture, and Cowan offered to pay NMC five thousand dollars as an honorarium. Maddy, though, wanted assurance that the picture would show off the camp in the best light, so he secured an agreement giving him the right to approve the story. Maddy was listed as the cofounder of the camp in the agreement, but at the time, he was in the midst of his feud with T. P. Giddings, so Giddings was not part of the agreement and was not a character in the film.

As Maddy looked at the first script, he realized that a love story, central to the film as it was being developed by the writers, created a problem for him. The predicament was that the first script, written for Deanna Durbin, then revised to suit Mickey Rooney and Judy Garland (the most popular stars of the time), included a romance between two high school students at the camp. Maddy was distressed at the thought of a potential romantic encounter among his young campers. He was further chagrined that the plot included scares involving wild animals.

Since Maddy was sure that real-life parents of his campers would not approve, he rejected this story. Cowan then devised a new story line that featured the Maddy character as the romantic lover. Maddy was appalled, saying it was bad business for the director of the camp to be romantically involved. Maddy rejected this script, too, and insisted that the romantic parts be confined to adults other than himself.[97]

Finally, Cowan decided to create a fictitious character named Michael Maddy, who would be Maddy's son and the principal lover in the film. Making Michael a main character seemed agreeable since, according to Maddy, Allan Jones, who eventually played the son, refused to take the part of Michael Maddy if he were not the most important person in the movie. The final plot centers around Toodles LaVerne, a young girl working in burlesque in New York. LaVerne, played by Susanna Foster, must leave New York because the police have raided the burlesque show. Michael Maddy, about to take over the camp during Joe Maddy's illness, comes to the girl's aid by enrolling her at NMC. When Michael Maddy meets camp accountant Sylvia Worth, played by Margaret Lindsay, they portray the love story that troubled Maddy in the first scripts. With minor reservations, Maddy finally approved this story.[98]

In the movie script, Cowan made the Joe Maddy character older and "on the shelf." The Maddy character, played by William Collier, Sr., was to be an old grouch, a characterization not very pleasing to Maddy. In the movie, NBC's music critic Deems Taylor, playing himself, explains over a radio broadcast that Joseph Maddy is "temporarily ill" and that his son will replace him as director of the camp during his illness. The elder Maddy's infirmity lasts throughout the film, so Collier makes just two brief appearances. Maddy approved these episodes, reasoning that nearly every audience would "contain one or more of my friends" and that they would understand why he sanctioned the script.[99] Maddy succeeded in getting two of his favorite subjects into the opening broadcast scene. First, Taylor lauds NMC, and second, he comments that more phonograph records are sold for classical music than for popular music.[100]

Producer Andrew Stone, a veteran director of many Hollywood comedy films, reworked the script into a musical for Paramount Studios and hired a popular song composer, Ann Ronell, to write the music and lyrics. Maddy admired Ronell's work, particularly one original song written for the Interlochen movie, "Fireflies on Parade." Stone contracted Jones and Foster, who had been featured as the lead singing actors in an earlier movie, called *Life of Victor Herbert,* to star in the film.

Maddy was to be the technical advisor, but Stone, fearing Maddy would cause more trouble over the script, kept him away from the filming. Maddy recalled that his job drew a good salary for doing "absolutely nothing except staying away from Hollywood while the picture was being made."[101] Surprisingly, Maddy was not offended, because he believed that Stone was already burdened with managing temperamental actors and maintaining a somewhat true-to-life story. Maddy wanted Stone to produce a film complimentary to the camp, so he did not object to being left out. Nor did he seem to mind being portrayed as an old grouch, if that pleased Stone.

Cowan proposed that the picture be made at Interlochen while the 1940 camp was in progress. Maddy was aghast and complained, "My boys and girls come here to study music, not to be motion picture extras."[102] To meet Maddy's objections, Stone shot the film at a camp in Lake Arrowhead, California, and substituted the Peter Meremblum Junior Symphony Orchestra of California for NHSO. The scenery does resemble the wooded atmosphere of northern Michigan, but those who have attended Interlochen will notice a few differences: the girls in the movie wear jumpers instead of knickers, and the stage of the film's Interlochen Bowl is framed by Greek columns rather than by the actual shell made of pine logs.

A written announcement at the beginning of the film declares, "The children in this picture actually performed the musical numbers as shown." Five young actor-musicians—a singer, a pianist, and three violinists—play themselves in the movie. Most prominent is Heimo Haitto, a Finnish conductor, whose appearance in 1941 would have evoked for the movie audience the memory of the young conductor Lorin Maazel, the conductor of the camp orchestra during its tour to New York in 1939. The featured student violinist, Patricia Travers, enjoyed a concert career in the early 1940s. The pianist, listed as Dolly Loehr in the film, became a popular film star named Diana Lynn. She costarred with Ginger Rogers and Ray Milland in *The Major and the Minor* in 1942. None of the actor-musicians, though, were Interlochen campers.[103]

Four opera stars perform in the grand finale of the movie. In the story, the NMC students tour to New York to appear at an opera house called the Manhattan Opera Company. The film concludes with a vocal competition between the opera cast, headed by Richard Bonelli and Irra Petina, and the Interlochen students, led by Jones and Foster.

The movie was originally entitled *Interlochen*. After the picture was completed, the title was changed to *There's Magic in Music*. But before Paramount released the picture, Susanna Foster demanded that the title be altered to focus on her part, which highlighted the arrogant New York girl who raged into the rural Michigan woods. To placate her, the movie was renamed *The Hard-Boiled Canary*. Paramount mounted an extensive promotional campaign using the new name. A flyer promoting the film declared, "Wait'll you thrill to her one-kid invasion of the famous music camp at Interlochen."[104] Allan Jones was unhappy with a title that referred to Susanna Foster instead of to himself, but the studio distributed the film with the new appellation nevertheless. Maddy was also troubled, and he sided with Jones, observing, "In show business top billing is the all-important thing, and Jones had a right to kick."[105]

In early 1941, Paramount released *The Hard-Boiled Canary* in two metropolitan areas, Dallas and Los Angeles. After the first showing, Maddy's friends in music education, music clubs, and women's clubs in both Dallas and Los Angeles wrote letters to Paramount Studios protesting the title as uncomplimentary to the reputation of the camp. Paramount was besieged with complaints and withdrew the picture shortly after its opening. The studio immediately returned to the earlier title *There's Magic in Music* and began a new advertising campaign. To help with this promotion, Maddy asked friends in the National Federation of Music Clubs to sponsor openings of the picture in several cities. A completely new premiere took place in Atlantic City in May 1941.[106]

Maddy thought that Stone did a superb job and that the picture, replete with good music and light comedy, achieved a complete triumph in promoting NMC. Interlochen reaped extraordinary publicity from the movie, attracting students who had not known about Interlochen before, although some campers probably arrived hoping to see Doric columns in the Interlochen Bowl, as depicted in the picture. The publicity proved critical, because when World War II broke out six months after the movie's opening, the number of potential applicants for the camp dwindled.

The movie was a moderate financial success, and Maddy was sorry he had not secured a more lucrative agreement for the film. The triumph of *Boys' Town* had generated a sequel, and Maddy hoped his movie would spark corresponding interest. But there was no sequel. Though the movie is now known only to film-history buffs, students in the first years of the Interlochen Arts Academy recall viewing *There's Magic in Music* twenty years after the movie was made.[107]

Part 4

Swan Song for Free Music

The more free music the radio stations program, the fewer professional musicians will be needed.

—James Caesar Petrillo

I think we owe it to America to break Petrillo's dictatorship over American music.

—Joseph E. Maddy

James Petrillo and the Musicians' Union

In 1928, while preparing for his very first NHSO broadcast, Maddy had his initial confrontation with James Petrillo, then president of Chicago's Local 10 of the American Federation of Musicians (AFM), the musicians' union. This encounter was the beginning of a lifelong feud between the two men, occurring just when broadcasters and record producers were starting to experience disagreements with professional musicians, a situation that accelerated because the musicians feared losing their jobs to recordings and radio performances. For the next thirty years, Maddy and NMC would play a pivotal role in a labor-dispute drama that reached the Supreme Court. The consequences would be startling for public music education, professional musicians, and the labor movement in the United States.

Maddy was a longtime member and supporter of AFM, which he joined in 1909, several years before Petrillo joined. At age eighteen, Maddy had become a member on his appointment to the Minneapolis Symphony Orchestra, just thirteen years after professional musicians organized the union in Indianapolis. Maddy had always championed AFM and was a friend of Joseph Weber, the national AFM president, so he resented Petrillo's interference with the students' broadcasts.[1]

Petrillo would not approve the April 18, 1928, NHSO broadcast. He believed that the employment of amateur musicians, particularly for radio broadcasts, took jobs from members of AFM. Then, two days before the scheduled broadcast, Petrillo phoned Maddy to say that he would be able to broadcast the NHSO concert if MSNC employed a professional standby orchestra of fifty union musicians at twelve dollars per player.[2]

Maddy considered these featherbedding conditions draconian. He was particularly disturbed because he had already notified parents and friends about the broadcast and knew that listeners would gather around their radios to hear the children play. Rather than facing their disappointment and his humiliation, Maddy, with Giddings's concurrence, agreed to pay the cost of the professional musicians from their own school funds. However, because of his anger at Petrillo, Maddy told Giddings that he would announce the union's conditions during the concert broadcast. When officers of MSNC heard about Maddy's plan, they were not pleased. Most officers were themselves members of AFM, and they did not want to create a public fuss over the confrontation. The officers agreed that MSNC would pay the six-hundred-dollar fee if Maddy would cancel his announcement about the AFM conditions over the air. Grudgingly, Maddy acquiesced to his colleagues, but he never forgave Petrillo for marring his first radio program.[3]

In the spring of 1930, the Grigsby-Grunow Company offered to sponsor eight radio programs in a series called *The Majestic Hour*, over CBS. Maddy appealed for approval to President Weber and the national office of AFM, then traveled to Boston to appear before the AFM International Executive Board, where he proposed to pay a seventeen-piece union orchestra in New York for each broadcast so that the camp could accept this engagement. The union granted the permission, with the understanding that no precedent was established. On each program the announcer stated, "This program is presented in cooperation with the American Federation of Musicians in the interests of living music." Since the camp was paid sixteen thousand dollars for the series, Maddy felt he could accommodate this arrangement with AFM.[4]

Maddy began to bristle at the intrusion of the CBS union orchestra into his student broadcasts, so when the Grigsby-Grunow Company canceled a prospective second year of programs from Interlochen, Maddy immediately sought and secured a noncommercial radio series over NBC. Maintaining that the musicians' union had no right to demand standby orchestras, Maddy fought Petrillo and advocated noncommercial radio for the rest of his life. Though other opportunities to broadcast commercial radio programs from Interlochen arose over the years, none materialized until after Maddy's death, when relations with AFM improved. The 1931 NBC series was very successful for both the camp and NBC, and major concerts from the camp continued to be broadcast continent-wide for eleven seasons. Weber and most of the leadership of AFM remained untroubled with this arrangement in the early years of NMC broadcasts.[5]

In Chicago, however, Petrillo was distressed about Maddy's arrangements with the national union. He and Maddy confronted one another a second time in 1933. Maddy, representing MSNC, took charge of the music education programs for the Century of Progress Exposition, the Chicago World's Fair of 1933. As a condition, Petrillo's Local 10 required that a large union band play throughout the fair. For his part, Maddy featured student groups from throughout the country. Taking advantage of his MSNC position, Maddy had scheduled his campers to perform for the fair at the conclusion of their Interlochen summer. But late in the spring, fair officials suddenly canceled the union band and all other music programs because of looming financial difficulties. Helped by this situation, Maddy expanded the number of performances by his nonpaid students. Petrillo, not to be completely outdone by Maddy, secured a paid engagement for his union musicians at the final event of the fair. This time, Maddy and Petrillo met in harmony in a musical finale. But the fair set the stage for bitter fights during the following years.[6]

In 1936 Maddy arranged for classroom orchestras from across the country to play on his noncommercial program *Music and American Youth,* broadcast over NBC's Red Network. The school orchestras demonstrated the achievements of school music groups in various sections of the country. Each program originated in a different city, and most local AFMs in each city were cooperative and demanded no standby musicians. But during the entire three winters when Maddy conducted *Music and American Youth* from NBC's Chicago studios, Petrillo required the network to pay the union twenty-five dollars whenever a pupil played a few notes over the radio. Furthering his humiliation, AFM member Maddy was treated as a nonunion musician by Petrillo, who forced NBC to hire a standby union music director.[7]

James Caesar Petrillo was born in Chicago on March 16, 1892, five months after Joe Maddy. As a boy, Petrillo studied the trumpet at the Hull House Settlement School of Chicago, founded by the legendary Jane Addams. As a teenager, he played in the *Chicago Daily News* Band, and he led his first dance band at age fourteen. In 1914, at age twenty-two, he was elected president of the American Musicians Union in Chicago, a rival union to AFM. When he was defeated for reelection in 1917, he joined AFM, rose through the ranks, and became president of the Chicago AFM Local 10 at age thirty. Petrillo then gained prominence on the national AFM board, and on the retirement of President Weber in 1940, Petrillo became president of the national AFM. He remained national president until 1958, when he returned to head the Chicago Local 10 until his retirement in 1962. He died in Chicago on October 23, 1984, at age ninety-two.[8]

Petrillo was very popular with the vast majority of the AFM membership. Throughout his eighteen-year presidency, the membership voted overwhelming support for him and his proposals. Had he wished to remain, he could have continued as national president beyond 1958. Under his leadership, AFM increased both the income of professional musicians and the number of jobs available to them, well beyond their greatest expectations. Because of Petrillo's relentless negotiations with the executives of the radio and recording corporations, many performing musicians earned full-time wages for the first time.

Petrillo was driven to find more and better jobs for his musicians. He believed that without union pressure, the recording and broadcasting industries would replace live musical performances with records whenever possible. So, with his power, he pressed radio stations and networks to hire a union-determined number of musicians to perform live on the air. Unlike Maddy, Petrillo believed that amateur musicians, including school band and orchestra members, were taking jobs away from his union members, and because many radio stations refused to pay his members, he believed he should stop school organizations from performing on radio.[9]

In the two years after his 1940 election to the national presidency, Petrillo enrolled thousands of new musicians into AFM, particularly in the field of popular music. Shortly after his election, he also began wooing the most celebrated classical musicians. Many of Maddy's colleagues joined, including Howard Hanson, who wanted to maintain a professional conducting career. Petrillo's crusade to recruit all major symphony orchestra members finally culminated when members of the Boston Symphony Orchestra joined the union in November 1942.[10] The increased number of members now gave him the power to press both the recording and the radio corporations for better jobs, working conditions, and wages for performing musicians.

Maddy experienced Petrillo's emerging power in the summer of 1941. With the help of NMC instructor and renowned composer Ferde Grofé,

Maddy had persuaded Paul Whiteman to bring his famous seventeen-piece jazz band, expense free, to Interlochen for a performance on July 11. Students were excited because NHSO was to join Whiteman's band in an NBC broadcast of George Gershwin's *Rhapsody in Blue* and Ferde Grofé's "Mardi Gras" from the *Mississippi Suite* (Grofé was notable for orchestrating the original Gershwin *Rhapsody* for its New York premier). The Whiteman concert, the first to feature jazz at the camp, was well publicized, and Willis Pennington joined other prominent Interlochen citizens in praising Maddy for adding jazz to the summer concerts.[11] Unfortunately, the Whiteman concert proved to be the last camp concert emphasizing jazz until after Maddy's death.

Three days before the scheduled concert, Petrillo notified Whiteman that he could not donate his service or the services of his band. Maddy offered to pay union scale for the band's services, including the broadcast fees. Petrillo responded with approval of the performance, but he insisted that the camp pay the Whiteman band members three times the union scale for the broadcast. Petrillo also demanded that he receive a personal copy of the contract, to guarantee the arrangements. Unable to pay Petrillo's fees, Maddy appealed to his friends on the AFM International Executive Board to reverse Petrillo's demands, but each board member agreed that the decision was Petrillo's. Maddy lost the fight, and though the Whiteman band and NHSO performed as scheduled, NBC did not broadcast the concert.[12]

NBC, Petrillo, and Maddy were all dejected with the outcome of the Whiteman broadcast incident. From Maddy's point of view, the Whiteman broadcast was of educational benefit for the campers, but for Petrillo the concert exploited union musicians, who, he believed, ought not perform on radio with the nonunion campers. Petrillo then demanded the cancellation of Interlochen's remaining 1941 broadcasts. NBC, shocked by Petrillo's last-minute interference, pleaded that commitments for the Interlochen broadcasts had been completed and that Frederick Stock, esteemed conductor of the symphony in Chicago (where Petrillo headed Local 10), was to be the featured conductor in the concluding broadcast of the camp season. Not wanting to offend Stock, Petrillo relented and approved the remaining broadcasts in 1941, with an understanding that NBC would reopen negotiations with the union before scheduling NMC broadcasts for the 1942 season.[13]

Though Stock was featured at Interlochen in 1940, 1941, and 1942, his most memorable camp concert was the 1941 broadcast, for it was the last live NBC broadcast from Interlochen and drew a large crowd. The *Traverse City Record Eagle* glowingly reported, "Several hundred people, comprising the largest audience to visit the National Music Camp for a single performance since the starring of the late John Philip Sousa, attended the special concert at the Bowl last night."[14]

The 1941 camp season marked the end of an era. U.S. involvement in World War II commenced the following December, the University of Michigan took over the camp's College Division (later named the University Division) in the summer of 1942, and the radio industry changed significantly, altering Maddy's professional career and the camp's future broadcasts. Following NMC's season of 1941, the Federal Communications Commission (FCC) ruled that a single company, such as NBC, could no longer own more than one network. To comply with the FCC ruling, NBC kept its Red Network but sold the Blue Network. Edward Noble purchased the Blue Network two years later, and after another sale in 1945, it was renamed the American Broadcasting Company (ABC). During these changes, noncommercial educational radio, pioneered in part by Maddy and NBC, vanished from the airwaves.

Yet the 1942 NMC opened with Maddy believing that the NBC camp broadcasts would continue. Producers and technicians prepared for the first July broadcast, and Petrillo, on his part, thought that NBC would negotiate the 1942 broadcast season with the AFM board. But NBC chose not to initiate any negotiations.[15]

On July 10, 1942, Petrillo notified NBC that AFM would not authorize the broadcast of the first camp program on the following day. Moreover, the union would not allow NBC to broadcast the remaining programs of the Interlochen season. On the night of the first scheduled broadcast, and without an announcement over the air, an NBC studio orchestra program directed by Leopold Spitalny was substituted for the NMC concert.[16]

An angry Maddy telephoned his friends and colleagues in the union, seeking to overturn Petrillo's command. However, many colleagues disagreed with Maddy or would not speak openly against Petrillo's decision. One told Maddy, "Of course we do not favor the banning of broadcasts from Interlochen, but we dare not say so in public for fear we will be thrown out of the union."[17] Maddy aroused the indignation of the campers, and they wrote letters to Petrillo, appealing for a change in his decision and asking his reasons for banning the broadcasts. In response to

Maddy's entreaties, teachers at the camp and educators across the country spoke out against the union's action, saying it discouraged children and hindered music education without benefiting the professional musician. Maddy even invited Petrillo to visit Interlochen to see the campers in action, but Petrillo did not respond.[18]

Despite Maddy's efforts, AFM abruptly terminated all live network broadcasts from Interlochen, and no major network would ever again broadcast a similar series from Interlochen. NMC was Petrillo's first and most important target in his plan to halt broadcasts of other student organizations in the 1942–43 school year. In the fall of 1942, Petrillo and AFM forced the cancellation of high school band broadcasts in Chicago, Cleveland, Washington, Milwaukee, St. Louis, and San Francisco. The union also compelled the Cincinnati Conservatory of Music's student orchestra to terminate its ninth season of broadcasts over CBS.[19]

But when AFM canceled the Eastman School of Music's student broadcasts, Howard Hanson, who was conducting at Interlochen when Petrillo canceled the camp broadcasts, advised a different response. Hanson urged every student to join the union, after which AFM approved all subsequent broadcasts of the Eastman ensembles.[20]

Most schools were forced to end their broadcasts. The Juilliard School of Music (now Juilliard School) alone was unaffected by the cancellation of broadcasts, since the Juilliard orchestra aired over WNYC, a noncommercial radio station in New York City that did not recognize AFM's authority.

Petrillo and AFM blocked efforts to broadcast national programs from Interlochen for almost two decades. Stock and Hanson were the last professional conductors to direct Interlochen concerts in a series on network radio. The battle line between Maddy and Petrillo was drawn, and a distraught and furious Maddy wrote:

> It matters little whether we broadcast again from Interlochen. But it is of the utmost concern to every American that the use of radio—the greatest avenue of communication and culture ever devised by man—shall not be denied our children—and their children—and their children's children.[21]

Petrillo's prohibition of student broadcasts was part of his comprehensive plan to improve the lot of AFM musicians. On August 1, 1942, less than two months after canceling radio broadcasts from Interlochen, AFM called a strike against both the broadcasting and the recording industries. Claiming that radio and recordings were earning huge profits, Petrillo demanded more jobs and better salaries for members of his union. AFM declared, "members of the American Federation of Musicians will not play or contract for recordings, transcriptions, or other forms of mechanical reproductions of music."[22] By striking both radio and recordings, AFM brought the music entertainment industry to its knees.

Before the strike, many radio administrators had not acknowledged the union or engaged in collective bargaining. In fact, when stations or the networks aired educational and cultural programming as a community service, the producers rarely paid the musicians. Stations would often use AFM musicians to avoid the costs, hassle, and notoriety of confronting the union, but the union was not the official labor representative for the musicians. Through their strikes, Petrillo and AFM gained recognition and higher earnings for performing musicians, and the membership showed its gratitude by supporting Petrillo in protracted strikes and negotiating sessions.[23]

NBC, Interlochen's broadcast network, proved the most formidable adversary for the union. At the time of the strikes, NBC was the largest, wealthiest, and most popular network. CBS was a strong second, followed by the new ABC and, finally, the Mutual Broadcasting Company. Over the following two years, each network signed an agreement with AFM. NBC, the last to bargain with the union, finally signed an agreement on November 11, 1944, and joined the other networks in broadcasting live music. Simultaneously with the broadcast ban, AFM had prevented recording companies from making phonograph recordings and transcriptions using union musicians. Then, also in the fall of 1944, the recording companies came to agreement with AFM. The union won most of its goals, including better pay, more jobs, and a prescribed number of musicians to be paid for each radio program and recording.[24]

Petrillo wanted to stop all nonunion musicians from securing broadcasting jobs. The union granted few exceptions, usually when stations employed standby musicians. In December 1940, near the beginning of his AFM presidency, Petrillo had once prevented the army bands from performing on radio, though, under government pressure, he finally relented and declared that radio stations could hire army bands if no studio musicians lost their jobs. With the force of the AFM strikes, Petrillo expanded his demands.

The Interlochen controversy stirred a debate about whether or not non-commercial broadcasts would be subject to closed-shop rules, according to which all radio musicians must belong to the union. NBC and AFM had such a closed-shop agreement, and Petrillo thought that the distinction between NBC's commercial and noncommercial radio broadcasts was irrelevant to the union's goals of increasing musicians' jobs and wages. He sought to protect professional musicians from amateur intrusions anywhere, and he reasoned that since the number of weekly broadcast hours was fixed, union musicians would get fewer hours of work if the networks allowed the Interlochen campers to perform during any of those radio hours. Petrillo argued that music was already an overburdened profession and that in some of the locals, unemployment had reached 60, 75, or even 90 percent. He declared, "it's easy to understand that the more free music the radio stations program, the fewer professional musicians will be needed." If the trend continued, he complained, campers would choose not to become professional musicians, because they would find themselves in a starving profession. He predicted that ten years later, the campers, as professionals, would resent Interlochen students for taking their "bread and butter under the guise of educational purposes."[25]

The union's stopping of the Interlochen broadcasts crushed not only Maddy's plans for the camp but also his attempts to revive his recording project for the National Committee for Music Appreciation, since symphony orchestras could no longer make records for distribution. Because of the strike, teachers were deterred from using recordings in the classroom, and promoters of concert music were paralyzed.

Following the union's ban of transcriptions and recordings, NMC was besieged with requests to make recordings and transcriptions of performances by the camp musicians. Maddy dismissed these requests, saying that Petrillo's canceling of broadcasts by school bands and orchestras was unrelated to his forbidding union musicians from making transcriptions and recordings. Maddy was unwilling to take any action against what he believed were the best interests of the union musicians. He supported the union in this case, stating publicly that he was in complete sympathy with the efforts of AFM to obtain maximum employment for its members and that he himself had been a union member in continuous good standing for thirty-five years. For twelve of those years, he had earned his living as a professional musician, playing violin, viola, and clarinet in symphony orchestras. He had also played saxophone in a leading dance orchestra in Chicago.

Maddy may have resented Petrillo's ban on Interlochen broadcasts, but he agreed with Petrillo's desire to gain more jobs and better salaries for his professional musicians.

Maddy's anger in the Interlochen matter was focused on Petrillo's assertion that the campers took jobs from AFM musicians. Maddy believed that noncommercial broadcasts with students deserved special consideration, and he contended that no radio stations or networks hired amateur musicians to avoid paying AFM musicians. He challenged Petrillo to cite one instance where banning Interlochen and other school music groups from the air had resulted in a "single dollar of additional income to a member of the musicians' union."[26] Maddy argued that with the exception of the first season on CBS, Interlochen concerts had always been noncommercial programs for which the network and affiliated stations received no income, and since a standby orchestra was always in the New York NBC studios for all Interlochen broadcasts, there was no basis for Petrillo's claim that the Interlochen broadcasts interfered with employment of union musicians.

Maddy also disputed Petrillo's claim that all members of AFM were professional musicians. Moreover, Maddy observed that membership in the union was no guarantee of musicianship or performing ability, since the union admitted anyone who was willing to pay the initiation fee and dues. He claimed that there were no permanently unemployed *good* musicians and that many members of the musicians' union did not expect or wish to obtain full-time employment through musical performance. According to Maddy, the number of good musicians was similar before and after Petrillo was AFM president, so banning school music from the air would not change the number of good and bad musicians in AFM.

In a massive campaign against Petrillo, Maddy spoke to service organizations and wrote articles proclaiming that the Interlochen broadcasts were serving a national cultural need. He reported that music educators' organizations and union musicians from three states had adopted codes of ethics so that student musicians could perform on radio. Following this assertion, Petrillo, together with the AFM Executive Committee, overruled the codes in Ohio and New York by prohibiting student broadcasts from the Cincinnati Conservatory of Music and the Eastman School of Music.

In 1944 Maddy directed his campaign to the U.S. Congress, asking representatives to regulate AFM so that the union would not monopolize radio over what Maddy called the "public welfare in music education." As he said, broadcasting was similar to city streets, which are used for commercial purposes by taxi drivers and for noncommercial purposes by the general public. If taxi drivers forbade the general public to drive on the streets of the city unless they joined a taxi union, the public would be in a position similar to the amateur broadcaster during the strike of the musicians' union.[27]

Petrillo's argument about the irrelevance of commercial versus noncommercial radio did not seem to succeed with the public or the government, so he began a new tactic. Asserting that Interlochen was in a different category from other educational institutions, he declared that NMC was a commercial enterprise. Petrillo stated that Interlochen, by charging tuition, was "squarely on a commercial basis" and that the radio concerts were used to advertise and attract more students. He explained that children in public school bands and orchestras receive their tuition free, while children at Interlochen paid $275, plus additional fees for private lessons and other items, for a period of eight weeks. He further declared that radio advertisers paid musicians and all other participants a salary for advertising their commodities; thus the same rule should apply to NMC.[28]

Responding to the accusations, Maddy countered that charging tuition did not make Interlochen any more commercial than colleges or universities that charged tuition. NMC was legally a nonprofit educational corporation, exempt from taxation by either the state of Michigan or the U.S. government. He cited the camp's affiliation with the University of Michigan, which supervised many instructional programs. Furthermore, he said that ever since 1939, the Michigan state legislature had recognized the camp's nonprofit status and had appropriated funds for activities at NMC. And guest conductors, such as Frederick Stock and Walter Damrosch, he continued, had been conducting NHSO without fees because the camp was nonprofit.[29]

In 1943, to quell any legal objections that might jeopardize the NMC's nonprofit status, Maddy and his staff reconstituted the camp's board of control and board of incorporation, officially reincorporating them into one new board of trustees. The officers remained the same. Joseph Maddy was president, T. P. Giddings was vice president, and Charles Tremaine was treasurer; in addition, staff members George Mackmiller and Margaret Stace were elected assistant treasurer and assistant secretary. Other members of the new board included Ohio State University's head of educational and radio research W. W. Charters; Franklin Dunham, then chief of radio at the U.S. Office of Education; Joseph Herbert, a prominent lawyer on the board of trustees at the University of Michigan; and Judith Waller, NBC public affairs representative from Chicago.[30]

Dunham replaced Howard Hanson on the board at Maddy's request. Not only had Maddy been upset by Hanson's contrary response to Petrillo, but he had also grown tired of Hanson's lack of attendance at board meetings, where the conductor, when he did attend, seemed to believe, according to Maddy, that "he should look wise and say nothing." Maddy had been greatly perturbed when Hanson had burned a hole with his cigar into a legal document that Maddy's secretary, Helen Hollingsworth, had sent Hanson to sign. According to Maddy, Hanson had not even apologized but instead had suggested that Hollingsworth should save the now valuable document and have it framed.[31]

To fight his battle with the union, Maddy enlisted the help of Senator Arthur Vandenberg of Michigan, a staunch supporter of NMC. Vandenberg's daughter, Betty, had attended the camp and starred as a piano concerto soloist, playing for President Hoover on the 1930 NHSO tour. Senator Vandenberg persuaded James Lawrence Fly, chairman of FCC, to write to Petrillo on July 22, 1942, requesting information about the Interlochen broadcast cancellations. Petrillo answered Fly in a lengthy letter, which he also published in *International Musician,* the monthly magazine of the union, and distributed to the national press associations. In his response, Petrillo wrote that he resented Maddy's calling him a "czar," because the entire AFM membership, at their 1941 convention, held in Seattle, Washington, had voted for the broadcast ban against Interlochen. Contradicting Maddy, he said that the union had always supported school musicians, as evidenced by AFM members instructing high school bands and orchestras in "thousands of schools across the nation."[32]

Maddy was ecstatic to have gained this public forum, so he encouraged FCC to investigate Petrillo's charge that Interlochen was commercial. As Maddy hoped, the FCC investigation declared NMC a nonprofit educational institution. According to FCC investigators, camp tuition barely covered expenses for the eight-week camp season, and the camp continued to pay for original construction costs, maintenance of buildings and equipment, insurance, and interest on indebtedness. Maddy thought he had defeated Petrillo on the commercialism issue.

In August 1942, Vandenberg introduced and the U.S. Senate passed a resolution to begin a Senate investigation of AFM. It was one of the first congressional investigations of any American labor union, but despite congressional pressure, AFM maintained its ban on student orchestra broadcasts.[33]

At Vandenberg's urging, Thurman Arnold, head of the U.S. government's antitrust division, initiated an injunction against AFM in October 1942, citing the union's strikes against the radio and recording industries. To sway the court, Arnold recounted the union's prohibition of broadcasts from Interlochen and other music schools, thus stressing the union's damage to school music programs in the United States.

Arnold derided the union's musician quotas for each radio station, and he berated AFM for forcing radio executives to hire only AFM members and standby musicians. He explained that networks and stations refusing to comply with the union encountered three pressures. First, he said, AFM's most popular musical organizations could not play for noncooperating networks or stations. Second, union studio musicians could not play for stations that did not comply with union demands. And third, the union could strike, with costly results for the radio industry.[34]

Joseph Padway, lawyer for AFM, countered effectively that "prohibiting the union from boycotting employers using amateur performers would encourage the use of free labor in competition with paid labor." He contended that public policy had always supported paid labor over free labor or even prison labor. In a forceful rebuttal, he quoted the Norris–La Guardia Act of 1932, which declared that a court could not issue an injunction in a labor dispute, and he claimed that AFM and the radio and recording industries were clearly in a labor dispute.[35]

The hearing was highly publicized. In the end, Padway convinced the court that the Interlochen broadcast ban was a labor dispute, and the judge dismissed the lawsuit in November 1942. Petrillo and the union had won all legal points. AFM prevented NBC's broadcasting from Interlochen. AFM could also strike a network or a record company over union wages, hours, or working conditions, and AFM could insist that radio stations employ more AFM members where, in the opinion of the union, a sufficient number were not employed.[36]

Despite the AFM victory, Maddy's publicity campaign had stirred the public against Petrillo. The furor over the Interlochen broadcast ban was intense in the fall of 1942. The camp's publicity office tallied the publicity and found that the ban had spawned 2,283 news items across the country. Newspapers and magazines had published 462 editorials, seventeen cartoons, nineteen feature stories, 180 pictures, and forty-five letters to the

editors. To Maddy, the flood of public indignation against the ban of Interlochen broadcasts was "indicative of the attitude of the people of the
United States toward the curtailment of the freedom in broadcasting." Still,
Maddy was bitter over the loss of the Arnold case. He wrote, "No man can
deny that this ruling is in direct violation of the law governing radio broadcasting, which states that all broadcasting should be in the public interest,
convenience and necessity."[37]

Again, Maddy turned to Vandenberg and other friends in Congress. But
they said that nothing could be done to restrict Petrillo, and they advised
him to compromise and come to a reasonably satisfactory arrangement
with Petrillo, as Howard Hanson had done.

Maddy balked. He would not talk with Petrillo and said that he was not
interested in a "reasonably satisfactory arrangement." He noted that
Chamberlain and Hitler had worked out a reasonably satisfactory arrangement at Munich, with fatal results. Maddy preferred never broadcasting
educational programs over seeking permission from Petrillo or "any other
dictator."[38]

Though Maddy was outraged, the issue soon died down with the public,
who accepted the decisions of the court. Then, a year later, Petrillo miscal-
culated. He was so confident of his winning position that he gloated in
International Musician: "However, when all the shooting was over and we
came to the summer of 1943, there was no Interlochen high school student
orchestra on the air. Nor was there in the year 1943 any other school band
or orchestra on the networks and there never will be without the permission of the American Federation of Musicians."[39]

Maddy, hoping to revisit the ban issue, responded quickly by mailing
Petrillo's statement to Vandenberg and the U.S. Senate Committee on
Interstate Commerce. Offended by Petrillo's arrogance, a Senate subcom-
mittee convened and invited Maddy to appear before the members on
March 20, 1944. Senator Clark of Idaho chaired the meeting, and Senators
Vandenberg and Ferguson of Michigan, McFarland of Arizona, and Tun-
nell of Delaware attended. Maddy was accompanied to the subcommittee
meeting by Interlochen board member Joseph Herbert, a Manistique,
Michigan, attorney and prominent Republican regent of the University of
Michigan. With this meeting, Herbert and Interlochen lawyer George
Burke began many years of battle with AFM.[40] But at his death in 1956,
Herbert had not witnessed the end of Maddy's dispute with the union.

Just prior to the Commerce Subcommittee meeting, hoping to keep pressure on Petrillo, Maddy marshaled the forces of MENC to adopt the following resolution at their St. Louis convention in March 1944.

> While we are in sympathy with the aims of the American Federation of Musicians in its efforts to obtain maximum employment for its members, we do not recognize the claim that the American Federation of Musicians or its officers have the sole right to determine who shall be allowed the use of the air waves in broadcasting. We, therefore, urge adoption of an agreement or code of ethics between the Music Educators National Conference and the American Federation of Musicians which will permit the continued development of music education to whatever extent such development does not result in actual loss of employment to members of the American Federation of Musicians.[41]

Petrillo was very irritated with this turn of events, because, while he was winning with the radio networks and the recording companies, Maddy and other music educators had become troublesome with their appeals to Congress. Unbending, however, Petrillo continued to oppose the educators' resolution, and when MTNA met later that year in Chicago, he prevented student performances at the convention headquarters, even though the performances did not replace services of union musicians.

NBC signed an agreement on the union's terms on November 11, 1944, ending the last network strike and gaining ground for Petrillo. With the agreement, union musicians secured new jobs at excellent salaries in network and local radio. At the same time, Decca, RCA Victor, and Columbia Records each yielded to AFM and agreed to pay the union between one-quarter cent and five cents for each issued recording. Professional musicians could record again and could earn good money in an expanding industry. Because of this record agreement, the union received more than four million dollars from the recording companies in the year following the agreement.[42]

Because his strike tactics were so successful financially, the AFM membership lavishly praised Petrillo, rewarding him with reelection each term until he chose to retire in 1958. His support from appreciative members of the union was broad and enthusiastic, for he had led them to prosperity and respect in less than five years. Members were finally treated as professionals, and work was plentiful.

But Maddy did not give up. In the fall of 1944, he persuaded Vandenberg to introduce a bill in the Senate that would prevent the union from stopping noncommercial broadcasts featuring students. In December, the Vandenberg Bill (S. 1957) passed in the Senate but died in the House of Representatives. Vandenberg was not to be denied, though, and in the next session, he introduced a similar bill that passed in the Senate on January 15, 1945. Following quickly on this bill's passage, Congressman George Dondero of Michigan introduced a companion bill in the House of Representatives on January 22. Maddy's relentless attacks on Petrillo during the congressional hearings were about to pay off.

Passage of some form of anti-union legislation seemed inevitable in 1945. Striking out against Maddy, Petrillo persuaded the AFM leadership to place Interlochen on the National Unfair List. This list included all organizations and promoters for which union musicians were not allowed to work. The list also included musicians who had performed for these organizations or promoters and thus were banned from union employment. *International Musician* posted the following notice in its February issue.

Re: National Music Camp of Interlochen, Michigan

The National Music Camp of Interlochen, Michigan, has been placed on the National Unfair List of the American Federation of Musicians. This action was taken by the International Executive Board at its meeting in New York, N.Y., on January 19, 1945, due to the fact that the National Music Camp through its officers has adopted means and methods and indulged in activities highly detrimental and antagonistic to the Federation.

Under the laws of the American Federation of Musicians its members are prohibited from rendering services for anyone or any establishment on its National Unfair List. This of course means that members cannot teach, coach, conduct or play an instrument etc. at the National Music Camp of Interlochen, Michigan.

Members will therefore govern themselves accordingly.

Leo Cluesmann,
Secretary, A. F. of M.[43]

Maddy was traumatized. The camp had been founded on a policy of hiring professional union musicians to work closely with the students. Now, engaging prominent conductors, such as Hanson, Grofé, and Whiteman, came to an unanticipated end. Celebrities such as Walter Damrosch, Edwin Franko Goldman, and Ossip Gabrilowitsch could not have come to NMC had the union acted in this manner a decade earlier. Even Maddy, who was a member of the union in good standing, could not now conduct at the camp.

To complicate matters, many of his friends and associates presently became critical of Maddy's tactics with Congress. Many musicians who had worked at the camp in the early days supported Petrillo instead of Maddy, citing the financial and professional gains they attained under Petrillo. Burnet Tuthill, NMC's former registrar and the executive secretary of the National Association of Schools of Music, wrote to Maddy: "Why not talk things over with Petrillo instead of 'defying his wrath.' We who have to be in the Federation would also like to be back at Camp some day and fighting alone won't solve the problems."[44] But Maddy had made the fateful decision, and the camp could no longer host union musicians.

Interlochen and the Lea Act

Petrillo's methods of negotiating, particularly in wartime, increased public resentment not only toward AFM but also toward the parent American Federation of Labor (AFL) and all unionism. Maddy, the radio executives, and the record company owners attacked Petrillo's actions relentlessly, so that eventually the public was aroused against the musicians' union, and Congress increased its scrutiny of AFM.

Representative Clarence Lea of California, chair of the Committee on Interstate and Foreign Commerce, began investigative hearings on AFM on February 22, 1945. Petrillo defiantly refused to attend or to send a union representative. The hearings dragged on for months, continuing until after World War II ended on September 2, 1945. On November 19, 1945, the Commerce Committee reported favorably on what became known as the Lea Act.[45]

The Lea Act, remembered also as the "Anti-Petrillo Law," was passed by the Senate, then signed by President Harry S. Truman on April 16, 1946. The act thwarted many of Petrillo's recent initiatives, so the union could no longer compel radio executives to

1. employ a prescribed number of persons;
2. pay fees when union persons were not hired;

3. pay more than once for a previously produced broadcast;
4. pay for performances not broadcast;
5. remove noncommercial educational programs from the schedule;
6. remove programs produced outside the United States from the schedule.

The Lea Act also prohibited the union from

1. requiring station or network fees to broadcast records;
2. restricting the production of recordings;
3. requiring additional payments for extra broadcasts of recorded programs.[46]

The passage of the Lea Act affected not only AFM but also other labor organizations, such as railway and coal workers' unions. Other unions could no longer engage in featherbedding or in required hiring, so Petrillo's counterparts in AFL were also enraged at Maddy and Interlochen. Petrillo's hatred of Maddy deepened as the new sanctions against AFM took effect.

During the 1945 camp season, though prevented from hiring union musicians for the camp, Maddy defiantly conducted NHSO himself. Early in 1946, AFM ordered him to appear before its International Executive Board to show why he, a member of the union, had conducted at NMC, which was on the National Unfair List. Though Petrillo did not participate in the hearing, the union board expelled Maddy.

Maddy wrote to Giddings:

> Yep, I'm out. I'm no longer a musician, which gives me a feeling of freedom at last. The 'trial' was a farce of course and almost turned out to be a trial of Petrillo. Of course that is what it really was—in the public judgment, which is what I went to Chicago for. My lawyer, George Burke, tangled with Padway and two other AFM attorneys and we got the best of it—which means nothing unless we should get into court sometime when the transcript of the fake trial will prove damning to AFM.
>
> I get heaps of fan mail and congratulations every day. This fight is making friends for NMC in a big way. Also some cash. About $2,300 has come in in donations this winter—about enough for the two

class-practice buildings. Am going to Interlochen Saturday to drive stakes in the snow. The sawmill is working and we will have lumber enough for the dormitories but plumbing material is very scarce. It will be another scramble and I hope we will be able to handle the crowds. Enrollments come in in gobs—10 a day for awhile.[47]

Petrillo would not accept the restrictions of the Lea Act and, after checking with Padway and the AFM International Executive Board, he decided to test the act's constitutionality. As the first test in his plan, he demanded that radio station WAAF in Chicago hire three additional musicians. The station refused, and consequently AFM called a strike. Other labor unions lined up with AFM, and AFL, at its convention of 1946, voted to support AFM in fighting the Lea Act.

As expected, the national government and WAAF sued AFM for violating the Lea Act. At the U.S. District Court in Chicago, the government charged that AFM was a racketeering organization that extorted millions of dollars from the radio industry. But Judge Walter La Buy ruled in Petrillo's favor, declaring the Lea Act unconstitutional. Feeling vindicated, Petrillo was euphoric.

The government then appealed the case directly to the U.S. Supreme Court. In a dramatic reversal, the Supreme Court overruled the district court on June 23, 1947, upholding the Lea Act in a five-to-three decision and giving Maddy what he thought was his final victory. Though deflated, Petrillo accepted the court's ruling, saying, "The Supreme Court has spoken, and I bow to its dictates."[48]

Maddy's jubilation at the latest decision would prove to be premature. On May 14, 1947, three weeks before the Supreme Court ruling, Representative Carroll Kearns, chairman of the House Subcommittee on Education and Labor, convened a meeting to investigate AFM. Because he was a member of AFM and a former music educator, Kearns seemed uniquely qualified to resolve the schism between the union and music educators. He was also a skilled negotiator and conciliator. This meeting in Chicago included George Jennings, director of the Chicago Board of Education's FM radio station; NMC secretary Clyde Vroman; NMC lawyer George Burke; and Maddy.

At the meeting, Maddy sought to strengthen his case against Petrillo. To both outwit Petrillo and gain Kearns's goodwill, Maddy invited AFM member Kearns to conduct NHSO two months later. When Kearns said he might accept the engagement, Petrillo fumed and threatened the representative with AFM expulsion if he conducted at Interlochen. Not wishing to be a point in the battle between the other two men, Kearns declined Maddy's invitation.[49]

Kearns held his subcommittee hearing on July 6, 1947, three weeks after the June Supreme Court ruling. The evening before the hearing, Kearns invited Maddy to speak with him. Maddy was pleased, because he understood from the talk that he would be the key witness against Petrillo on July 8.

But on July 8, just prior to the time scheduled for Maddy's appearance, Kearns called Maddy to say that Petrillo had made concessions. Under an agreement with Petrillo, Kearns would negotiate terms between the union and all music educators. He assured Maddy that the terms would include union reinstatement for both Joe and the camp. Emphasizing that the Petrillo negotiations were delicate, Kearns requested that Maddy not issue any press releases antagonistic toward Petrillo.[50]

Kearns scheduled a meeting of the involved parties for July 22, to consider a joint code of ethics between the union and music educators. Maddy felt vindicated, because he had proposed just such a code in 1936, when he was president of MENC. During his term of office, he had made improved relations between union musicians and music educators a stated goal; a national code of ethics would finally clarify the relationship.

A decade earlier, MENC officers had fostered greater cooperation between music educators and AFM by asking union representatives to address the MENC national conventions. As MENC president, Maddy claimed to have helped Joseph Weber, Petrillo's predecessor, settle several misunderstandings between union musicians and school music groups. Urging a spirit of cooperation in 1936, Maddy had proposed a national code of ethics patterned on agreements between local unions and educators in several states, noting that his friend Will Earhart had secured the first state code, in Pennsylvania in 1935. In June 1937, armed with this MENC-approved ethics code, Maddy had met with the AFM International Executive Board in Louisville, Kentucky, where he had proposed that the two organizations agree jointly to protect union musicians from competition with school musicians.

In Maddy's proposal, the field of entertainment would be the province of the professional musician. Students could perform in school events, community educational programs, charity performances, and broadcast demonstrations, but no student concert could usurp the rights and privileges of local professional musicians.

Following the 1937 meeting, the union had sent Maddy a telegram stating that the national AFM would take no action on the code and that the relationship between union musicians and music educators would be determined by the local unions. According to Maddy, board member Petrillo, not yet president, had pushed for this decision. After this national rejection, state music educators in Ohio and New York, copying Maddy's agreements, adopted codes with local unions. Though revised many times, these state codes endured over a decade, and Maddy was proud of his role in devising them.

Because of his background in writing these codes, Maddy looked forward to Kearns's meeting, where he could help to create a new national code. But despite writing assurances to the contrary, Kearns did not invite Joe to the meeting. Those in attendance, besides Petrillo, were the officers of MENC and Superintendent W. H. Lemmel of Baltimore, representing the American Association of School Administrators, the third organization to co-sign the code.[51]

The group came to an agreement on a code of ethics that closely resembled Maddy's proposal of ten years earlier, but the relationships of NMC and Maddy to the union were ignored. On July 23, 1947, the press quoted Kearns as saying that he "did not believe Interlochen to be strictly an education institution and therefore not within the scope of Petrillo's lifting of his broadcast ban."[52] The words clearly reflected Petrillo's position, which Maddy thought Kearns had repudiated.

Enraged, Maddy released a statement to the press on July 26, 1947: "Petrillo has nothing to do with allowing us to air our music. Congress passed the Lea Act prohibiting the union from interfering with any non-commercial broadcasts by education institutions and this law was upheld by the Supreme Court on June 23, 1947. Any attempt to give Petrillo credit for graciously allowing school children to broadcast is merely whitewash." Unfortunately, according to Maddy, some papers substituted the word *eyewash* for his *whitewash,* and Kearns, in turn, became angry at Maddy.[53]

Maddy and Kearns telephoned one another several times over the next days, seeking to patch their public argument. During these conversations, Maddy concluded that Kearns's settlement with Petrillo would not help Interlochen. Frustrated, he turned again to Senator Vandenberg for help. The senator obliged by issuing a statement on July 28, 1947.

I hope the Supreme Court and the subsequent Petrillo consideration means that Interlochen is once more a free American community. ... Any notion that it is not strictly educational in concept and operation is fantastically wrong.[54]

Kearns was offended. He disapproved of the press release and resented even more that Maddy had gone publicly to Vandenberg, possibly undermining Kearns's negotiations with Petrillo. Not wanting to provoke Kearns further, Maddy decided to follow the representative's advice. He swallowed his pride and sought peace with Petrillo. On August 10, 1947, he wrote a letter to Petrillo, saying, "May I extend a personal invitation for you to be our guest at the final concert [at Interlochen] on Sunday, August 17." To help secure the peace, Maddy asked Charles Tremaine to write a similar invitation to Petrillo. But either because of fury or because he thought he had won the negotiations, Petrillo did not respond to either Maddy or Tremaine.[55]

MENC and Petrillo scheduled a meeting in Chicago on September 20, 1947, to formalize the proposed code of agreement between the educators and the union. Fearing he would be left out, Maddy pressed his longtime friends, the MENC officers, for an invitation to the meeting. On August 30, he traveled to Denver to secure MENC vice president John Kendel's support, and Tremaine went to Richmond, Virginia, to see MENC president Luther Richman.

Despite Maddy's pleas, he was not invited to the meeting, but a determined Maddy and Tremaine traveled to Chicago to be available anyway. Late in the afternoon on Saturday, September 20, MENC secretary Clifford Buttelman called Maddy to meet immediately with the MENC Executive Committee. Speaking for the committee, Buttelman told Maddy that MENC and AFM had just adopted a code permitting public school children to appear on radio. He also said that MENC, at Petrillo's insistence, had negotiated only for public school teachers and that agreements between the union and camps or institutions of higher education would be mediated in the near future. Buttelman and Kendel promised that when Kearns arrived, Kearns would meet with Maddy and Petrillo to resolve differences between the union and the camp. Meanwhile, they urged Maddy not to instigate negative publicity or antagonistic statements toward Petrillo, who was now working positively with the music educators.[56]

On the next morning, Buttelman called Tremaine to say that Kearns would be in Chicago at four o'clock on the following day to hold a press conference with Petrillo and MENC officers. Buttelman assured Joe that, following the press conference, he would ask Kearns to meet with Maddy about the camp.

NMC attorney George Burke advised Maddy to ask a friend to attend the press conference to inform Joe of events beyond the newspaper reports. Maddy called *Chicago Tribune* reporter Norma Lee Browning, who would later become Maddy's biographer, but she was unavailable. So her supervisor, Phillip Maxwell, promised to send a reporter who would then contact Maddy following the press conference. According to the reporter, Petrillo publicly stated that NMC was a commercial institution, and none of the music educators contradicted Petrillo.

Following the press conference, Buttelman did not call Maddy until eleven o'clock that evening. He confided that Kearns was irked at Maddy for sending the *Tribune* reporter "to heckle him and Petrillo" and that Kearns had declined a meeting and returned to Pennsylvania. Buttelman firmly suggested that Maddy needed to appease Kearns. So, though he was distressed with the outcome of the new code, a chastened Maddy asked Tremaine and Burke to draft a statement saying that Maddy was pleased with the adoption of the code, which had been based on his proposal to MENC ten years earlier. He then wrote a letter to Kearns, concluding, "Please let me know when and where I can talk with you this week or next. Please wire me collect at Interlochen."[57]

Feeling betrayed, Maddy blamed Kearns and the MENC officers for the outcome. The officers, though aware of Maddy's opposition, had gained broad support from the MENC membership before the Petrillo negotiations. The September 22 code signing had been affirmed by a combined session of the MENC Executive Committee and the presidents of six MENC divisions, representing membership throughout the United States. The signing was lauded widely by the membership and in *Music Educators Journal*. Though initially approved for one year, the code became a long-lasting formal arrangement that remained in effect for several decades. Although AFM reached the code agreement with MENC, AFM retained NMC on the union's National Unfair List, and when the union lifted the ban on student broadcasts in 1948, Interlochen alone among educational institutions could not broadcast.[58]

A week after the Chicago press conference, Maddy was annoyed that Kearns had not responded to his letter. A furious Maddy held his tongue

with Kearns, but he wrote Representative Albert Engel from the Interlochen district, asking him to arrange a meeting to include Maddy, Representative Fred Hartley (later coauthor of the Taft-Hartley Act restricting
labor union activities), and the House Labor Committee attorney. Maddy
wrote to Giddings October 1, 1947, that he planned to see both members of
Congress and "open the fight that I have been honing for—and let the chips
fall where they may." But Engel was in South Dakota for the week, so
Maddy continued to wait.

Maddy wrote Giddings, "I'm through taking advice leading to appease-
ment. I don't care a damn if we never broadcast over a network, nor if we
ever have union teachers or students. I think we owe it to America to break
Petrillo's dictatorship over American music and to expose anyone in the
government who tries to make a deal with such a scoundrel, especially a
deal which penalizes a legitimate institution like Interlochen. I am sure I
have enough ammunition to blast Kearns out of politics, also to eliminate
CVB [Clifford Buttelman] from the MENC and break the control over
music education that he now exercises, and at the same time boost Petrillo
out of the AFM. I've spent years building up this case and now is the time
to fight it out once and for all, even if the trustees throw me out for doing
it."[59] However, Maddy's efforts over the next weeks were fruitless, and
Kearns never met with him.

The fight between Petrillo and Maddy was far from over, for Maddy
continued to fight in the press and magazines, even though Petrillo won
the battles. Early in 1948, Judge La Buy of Chicago added salt to Maddy's
wounds when he acquitted Petrillo in the WAAF case, which tested the
Lea Act.

Furthermore, even after the passage of the Lea Act, Maddy seemed
unable to arrange a radio network broadcast from Interlochen. Then, in
1948, Maddy made a breakthrough when the Mutual Broadcasting Company agreed to broadcast the following summer's NMC programs. He was
elated to claim this victory over Petrillo, and he reasoned that the public
needed to know how he won. With the help of editor Douglas Ingells,
Maddy wrote "How I Beat Petrillo," an article that appeared in the March
1948 issue of *Coronet* magazine. He related his version of the creation of the
MENC and AFM code of ethics. The article ended:

> Such is the story of how a seemingly insignificant incident in a Michi-
> gan village aroused the citizens of America to fight for the things their

country stands for. It means that this summer, when Interlochen returns to the air, there will be free music in the woods and on the air, for all Americans to cherish and enjoy.[60]

Avoiding any antiunion statements in the article, Maddy emphasized that his argument was with Petrillo alone. A draft of Maddy's article was so strong that his lawyer suggested that to avoid a libel suit, he remove the following sentence: "[Petrillo] ignored wartime patriotism with strikes and other rebellious acts." But Ingells was impressed and said, "I am left with the feeling personally, and very deeply, that all of us owe you a great debt of gratitude for having the courage to fight for such a fine ideal." The managing editor of *Coronet* also lauded Maddy for sharing "[h]ow you built Interlochen into the greatest single center of youth culture." He said that the account of how Maddy surmounted Petrillo's obstacles created a "story of interest and significance to millions."[61]

Maddy gloated because, though Interlochen was still on the National Unfair List, the camp concerts would be broadcast that summer. But Petrillo was not finished battling. Shortly after the *Coronet* article was published, a storm of protest burst among the top executives at Mutual, and the broadcaster reversed direction. Phillips Carlin, vice president for programming at Mutual, wrote a letter to Maddy, sending a copy to the *New York Times*.

> Mutual's conversations with you were for the sole purpose of arranging for the broadcast of music from your camp. Instead, we find you have issued statements to the press without consultation with us in which you involved our network as an instrument to further your controversies and intimating that in scheduling such broadcasts we are in support of your differences with the union and other networks. That was not our object and we feel that you have taken undue advantage of Mutual. In view of this we cannot offer the time you requested.[62]

When Mutual canceled the prospective 1948 camp broadcasts, Maddy's efforts to reinstate Interlochen national broadcasts crumbled. His defeat was staggering, because the union banned Interlochen's broadcasts and kept the camp on the National Unfair List until the year following Petrillo's retirement as national president ten years later, in 1958.

Union Musicians Banned for Fifteen Years

In the fall of 1942, following AFM's broadcast ban on the camp, Maddy returned to the University of Michigan to find a rapidly changing environment for his work. NBC had canceled his educational programs over its airwaves, and male music students had left for war service. Maddy aired a weekly program featuring patriotic themes over local radio station WJR in Detroit, but increasingly commercial radio stations would no longer provide scheduled times for such educational programs. Over time, to replace his previous commercial station outlets, he nurtured educational and community radio stations throughout Michigan, and in 1945 he became the chair of the Michigan Community Radio Association.

During the 1942 camp season, Maddy had expanded his radio workshops, and NBC hailed them as the most practical in America. With the help of local stations, the workshops enabled the camp to produce its own radio programs. That summer, Maddy hired Kathleen Lardie as the first of many camp broadcasting directors.[63] From 1942 until 1950, Maddy broadcast his camp-produced radio programs on the noncommercial college station WKAR in East Lansing and the commercial station WTCM in Traverse City, which did not observe AFM's ban.[64]

In 1948, with Maddy's encouragement, the University of Michigan launched the educational radio station WUOM in Ann Arbor. When WUOM first broadcast recorded programs from Interlochen the next year, camp recordings were not yet of good technical quality. Henry Austin, then director of camp broadcasting, complained because the camp still recorded concerts on program discs; since the needle would bounce from the groove, the station could not air many of the programs. The eight programs produced by the camp's broadcasting director William Stegath in 1949, after the camp purchased a new high-fidelity tape recorder, were greatly improved in quality.

In 1950 Ralph Steetle, the camp's broadcast director, produced thirty-two audio-taped programs called *Music from Interlochen*. Maddy persuaded the Michigan state legislature to pay for tape duplication, and in the following winter, the National Association of Educational Broadcasters (NAEB) distributed the series to sixteen educational and classical music stations. Headquartered at the University of Illinois and licensed primarily to college stations, NAEB ignored the AFM broadcast ban, claiming exemption because of its educational charter. In 1951 thirty-nine stations, more than twice as many as in the first year, aired *Music from Interlochen,* produced that year by the camp's broadcast director Irving Merrill.

Though a smaller audience than NBC's, NAEB's radio listeners proved to be a select group, with classical musical experiences and cultivated tastes. Maddy boasted that the *Music from Interlochen* concerts were more varied than NBC's, since the camp producer scheduled three broadcast hours weekly of complete and lesser-known symphonies, instead of the shorter movements and familiar overtures previously aired over NBC.

By the 1953–54 season, a record 174 educational stations in thirty-eight states carried a thirteen-program series of half-hour *Music from Interlochen* concerts. Duplication for distribution became an impossible burden that year, so Maddy hired the Audio-Video Recording Company in New York to duplicate the tapes. Then, in 1955, the Michigan legislature no longer provided funds to pay for duplicating the camp's broadcast tapes, so Maddy, using precious camp funds, bought new duplicating equipment and opened his own dubbing services. By the late 1950s, both commercial classical stations and college educational stations were successfully reaching new concert music listeners, prompting NAEB to add more broadcast series from U.S. music schools to join the camp's *Music from Interlochen* series.

The radio industry changed dramatically between 1941 and 1961, the period when Interlochen could not broadcast nationally on commercial networks. By 1961 stations employed new tape recorders and transcription services, and radio receivers had become smaller and more reliable because of the invention of the transistor, first demonstrated by Bell Laboratories in 1947. For classical music fans, the invention of frequency modulation (FM) radio, with its clear signal, was undoubtedly the greatest step forward. The superior sound of high-fidelity tapes and, later, stereophonic recordings was coupled with the static-free FM signal. Keeping abreast of these technical improvements, Maddy embraced FM broadcasting as the next phase for his career in music education. In 1945 the FCC had set aside twenty FM stations for noncommercial and educational purposes, and Maddy envisaged these stations coming together as a music network to air his instrumental classes and concert broadcasts from Interlochen.

FM inventor Edwin Armstrong had established his first NBC FM station, with its tower on top of New York City's Empire State Building, in 1941, but the war intervened to slow the new medium's growth in popularity. Not until the 1980s, after FM radios became prevalent in cars, would

FM finally surpass amplitude modulation (AM) as the dominant radio medium. As a result, the 1950 *Music from Interlochen* series was heard on NAEB stations with AM signals, which diminished the excellent acoustical qualities of the camp recordings.

Commercial network programming also changed following the war, as CBS became the most popular network by persuading NBC comedians to move their programs to CBS. Moreover, with new transcription services, local programs became more economical than network programs. Competition among radio stations became so fierce that more than two hundred commercial FM stations left the air in 1949. Then, by 1952, television had gained so many evening viewers that local radio stations dropped membership in the networks and aired the least expensive programming, recorded music. Each station began to feature one style of music, usually popular hits, though some stations aired country or classical music. This mode of broadcasting to special listener groups, called block programming, also prospered at the network level, when Paul Whiteman, whose 1941 jazz concert had precipitated Maddy's AFM feud, hosted an NBC series of recorded classical music. By 1956 television dominated evening programming, and most network radio programming disappeared from the air.[65]

During the years when Maddy could not broadcast the camp concerts, the total radio audience listening to classical music stations grew from nothing to almost 3 percent of the listeners. Though Maddy and other music broadcasters struggled to increase the total number of classical music radio listeners over the next half century, the percentage of classical music listeners, compared to all listeners, remains at approximately 3 percent in the 1990s.

While the radio industry evolved, Maddy stubbornly and relentlessly sought ways to counter Petrillo and AFM. In 1953 he again appeared before the U.S. House of Representatives Committee on Education and Labor, which was investigating restrictive union practices. Maddy told the committee, "I seek the right to employ union musicians to teach at the educational institution which I head." Maddy complained about the AFM punishment, saying that television stations were refusing to broadcast films from the camp. Motion picture theaters, he said, had rejected a newsreel-length film of campers playing Sousa marches, and Voice of America radio personnel had requested camp concert tapes but had never broadcast them.[66]

As late as 1958, when Petrillo was approaching retirement, Maddy was still feuding with him. NMC was to present two concerts for the dedication of the new Mackinac Straits Bridge on June 27, 1958. According to Maddy, an official representative for the Detroit Federation of Musicians threatened to send three thousand pickets to the dedication if the camp orchestra was permitted to play, so the dedication committee canceled the camp concerts. Maddy traveled to Washington, D.C., unsuccessfully seeking the help of Congress through Interlochen representative Robert Griffin, later a U.S. senator from Michigan. When the camp was banned from the dedication, Maddy reported that "a lot of talk and newspaper publicity was all one could expect from speaking to Congress."[67]

In 1958 Petrillo, still popular with the AFM membership after eighteen years, stepped down as president and returned to Chicago, where he remained president of AFM Local 10 until he retired in 1962. He recommended Herman Kenin as his successor.

Seizing the opportunity provided by Petrillo's departure, Maddy sought AFM negotiations to reinstate his membership and the camp's removal from the National Unfair List. Maddy asked Don Gillis to speak with Kenin on behalf of NMC. Gillis, a well-respected composer, had recently joined Maddy's staff to raise money for the camp and plan the opening of a winter school. He was well suited to negotiate a settlement with AFM, because, as a producer for NBC in New York City and Chicago, he had previously bargained with the union.

Gillis succeeded in his quest, and AFM removed the camp from the National Unfair List in March 1959, almost too late for Maddy to hire union musicians for the following summer. Both Maddy and Kenin agreed to make no public statements about past grievances or the conditions of reinstatement, which simply enabled NMC to be treated like other educational institutions and allowed Maddy to rejoin the union.[68]

Following his reinstatement, Maddy entered wholeheartedly into the union's activities. He wrote Kenin, expressing his appreciation for the reinstatement, offering his services for the union's International Congress of Strings project, a six-week summer camp for student players of stringed instruments, first held in 1959 at Greenleaf State Park in Oklahoma; and he invited Kenin to visit Interlochen in 1959. Kenin accepted the invitation that summer, and the quarrel between AFM and Interlochen ended. In the following year, Maddy wrote to Kenin again, suggesting that AFM, comparable to the actors' union, ought to collect and distribute royalties to musicians in motion pictures, but the idea did not take form. Pressing the new peaceful relationship, Gillis sought AFM funds to pay for a new scholarship lodge at the camp, but the union turned down the request.[69]

Finally, in 1961, after twenty years of dissonance, AFM granted Maddy permission to broadcast over NBC a taped Interlochen radio series called *The Best From Interlochen,* and the Petrillo controversy ended.[70] The Interlochen dispute with AFM was an unfortunate episode for music in the United States. Interlochen suffered the loss of national broadcasts for twenty years, considerably longer than the five-year ban levied against MENC schools. Of even greater consequence, according to Maddy, the loss of union musicians as camp teachers for fifteen years lessened the educational and artistic experiences of the campers during that time.

Following the passage of the 1946 Lea Act, radio station managers and network executives had no longer needed to maintain the musician employment levels demanded by the union, so many studio musicians nationwide were fired. The Lea Act also was responsible for ending the big band era; the act relieved managers from hiring union-prescribed numbers of musicians for concerts, and dance orchestras dwindled.

AFM's school broadcast ban was ultimately an unsuccessful way to increase musicians' employment, because AFM jobs never replaced the small number of banned broadcasts. Still, even in 1984, the year of his death, Petrillo insisted: "With children you always lose—but I was right. They took jobs away from professional musicians."[71]

Petrillo bristled because Maddy, helped by the press and Congress, had broadened the affair from an internal squabble among musicians and music educators to a national fight between corporate administrators and labor unions. The Interlochen dispute magnified many longtime union practices that offended important members of Congress, who then fanned public disapproval of AFM and AFL. All unions suffered loss of negotiating power, first with the Lea Act and then with the subsequent passage of the still more restrictive Taft-Hartley Act.[72]

Throughout the 1960s, the weakened AFL unsuccessfully lobbied Congress to repeal the Lea Act. Following another failed effort in 1973, AFL finally persuaded Congress to revoke the act in a bill signed by President Jimmy Carter in December 1980. The Lea Act had curbed all unions for almost thirty-five years, but Maddy could not have foreseen how significantly it would alter the lives of so many musicians and broadcasters, whether Interlochen students or not.[73]

University of Michigan to the Rescue

The University of Michigan, through its leaders, was the most important collegiate institution in the Interlochen story. The university never governed Interlochen, but its administrators supported Maddy and his successors financially, academically, and artistically in many ways. First, as a professor in radio and music, Maddy could pursue his Interlochen dream without fearing his personal financial failure. Second, his supervisors allotted Maddy the time to start and manage the camp. Third, the university lent or contributed funds to a variety of Maddy's projects, some administered by the university's School of Music and some administered by the Interlochen staff.

During World War II, the University of Michigan and NMC formed a partnership of mutual need. Prior to the war, the university's School of Music had reorganized, an action that benefited both Maddy and the camp at Interlochen. In the summer of 1940, the University of Michigan Board of Regents separated the School of Music from the University Musical Society (UMS). School of Music head Earl Moore, who had taught at Maddy's camp in the first season of 1928, now reported to university academic executives rather than to UMS's Charles Sink. Severing his ties further, Moore resigned as conductor of UMS's Choral Union Chorus, a position he had held since 1922. Following the separation, UMS moved to the Burton Memorial Tower and concentrated on presenting professional concerts and choral programs. The young Thor Johnson, later an internationally acclaimed symphony conductor and a major figure at Interlochen, replaced Moore as conductor of the Choral Union Chorus.[74]

Maddy, a conductor of many UMS youth chorus programs in Ann Arbor, had hired a number of camp teachers and celebrities as a result of his associations with UMS concert performers. The society also commissioned composers, including many who were associated with the camp. Normand Lockwood, for instance, was commissioned by UMS to write choral works. Lockwood, whose father was a School of Music violinist, had taught at the camp in its early years. In 1953 UMS commissioned Lockwood to write his composition *Prairie,* dedicated to Charles Sink, followed in 1976 by *Life Triumphant,* a choral and instrumental work composed in memory of Thor Johnson shortly after his death.

In the 1940s, Maddy established a close relationship with UMS board

members from Ann Arbor. UMS was important to NMC's history, as three
of its board members became pivotal at Interlochen. University of Michigan president Alexander Ruthven, who had enabled Maddy to expand his
radio career in 1930, served on the camp advisory board for many years.
Thor Johnson, who replaced Earl Moore on the UMS board in 1940, conducted NHSO at the camp and directed the Interlochen Arts Academy for
three years in the 1960s. UMS board member Roscoe Bonisteel, a prominent Ann Arbor lawyer and regent of the University of Michigan, later
chaired Interlochen's board of trustees in the leadership transition following Maddy's death. These prominent board members guided UMS until
1968, when Ruthven and Johnson became emeritus members. Bonisteel
served on the UMS board from 1938 until his death in 1972. Even following Maddy's death, Interlochen maintained a close working relationship
with UMS, when William Brittain, UMS board member in the early 1970s,
joined the camp board.[75]

Following the separation of UMS and the School of Music, the university contributed funds to NMC to construct camp buildings and install
plumbing, relieving facility shortcomings that had plagued Maddy since
the camp's first season. In 1940, the camp still occupied the original Pennington lands, and a pen enclosing native deer greeted visitors at the camp
entrance. Though the Interlochen Bowl was a large structure, all other
camp buildings were quite small, and the entire campus was much less
extensive than it is now.

Late in 1941, after NMC had substantially paid Willis Pennington's ten-
year mortgage on the original camp's land, Maddy and Tremaine conceived of a plan to expand camp housing and provide scholarships for additional campers. Under this plan, donors would build cottages that, when
rented, would provide funds for camp scholarships. Canfield Lodge on
Green Lake, near the camp hotel, became the first of forty-seven such
scholarship lodges built over the next twenty-five years. Canfield Lodge was
followed by Nesbit Scholarship Lodge in 1944, Langford Lodge in 1948,
and Tremaine and Greenleaf Lodges in 1949. The plan was so successful in
attracting contributions that thirty-three lodges had been built by 1957.[76]

The Pennington family suffered severe financial hardships in 1942, and
Maddy took advantage of this opportunity to acquire property next to the
original camp, enabling him to triple the NMC campus size over the following two years. Because of the war, enrollments at Willis Pennington's

camp declined, forcing him, under a new mortgage, to sell his twenty-year-old Camp Penn Loch for Boys to NMC. With this added land, Maddy opened an NMC Junior Division for younger boys and girls.

A second opportunity to acquire land formed in the fall of 1943. Christina Pennington, Willis Pennington's sister-in-law, owned Camp Interlochen, a girls' camp on land next to NMC. Christina and others in the Pennington family had always been very protective of the Interlochen name. But unfortunately, publicity for Camp Interlochen, founded in 1918, was sometimes confused with publicity for NMC in music circles. The Penningtons had often chastised Maddy and his staff about the confusion, for in their minds, the fact that NMC was better known was no excuse for usurping the Interlochen name. While he was negotiating with Maddy over the Camp Penn Loch sale, Willis Pennington wrote to Maddy that he should chide his new secretary, Margaret Stace, for referring to the National Music Camp as "Interlochen."[77]

Christina Pennington's Camp Interlochen, with dwindling enrollments and financial difficulties caused by the war, was deteriorating, and because of failing health, she had wanted to sell her camp to Maddy for several years. When she died on August 26, 1943, she willed Camp Interlochen to her husband Parker Pennington, who persuaded Maddy to buy it immediately. On October 26, 1943, Maddy borrowed money and purchased Camp Interlochen, adding eight hundred acres of lakefront property and twenty-one buildings to NMC holdings. This new land enabled Maddy to enlarge the Junior Girls' Division the following summer, expand the University of Michigan offerings, and begin an intermediate-age camp division in 1947.[78] So, after 1943, whenever Maddy referred to NMC as Interlochen, he offended only the residents of nearby Interlochen village, who continue to harbor this resentment.

Following Maddy's Pennington land purchases, NMC building construction mushroomed, first with new scholarship lodges and then with classroom and concert buildings. Expansion occurred first along the lakefronts, then proceeded inland, producing structures in the middle of the isthmus to unite the campers in the two NMC lake communities more fully than in previous years. This larger campus evolved as an arrangement of dwellings and instructional buildings along parallel roads, patterned after the layout of Midwestern American cities. In 1946, further uniting the two lakefronts and capping a twelve-hundred-acre campus, Maddy bought

Willis Pennington's house and the entire site of Wylie Village for six thousand dollars. The Wylie Village houses provided summer residences for many faculty members.

With such increased acreage, Maddy became the manager of a small city. He established a transportation department and began to hire year-round personnel to tend to the expanding work. Following the war, he bought on sale seven war surplus buses and several trucks, vehicles that Interlochen rebuilt continually and pressed into service for many years.[79]

During World War II, NMC had to adapt to the loss of college-age men, to restrictions on travel, and to rationing of food, gasoline, and building materials. To fill spaces in the newly acquired property and replace reduced enrollments, Maddy hosted educational and musical conferences at NMC. In 1941 Maddy even offered to pay a 10 percent commission to Willis Pennington for each camper he recruited to NMC.[80]

Maddy supported the war effort by staging patriotic music programs at both Ann Arbor and Interlochen. At the behest of Michigan governor Murray Van Wagoner, Maddy organized an eight-week laboratory session on wartime music in the summer of 1942. With music scores gathered from this laboratory and similar material from MENC's American Wartime Music program, he published a book of patriotic songs, angering publishers whose copyrighted materials appeared in the book. Among other thrusts, Maddy advocated patriotic music through the University of Michigan Extension Service, under which he established the Michigan Civic Orchestra Association. Later in 1942, when he became conductor of the Ann Arbor Civic Orchestra, he again fostered patriotism through music.[81]

Following the reorganization of the School of Music, Maddy had again approached Earl Moore with a request to move NMC's academic affiliation from Illinois State Normal College to the University of Michigan. Finally, in the fall of 1941, the University of Michigan Board of Regents approved a summer college division at Interlochen, and Clyde Vroman, the University of Michigan's director of admissions, organized the new Interlochen division for Maddy. In the summer of 1942, the University of Michigan replaced Illinois Normal in giving collegiate credit for NMC classes in music, music education, and speech.

With the addition of both the college and junior programs, Maddy advertised six divisions, including college men and women, high school boys and girls, and junior boys and girls. Counting instrumentalists from all six divisions, he declared that NHSO grew to a record 185 performers in 1942.[82]

Russell Stover®

W e hope you enjoy this box of candy from America's #1 maker of boxed chocolates – Russell Stover. Our candy company started out small, but our story of success is built on making candy the old fashioned way.

In 1923, Russell and Clara Stover began hand dipping their unique chocolates in their Denver, Colorado home. Small batches of candy were made in their kitchen to maintain consistent quality and freshness. Today, over seventy years later, we still make our candy in small batches and are America's largest hand dipper of chocolates. We believe making things the old-fashioned way with fresh, quality ingredients is the only way to make Russell Stover candy.

Rest assured, a lot of things are changing in our world today, but Russell Stover Candies will never change.

Sincerely, All the Folks at Russell Stover®

www.russellstover.com

N ous espérons que vous aimerez cette boîte de confiserie vendue par le fabricant #1 de chocolats en boîtes en Amérique, Russell Stover. Notre compagnie de confiserie a débuté de façon modeste mais elle a toujours connu beaucoup de succès grâce à son procédé de fabrication à l'ancienne.

En 1923, Russell et Clara Stover ont débuté la fabrication de chocolats en utilisant un procédé unique, dans leur résidence de Denver au Colorado. Ils fabriquaient les chocolats par petites quantités dans leur cuisine, afin que fraîcheur et qualité soient maintenues. Aujourd'hui, plus de soixante-dix ans plus tard, nous fabriquons toujours nos chocolats en petites quantités et nous sommes le plus grand manufacturier de chocolats faits à la main en Amérique. Nous croyons qu'il n'y a qu'une seule façon de fabriquer les chocolats Russell Stover et c'est en les fabriquant à l'ancienne avec des ingrédients frais et de qualité.

Bien sûr, beaucoup de choses changent dans notre monde d'aujourd'hui, cependant Russell Stover ne changera jamais.

Sincèrement, La grande famille Russell Stover®

Nutrition Information Nutritives

Serving Size/Portion: 3 pieces/morceaux (40g)

Servings per 7.75 oz. container:	About 6
Nombre par paquet 220g: Approximativement 6	
Servings per 1 lb. container:	About 11
Nombre par paquet 454g: Approximativement 11	
Servings per 2 lb. container:	About 23
Nombre par paquet 908g: Approximativement 23	

Amount Per Serving/Quantité par portion

Calories 190
    Calories from Fat/Calories provenant des graisses 70

% Daily Value*/Besoin quotidien*

Total Fat/Graisses Total 8g	**12%**
Saturated Fat/Graisses saturées 5g	**25%**
Cholesterol/Cholestérol <5mg	**2%**
Sodium 45mg	**2%**
Total Carbohydrate/Hydrates de carbone 27g	**9%**
Dietary Fiber/Fibres alimentaires 0g	**0%**
Sugars/Sucres 21g	
Protein/Protéines 2g	

Vitamin/Vitamine A 0%	•	Vitamin/Vitamine C 0%	
Calcium 2%	•	Iron/Fer 4%	

*Percent (%) Daily Values are based on a 2000 calorie diet. Your Daily Values may vary higher or lower depending on your calorie needs.
*Les pourcentages (%) en besoins quotidiens sont basés sur un régime alimentaire de 2,000 calories. Vos besoins quotidiens peuvent être plus élevés ou plus bas dépendant de vos besoins caloriques.

	Calories	2000	2500
Total Fat/Graisses Total	Less Than/Moins de	65g	80g
Saturated Fat/Graisses saturées	Less Than/Moins de	20g	25g
Cholesterol/Cholestérol	Less Than/Moins de	300mg	300mg
Sodium	Less Than/Moins de	2400mg	2400mg
Total Carbohydrate/Hydrates de carbone Total		300g	375g
Dietary Fiber/Fibres alimentaires		25g	30g

Calories per gram/Calories par gram –
Fat/Graisses 9 • Carbohydrate/Hydrates de carbone 4 • Protein/Proteines 4

Dark Chocolate   170-107/171-127/172-123/EB

Having salvaged the 1942 camp season with the addition of collegians and juniors, Maddy engaged composer Ferde Grofé to conduct NHSO. The University of Illinois's Austin Harding conducted NHSB. That summer, NMC staff members produced Gilbert and Sullivan's *H.M.S. Pinafore,* and, in a brilliant stroke, Maddy secured a U.S. Army leave for Thor Johnson to conduct the final NHSO performance of the season.[83]

Though enrollments in the University of Michigan School of Music were low during World War II, the war effort absorbed needed campus space in Ann Arbor. Because room for music classes became scarce in 1943 and 1944, Earl Moore turned to Maddy and Interlochen both to gain summer teaching quarters and to recruit high school students for the university. In return, University of Michigan personnel came to teach at Interlochen. Maynard Klein, Maddy's former student, who was then teaching at Tulane University, became the camp choral director, and the University of Michigan's William Revelli replaced Austin Harding as director of NHSB.

In the summer of 1943, Clyde Vroman moved the annual University of Michigan High School Instrumental Music Clinic, in its eighth year, from Ann Arbor to Interlochen. Revelli had started these band clinics in 1935, his first year at the university, to recruit talented Michigan high school students for his collegiate programs. He was a veteran NMC faculty member, who had begun teaching at the camp in 1929, when he was director of a national championship band at Hobart High School in Indiana. When the University of Michigan hired him as conductor of bands, he was the only member of the university's wind instrument faculty. But he brought his winning style to the university, where he and Maddy were kindred spirits who advocated competitive music classes as the means to train students. Revelli pushed his students hard, occasionally blistering individual students with verbal tirades for their errors in rehearsals. Though today's students and administrators would no longer accept his teaching techniques, Revelli could gain approval and respect from his students and colleagues because of his bands' outstanding performances.[84]

Revelli's influence on American bands was enormous, not only at the University of Michigan and Interlochen, but also throughout the United States. He began his career as a violinist with degrees from the Chicago Musical College and the Vandercook School of Music in Chicago. During his Hobart appointment, he organized America's first high school band booster club. At the University of Michigan, he founded the College Band Directors National Association and became president of the American

Bandmasters Association. In association with Maddy, Revelli would shape the next two decades of Interlochen band programs, and with the University of Michigan band, he would bring national and international acclaim until his retirement in 1971.

In 1944 the University of Michigan added an orchestra and choir to Revelli's high school band clinic. To improve supervision of the growing number of younger campers, Maddy and the university instituted a collegiate program to train clinic counselors. Also in 1944 conductor Vladimir Bakaleinikoff brought his prodigy, the young conductor Lorin Maazel, to the camp, and composer Howard Hanson returned to conduct for his twelfth summer. While Maddy continued to promote American music performances at NMC, he balked in 1944 because the publisher's fees for Gershwin's Concerto in F were so costly. Maddy claimed that gate receipts for the Gershwin concert were $56.50, whereas the venture cost him $221.50. Adding to his disgust, the Music Publishers Holding Corporation would not let him keep Gershwin's music for sight-reading by his now 240-piece orchestra. Responded Maddy, "Needless to say, we will never do that again."[85]

In 1945 the university's music clinics were renamed the Michigan All-State Program. Maddy was proud of the All-State Program, and he envisaged a plan to enroll a student from every Michigan high school, with local Rotary, Kiwanis, or Lions clubs paying each student's costs. He never completely realized the plan, but many Michigan service and charitable organizations have supported students in the All-State Program since the programs' inception.[86]

At the conclusion of World War II, Maddy could boast that former campers played in eleven of the thirty-five major U.S. orchestras and that each orchestra employed professional musicians who performed at higher standards than ever before. But he also was proud that many NMC alumni earned their living by teaching students in private music lessons or in school bands and orchestras, though not as performers. He claimed that six or seven thousand boys and girls had attended NMC since 1928, the best of almost two million public high school boys and girls who were members of bands and orchestras. Maddy predicted that 3 percent of the country's music students would become professional musicians and that the remaining 97 percent would, as adults, demand more and finer symphony orchestras and opera companies.[87]

When AFM put NMC on the National Unfair List in January 1945,

Maddy had less than six months to recruit a nonunion faculty, including celebrities. But he would not give up his dream, and he vowed to expand the camp programs. He hired instructors from universities, including the University of North Carolina (now University of North Carolina at Chapel Hill), the University of Texas (now University of Texas at Austin), Michigan State College (now Michigan State University), and Oklahoma A&M University (now Oklahoma State University), and from high schools in Chicago, Seattle, and Michigan. George Wilson, then teaching at Wichita State College (now Wichita State University) and later an Interlochen interim president, joined the faculty. William Knuth of San Francisco State College (now San Francisco State University) taught bassoon and conducted the University Division Orchestra. As an innovation for camp performers who were disappointed by the loss of union teachers, T. P. Giddings taught a performance class with stroboscope technology to help instrumentalists play in tune. An ambitious production of Mozart's opera *Così fan tutte*, sung in English, was staged in 1945. Departments besides music prospered, and the dance department, in its sixth year, taught ballet.[88]

Despite these innovative additions, the loss of AFM celebrity teachers was crucial for Interlochen, because the celebrities had set standards for the students and had brought universal musical connections to the students' world. With the departure of the union faculty, the remaining teachers and adult students in the University Division were thrust into the role of setting standards. As the years of the union ban dragged on and on, some faculty members and students sensed that the camp had become isolated from the mainstream of American artistic life. Though the number of campers grew each year, some believed that the quality of their experience at NMC had deteriorated.[89]

On July 1, 1945, despite the absence of union member teachers, NMC opened on schedule with a record-breaking enrollment of more than 700 campers, including 100 in the University Division, 400 in the High School Division, 100 in the All-State Program, and 110 in the Junior Division. There were fifty-one teachers and two hundred staff workers.[90]

Before the outbreak of war in 1941, NMC had enrolled 368 campers, but during the war years, because of the newly added College and Junior Divisions, the student population began to climb. At the end of World War II, prosperity, followed by the return of soldiers to civilian life, posed a countertrend to the tragedy of AFM's faculty ban in 1945. In fact, Maddy parlayed the publicity from his antiunion stand into increased NMC admissions. Undergraduate and graduate education enrollments at the University of Michigan School of Music escalated, and as a result, NMC's collegiate programs burgeoned. NMC benefited from the flourishing music programs in the public schools in the United States, and as the economy soared, students from all over the world flocked to Interlochen to study. From 1945 to 1960, NMC jumped from seven hundred campers to almost thirteen hundred, and the faculty increased from 51 to 120 members.[91]

In the summer of 1945, before the end of the war, Maddy needed lumber to build new buildings and repair old ones, so he bought a sawmill. In the previous year, the Michigan Federation of Women's Clubs had donated five thousand dollars for a new fine arts building. This structure was built mostly of stone, with beams of pine logs. With his sawmill, Maddy could construct new camp buildings and begin to winterize the NMC cabins. This building surge was the first evidence that he might eventually build a winter school. In 1946, with the war's end, Maddy commenced a blizzard of construction, building a library, a maintenance garage, fourteen dormitories and cabins, and new tennis courts. Since the campus sawmill crunched scores of Interlochen trees, Maddy and the staff, concerned about conservation, replenished the crop by planting 120,000 pine trees that summer.[92]

Two major buildings were constructed in the late 1940s. The Hildegarde Lewis Dance Building was completed in 1950, ten years after NMC started the dance program. Kresge Assembly Hall, a new outdoor performance arena, was planned to be sited next to the historic Interlochen Bowl. Some members of the board resisted Maddy's plans to build the performance arena, but Stanley Kresge, the noted variety-store head and a donor in 1944, agreed to help. In 1947, shortly after he and Maddy went deer hunting, Kresge sent Maddy a check for thirty-five thousand dollars to build the new pavilion, with a promise of another ten thousand. Without telling his board, Maddy started construction of the arena, later commenting that management "must do things even when the board interferes." In May 1948, he wrote Giddings that the girders were rising despite difficulties in getting the board's approval for the project. In the letter, Maddy wrote that benches for the new auditorium, costing $6.50 each, had been stamped out at southern Michigan's Jackson State Prison. So, in the summer of 1948, the original Kresge Hall was completed and "dedicated to the promotion of world friendship through the universal language of the arts."[93]

The late 1940s saw new footpaths and paved roads at the camp. To meet enrollment pressures, Maddy built a laundry for campers' bedding, the boys' corduroy pants, and the girls' knickers. Interlochen operated the laundry until 1993. Then the building was remodeled for staff offices, and the camp began sending sheets and towels to a laundry service in Traverse City.

Camp construction continued at a steady clip in the 1950s. Four cabins for girls in the All-State Program were built in 1951, and in the following year, an administration building, named for Joe Maddy, was completed. NMC enlarged twenty-five-year-old Grunow Hall to hold opera productions, built a new addition to the infirmary, and constructed a radio production building on the shore of Green Lake.

During the postwar years, NMC expanded in scope and size beyond music education to embrace radio, drama, script writing, art, dance, crafts, photography, physical education, and recreational leadership. Pushed by a more academically oriented faculty, Maddy started a student council, which wrote a Charter for Youth. A junior orchestra was formed under the leadership of Marcia Weissgerber Palmer, founder of the Atlanta Youth Symphony and later the first dean of girls at Interlochen Arts Academy. William Knuth conducted NHSO during this period. Many believe the general quality of music programs was not as high as in earlier or recent years, but stellar young performers attending the camp in the late 1940s succeeded in music careers. Unfortunately, certain areas, such as stage management, lauded in the days of weekly radio broadcasts, suffered in these years.[94]

NMC's Junior Division grew rapidly after the war. In 1947 Maddy added an Intermediate Division to correspond with the junior high or middle school years. Maddy had taught acoustics to his students in Richmond, Indiana, and advocated studying new musical ideas, so in 1947 he asked Roderick Gordon of North Texas State College (now North Texas State University) to launch a multiyear program called Electronics in Education. This project culminated in a 1951 film called *Seeing Sound: Electronic Music.*[95]

During the summer of 1947, following the Supreme Court's positive ruling on the Lea Act, Interlochen's negotiations with AFM and MENC burdened both Maddy and Clyde Vroman. Vroman, who had been elected secretary to NMC's board earlier in the year, soon found Maddy's confrontation with Representative Carroll Kearns and MENC's Clifford Buttelman too consuming. So, late in 1947, though remaining on the board, Vroman resigned as secretary. Orien Dalley, a member of the music faculty at the University of Michigan, was elected secretary. Besides his

board contributions, Dalley became one of the venerated orchestra conductors at NMC.

In 1948 the camp's conductors included Wolfgang Kuhn, George Wilson, and Maynard Klein. In that year, with Dalley's urging, NMC established honor recitals to encourage the most gifted students. Seventeen-
year-old Henry Charles Smith, subsequently the principal trombone in the
Philadelphia Orchestra, enrolled in the High School Division. Smith later
became resident conductor of Interlochen's World Youth Symphony
Orchestra (the successor of NHSO) in the 1980s and 1990s.

John Lowell, head of the music theory department at the University of
Michigan, supervised the University Division in 1948. According to former
University of Michigan music dean Allen Britton, Lowell often found himself in the middle of conflicts between Joe Maddy and Earl Moore. These
conflicts came about because Maddy maintained that NMC needed to be
an inspirational seasonal camp. He told NMC instructors that they were
not to change students' embouchures or bowing techniques or to criticize
the campers' home teachers, because these tactics would alienate those
teachers from NMC. In contrast, Moore, who headed a professional school
of music at the university, thought that NMC instructors should correct the
bad habits of campers who were ill prepared, thus improving camp performances and helping campers progress as rapidly as possible. Since NMC
was Maddy's camp, he prevailed in this argument.[96]

NMC successfully grew to 866 campers under seventy-two faculty members in 1948. Enrollment was now so large that stringed instrument and
piano repair were added to the programs. The number of concerts
expanded to 185, including performances of Handel's *Elijah* and Gluck's
Orpheus. Elated over the spurt in camper numbers, Tremaine wrote
Maddy: "I think we should have a stabilizing enrollment plan. . . . As you
know, many people think the Camp is too large and has lost the charm of
close personal relationships provided by smaller camps. . . . We can have a
much *larger enrollment without detriment* and with less sense of over
growth, if we develop the entity of each camp."[97]

At first Maddy resented Tremaine's suggestion, because Maddy had
already instituted new programs to increase income. For instance, NMC
hosted nine high school bands for two weeks following the regular camp
season. Copying the traditions of ensembles during the regular NMC sessions, these bands played new literature at sight on Tuesday nights and held
Sunday morning devotional services patterned after NMC services. Thus,

having already expanded the curriculum and secured badly needed tuition income, Maddy replied to Tremaine, "It is just possible that you might get the wrong slant on things occasionally and that I might have a fairly good perspective—being on the grounds most of the year and hearing all sides of every matter."[98]

Nevertheless, Tremaine pressed for his view, using 1948 camp figures for his base. He calculated what he believed was the optimum enrollment for each division, considering housing, lodging, ensemble sizes, and faculty loads. He reasoned that the University Division could grow by 75 students, that all other divisions could grow by 200, and that the camp could move from 866 total students in 1948 to 1,140 in the next year. Tremaine's figures were so convincing that Maddy embarked on recruiting visits to increase the numbers of students. Though the numbers did not increase at quite the rate Tremaine predicted, NMC enrolled almost thirteen hundred campers after ten years.

Maddy had already begun persuading the Michigan legislature to grant advertising funds to the camp. Between 1947 and 1954, the state gave NMC eight thousand dollars each year to promote Michigan and the camp for summer vacations. Maddy used the money to produce movies, purchase broadcasting equipment, create radio programs, and install local Interlochen broadcast lines. The publicity fed Tremaine's plan.

As enrollments increased, performance activity expanded significantly. In 1949 NHSO played eighteen symphonies in eight weeks, and instrumental soloists competed to play concertos with the orchestra. NHSB broadcast eight band programs over local radio stations and played in Traverse City's annual Cherry Festival parade. Maddy expanded the piano and organ department, establishing the first postcamp program in piano and purchasing a new electric organ. Kenneth Jewell, later a revered choral conductor, was first hired in 1949, as a piano tuner.

Expansion of the camp soared in 1950. In that year, Maddy preferred to conduct the huge NHSO, an ensemble of more than two hundred players. Orien Dalley, with Earl Moore's blessing, persuaded Maddy to divide the big NHSO into two orchestras, one for the most gifted students and another moving at a slower pace. Dalley conducted the orchestra of gifted students, called the Honors Orchestra. The Honors Orchestra exceeded all expectations of success, performing twenty-four major symphonies during the eight-week session.

Large productions in 1950 featured two performances of Gilbert and

Sullivan's *Mikado* and the University Orchestra and Chorus presentation of Haydn's *The Seasons*. Classes beyond music also sparkled, as the university speech department presented Shakespeare's *Twelfth Night*. The Sunday morning service inaugurated a tradition of brass choir performances that continues today. In its tradition of trying fashionable art forms, NMC mounted a roller-skating ballet on the new Kresge Hall stage, an innovation that was not repeated in following years. With the growing enrollment and number of performances, NMC hired more staff members each year. By 1950, performing ensembles needed twenty-four librarians to service the music library.[99]

The 1951 season brought Clyde Roller, an important conductor of the second half of the century, to conduct the University Orchestra for the first time. Eighty members of that orchestra and 450 singers in the Festival Choir sang two oratorios, and the University Opera performed Kurt Weill's *Down in the Valley*. Even the Intermediate Orchestra played one symphony each week, emulating the programs of NHSO in the early 1930s. Edward Downing, who would be director of the Interlochen Arts Camp (NMC's successor name) and then vice president for education during the last quarter of the century, first attended postcamp that year as a member of the Belleville High School Band.[100]

In 1952 the guest composer was Roy Harris, then widely known for his Symphony no. 3. Robert Murphy, a Benton Harbor sophomore who later became a pioneer faculty member at the Interlochen Arts Academy, enrolled in the All-State Program.[101]

Though NMC clearly missed its celebrity concerts and the influence of professional composers and performers after AFM put the camp on its National Unfair List, the campus size, programs, and enrollment numbers made remarkable gains during the postwar years.

Part 5

Variations on the Theme

We already have the year-around maintenance expense paid for by the summer operation.

—Joseph Maddy

End of the Giddings and Tremaine Era

Eighty-three-year-old T. P. Giddings suffered a stroke on May 31, 1953, just weeks before the camp opening for that season. Maddy, at work in Ann Arbor, fussed over the care given to Giddings, who was conscious in a Minneapolis hospital but unable to talk. Writing Giddings's doctor, Maddy said that he was the old man's closest friend, that he would pay his bills if needed, and that his brother, Harry Maddy, still in the Minneapolis Symphony Orchestra, would help the doctor with Giddings's rehabilitation.[1]

In July 1953, continuing without Giddings, Maddy supervised the educational programs, enrolled a large class of campers, and successfully prevented the state legislature from building a prison near Interlochen. In that year, NMC constructed Lochaven Cafeteria and Recreation Building on the shore of Duck Lake and a wishing well in the parking lot near the Maddy Administration Building. NMC claimed sixteen hundred campers and faculty members that summer. Barre Hill, in his seventh season with the University Opera, produced Bach's *Coffee* Cantata, Wolf-Ferrari's *The Secret of Suzanne,* and Pergolesi's *La Serva Padrona.* With newly added space in Grunow Hall, Hill's Opera Workshop mounted extensive productions of Puccini's *Madama Butterfly* and Bernstein's *Trouble in Tahiti.* At the end of the regular camp season, Interlochen appended a week of adult classes in chamber music, an offering that continues to this day.[2]

While never truly well again, Giddings recovered sufficiently to spend much of the next winter in Florida, where he owned property with citrus groves. Giddings died on March 4, 1954, in Clermont, Florida. Despite their 1939 quarrel, Maddy had always depended on Giddings for educational guidance, so he persuaded collaborator Charles Tremaine to be vice president of instruction and treasurer for one year while beginning a replacement search.

Always overshadowed by Maddy, Giddings had, however, shaped the order and discipline of NMC more than any other person. After his retirement from the Minneapolis schools in 1940, Giddings had devoted himself to Interlochen. Though he received only one hundred dollars a month from NMC following his stroke, Giddings did not die a pauper, and he willed half of his property to NMC.[3]

In 1954 Maddy began a three-year struggle to prevent the construction of an air base near Interlochen. Traverse City politicians and businesspeople sought the base to spur the local economy, but Maddy protested, saying that the droning of airplanes would drown out music performances. He persuaded Governor G. Mennen Williams of Michigan to visit NMC that summer to learn how the noise from the base could hurt the concerts. In his campaign against the base, Maddy endorsed several alternate sites, angering many area political leaders. Maddy ultimately won the dispute, for in 1957, the base was built near Kalkaska, Michigan, far enough away that campers could not hear the noise.[4]

In a major departure from the camp's rustic cabin architecture, NMC built two winterized dormitories, called Brahms and Beethoven, in 1955. These were touted as providing better faculty living spaces, which had always been quite primitive, but Maddy also contemplated using them for students in a future winter school. In that same year, the camp built the Walter E. Hastings Museum for environmental classes. Camp life continued to be busy six days a week, with a day off on Monday, when campers were taken on trips to the Lake Michigan dunes or to Traverse City for shopping, while the faculty played golf or picnicked at the lakes in the area. Each season, one festive Monday was named Maddy Gras, during which campers started such traditions as the junior boys' turtle races. The All-State Program added drama classes in 1955, and the Michigan Civic Orchestra Association sponsored meetings and concerts during the post-camp period. With his mentor Clyde Roller conducting, Donald Jaeger, later a director of the Interlochen Arts Academy, won the high school concerto competition on the oboe.[5]

David Mattern, director of the University Division, had a fatal heart attack in 1956, so Maddy and Earl Moore approached Allen Britton, music education professor at the University of Michigan, to replace Mattern. Britton, aware of conflicts between Moore and Maddy over educational methods, reluctantly accepted the University Division directorship on the condition that Maddy's philosophy prevail in any disagreements. Britton, later an Interlochen trustee, headed this division until Moore's retirement in 1959.[6]

Several new structures for girls led campus expansion in the late 1950s. In 1956, a large, multitiered sundeck was erected on Green Lake for high school girls. The Sundecker was a treasured sunbathing area for several decades, but it deteriorated, was condemned, and was torn down in 1994. The Pinecrest Cafeteria for junior and intermediate girls was built in 1957 and rebuilt following the roof's collapse from snow in 1990. After the original Pinecrest was completed, Tremaine suggested, unsuccessfully, that the Kresge Foundation replace the construction costs.[7]

In 1957 George Wilson, NHSO conductor and Giddings's successor, became a full-time vice president of Interlochen. Wilson, later an interim president of Interlochen, had been teaching and conducting at Interlochen since Austin Harding had brought him to camp as librarian in 1929. By 1957 the growing Interlochen campus supported more than two thousand campers, faculty, and staff, all busy presenting 320 concerts. Debt retirement seemed near, stimulating Maddy to establish the Interlochen Press to publish music composed and arranged by Interlochen personalities. That year Byron Hanson (no relation to composer and conductor Howard Hanson), a junior in high school and later music director of both the Interlochen camp and Interlochen Arts Academy, enrolled in the High School Division of the camp as a baritone horn player.[8]

The Interlochen Bowl Hotel, a structure on the original Pennington property, had been heavily used in the 1940s and 1950s, serving visitors, campers, faculty, and staff. Various renovations had taken place over the years. In 1945 Maddy had built a new kitchen in the hotel, and early in 1948, he planned to build classrooms in the hotel basement. Giddings objected and wrote to Maddy that classrooms below ground level "resulted in Sing-Sing in self defense."[9] Ignoring Giddings, Maddy built the classrooms regardless. Inspectors condemned the hotel in 1954, forcing Maddy and Tremaine to fret over money to rebuild it. Tremaine proposed that they ask the University of Michigan for a loan of $227,000 to complete the hotel.[10] But Roscoe Bonisteel, both a regent at the university and an Interlochen trustee, opposed an appeal to the University of Michigan, because he thought the university would charge an exorbitant interest rate.

By 1958 Maddy and Tremaine could no longer delay hotel construction, because of the condemnation. Tremaine suggested that Maddy pursue his wealthy friends to refurbish the hotel as a memorial to Giddings. Maddy appealed to many, including Stanley Kresge, who contributed to both a scholarship lodge and the hotel renovation. The fund-raising progressed well, so Maddy renovated the hotel over the next two years. Attracted by this more modern lodge, new and greater numbers of tourists came to the Interlochen concerts. The hotel also benefited Traverse City's tourist business, thus improving Maddy's relationship with the townspeople, who had often resented NMC's growth. The renovated hotel became a new focus for Maddy's pride, and in the 1960s, he expressed his appreciation for Clement Stone's donations by renaming the hotel the Stone Student Center.[11]

Always interested in new technology, Maddy consulted with his colleagues at C. G. Conn to create the Stroboconn tuner between 1958 and 1960. Camp enrollment climbed to 1,289 in 1958, 150 more than Tremaine had planned as camp capacity ten years earlier. Each camper paid $550 for the eight weeks. The staff grew to 650, plus 114 faculty members.[12]

Personnel at the top of the University of Michigan School of Music changed significantly in 1959. Earl Moore retired, and his assistant, James Wallace, replaced him as dean. Allen Britton, head of NMC's University Division, became assistant dean and chair of music education. Then the university's Eugene Troth succeeded Britton as head of the University Division. Though previously unassociated with Interlochen, Wallace became very supportive of the camp, particularly the University Division. Before his tenure, student fees had financed the University Division's budget, but in the 1960s, Wallace created a fund at the music school in Ann Arbor to pay for many University Division services.[13] With the end of the AFM ban, the strong backing of the University of Michigan, and the declining deficits, NMC and Maddy sailed on calm waters in the late 1950s.

After a long tenure, Charles Tremaine stepped down as NMC treasurer in 1957. In the following year, at age eighty-eight, he retired from the board, and in 1959, the board appointed him trustee emeritus. Mark Osterlin, director of the Central Michigan Children's Clinic and NMC resident doctor since 1931, replaced Tremaine as treasurer. Until his death in 1963, Tremaine returned to Interlochen each summer, always donating the money for three camper scholarships.[14]

Through three decades, Tremaine had regarded his NMC role as lowering the deficits that Maddy accumulated. He had been successful by the time of his retirement. Interest on the debts had been nine thousand dollars in 1933, when Tremaine first became the NMC treasurer. By 1941 Tremaine had reduced the interest to three thousand dollars, but Maddy's purchases of Camp Penn Loch and Camp Interlochen, with initial mortgages of almost $150,000, forced NMC into debt again. To pay for the new land, Tremaine had mounted an ambitious three-year fund-raising campaign of sixteen thousand dollars per year, and to pay operating bills, he had sold bonds at 50 percent of their worth. Despite Tremaine's efforts, NMC's total debt still hovered at sixty thousand dollars in 1945, and his only consolation was that NMC owned land and 155 buildings worth $465,000. By 1952 Tremaine had reduced the indebtedness to twenty-six thousand dollars, and NMC listed well above one million dollars in assets.[15]

In 1956, the year before his retirement as treasurer, Tremaine finally paid the NMC property debt. But to Tremaine's chagrin, Maddy marked their accomplishment by promoting plans to open a winter school and operate the Interlochen property year-round. Margaret Stace, Maddy's longtime secretary, was not surprised by his plan, observing that Maddy believed he should deplete all project funds and always be planning the next stage of development.[16]

Tremaine was displeased with plans for a winter school, and he worried that with his impending retirement, no one could restrain Maddy's spending impulses. Maddy and Tremaine had often been at odds over administering finances of the camp, but they had tempered one another. Maddy often fumed at Tremaine, once complaining to Giddings, "He had a grand time advising what to do on matters that had already been done." On another occasion, Maddy complained about a fourteen-page letter from Tremaine with "the d—dest array of figures he had Mack [George Mackmiller, the assistant treasurer] prepare and which mean nothing . . . but which apparently entertain CM [Tremaine]."[17]

Tremaine, for his part, had tried various tactics to curb Maddy. He sometimes complimented Maddy's better financial decisions, such as contracting laundry services to Traverse City vendors in 1949, but more often he wrote Maddy long letters of cautionary advice. In 1958 Tremaine wrote that his lifework had always been to help others, not to lead, and that he wanted to advise Maddy on two issues. One was the prospects for the winter school, and the other was NMC's legacy when Maddy died.[18]

To begin his letters, Tremaine sometimes reminded Maddy of his weaknesses, saying "I, alone, can do it—because I am the only one who had the experience [with you]." Tremaine declared that Maddy had lacked financial interest and knowledge in the early days of the camp. Tremaine admitted that Maddy had acquired considerable financial knowledge over their thirty years together and had been making fewer mistakes in the 1950s. But Tremaine maintained that the proposed winter school posed financial dangers similar to those at NMC's beginning in 1928. He worried that if Maddy were to make mistakes in the late fifties, such as creating a winter school when NMC was finally large and solvent, the radical change in direction could be costly and disastrous for the camp.[19]

Tremaine thought that Maddy had always given too little attention to both sides of a proposed undertaking before making a final commitment. In 1958 Tremaine worried that the camp, though finally out of debt and with assets of two million dollars, was still not on a solid footing. He admitted that Maddy had unquestionably accomplished wonders, but he added: "so did Napoleon and Hitler and many others. Where did they end up— and what was the final net result of their accomplishment? They left nothing—except trouble for others and, in their own minds, the deep consciousness of failure. Ego is a glorious thing. It is the incentive for accomplishment—but it can be carried to excess and can also be the cause of downfall. Downfall is always POSSIBLE. IF it should happen to you after your great success, I doubt if your health would stand it."[20]

When Maddy, at a meeting, commented that board members should have faith in the creation of a winter school, Tremaine protested, writing on May 1, 1958, that he had been faithful "for close to thirty-two years!" Tremaine noted that he had proven his faith by purchasing NMC bonds to stop the price from "dropping rapidly below fifty percent" and to stimulate the price "back to one hundred percent." He added, "I gave the saving, represented in the varying discounts, to the camp."[21] Tremaine thought that Maddy, by planning a costly winter school, had lost his coalition of powerful supporters of NMC, and he predicted that Interlochen leaders would divide into two factions, champions for either the camp or the winter school. Maddy, said Tremaine, could not create an expanded Interlochen, because he had not yet stabilized the camp. Tremaine's last written advice to Maddy and the NMC board was to delay the inauguration of a winter school until at least 1960.[22]

Maddy wrote a measured response, "You may rest assured that I do not intend to throw the camp into a financial gulf by acting too quickly in the establishment of the winter school of the arts. There is no possibility of getting it started before 1960 and probably not that soon, however there are several things that might speed up the process."[23] The Interlochen Arts Academy actually did not open for two additional years, until the fall of 1962. But for the remaining four years of his life, Tremaine would not sanction Maddy's dream of a winter school.[24]

In his declining years, Tremaine also fussed at Maddy for not grooming their successors. Though two decades older than Maddy, Tremaine urged him: "Suppose you should die tomorrow! Exactly what would happen to the camp? It probably would continue, but would its service and influence continue to grow, or gradually diminish, or possibly change its character? It would depend considerably on the strength and stability of the organization you BUILD and LEAVE!"[25]

Maddy disregarded Tremaine's pleading to drop plans for the winter school, but Tremaine's prediction of divided constituencies for the camp and winter school materialized over the next decades, particularly after Maddy's death. Maddy had built the camp into a distinctive organization by putting NMC interests first. But when he inaugurated the winter school, with its separate commitments and requirements, the Interlochen Arts Academy's success became a primary objective of his, vexing many camp leaders.

Return of the Celebrities: The Interlochen Arts Festival

In 1960, when NMC could again hire AFM members, Howard Hanson was among the first to return and conduct NHSO. After fifteen summers without celebrities, Maddy welcomed them back, warmly repeating his belief that the presence of leading instrumentalists and conductors from well-known symphony orchestras attracted the most advanced campers, especially in the University Division.[26]

Hanson had charted his own course with the musicians' union and opposed Maddy's public fights with Petrillo, but he had always lauded NMC's programs. Though unable to conduct NHSO, Hanson had quietly visited Interlochen several times during the union ban.[27] The hot-tempered Maddy had pressured Hanson off the NMC board in 1943, but in 1959, after the AFM dispute was settled, the two men reconciled their differences, and Maddy persuaded Hanson to return to the board.

Maddy wanted to heal his relationships with the celebrities of NMC's pre-union-ban era, and Hanson was the most prominent among them.

Hanson's reputation had expanded greatly during and after World War II. He had won the 1944 Pulitzer Prize for his Symphony no. 4. He was active on the U.S. Commission for the United Nations Educational, Scientific, and Cultural Association, had testified before Congress, and had been a guest at White House dinners given by President Dwight D. Eisenhower. In 1954, with his *Chorale and Alleluia,* Hanson began to write concert band music for veteran Interlochen camper and conductor Frederick Fennell and his celebrated Eastman Wind Ensemble.[28] Following his official Interlochen return in 1960, Hanson's commitment to Interlochen deepened still further. In 1977, recognizing his years of work for NMC, the Interlochen Alumni Association commissioned Hanson's *A Sea Symphony* for NMC's fiftieth anniversary celebration.

Many faculty members who had taught during the AFM-ban years were dejected when the celebrities returned in 1960. Some lesser-known teachers departed, and Maddy chose not to retain others.[29] At the conclusion of each camp season in the early 1960s, faculty and staff members received letters of review. If the letter contained two paragraphs of information and appreciation, the faculty or staff member knew that he or she would not be asked to return the following summer. But if the letter contained a third paragraph, that paragraph would include a request to return the following summer. So each summer during the early 1960s, following the final *Les preludes* concert (Franz Liszt's *Les preludes,* traditionally performed at the end of each summer's camp season, provides the same function as commencement at the end of a school career—to remind students it is not the end of a venture but the beginning of a greater one), the celebrating faculty and staff adjourned to the local Hofbrau tavern in Interlochen, where they toasted "paragraph three."[30]

In the 1960s, with the return of celebrities and absence of Tremaine's restraints, Maddy planned major innovations for NMC. Using the student challenge system, he split NHSO into two orchestras, the more advanced National High School Symphony Orchestra and the less able National High School Concert Orchestra. In 1960, the acclaimed Joseph Knitzer taught violin, and Deems Taylor and Don Gillis were the resident composers.[31]

Maddy accomplished a major feat in 1961, when he persuaded music's reigning international celebrity to perform with NMC campers. Traveling to Kilgore, Texas, he asked Rildia Bee Cliburn to persuade her son, Van, to play a piano concerto with the camp orchestras. Van Cliburn's mother, a prominent piano teacher, had been Maddy's friend ever since several of her students had attended NMC, years before Van conquered the musical world by winning Moscow's 1958 Tchaikovsky International Piano Competition. Taking advantage of her friendship, Maddy convinced Rildia Bee to telephone Van, who was touring, and coax him into playing the concert. Van was busy with his booked engagements, and the proposed trip to Interlochen was inconvenient and expensive, so he wanted to decline Maddy's invitation. But Rildia Bee would not hang up until he agreed to perform at Interlochen. So in the summer of 1961, Van Cliburn played Tchaikovsky's B-flat Minor Concerto with the combined NMC orchestras of 180 instrumentalists.

The smashing success of Cliburn's visit in 1961 vitalized NMC, not only because the performance was stunning, but also because Maddy could present Cliburn as the most celebrated NMC performer in more than fifteen years. For his part, Cliburn was so moved by Joe Maddy and his Interlochen experiences that over the following decade and a half, he performed yearly benefit concerts with the NMC orchestra. In 1963, charmed by Maddy, Cliburn joined the Interlochen board of trustees, where he continues to serve.[32]

Cliburn returned in the summer of 1962 to play Rachmaninoff's Third Piano Concerto, and NMC stepped up its association with other celebrities. Margaret Hillis, director of the Chicago Symphony Chorus, conducted the NMC Festival Choir, assisted by piano accompanist Byron Hanson, who later became Interlochen's director of music.

Late in the summer of 1961, Maddy took the NMC orchestra and dancers to Washington, D.C., where they performed for President John F. Kennedy in the garden of the White House. Kennedy so expansively praised their presentation that Maddy called Kennedy the next day to suggest that the U.S. government fund an NMC music tour to Europe. Though he succeeded in talking personally to Kennedy, Maddy could not secure his European tour.[33]

Maddy, however, had not lost his touch with celebrities. In the spring of 1964, Joe, by then retired three years from the university, was awarded an honorary doctorate by the University of Michigan. Also receiving an honorary degree that day was President Lyndon B. Johnson, who delivered his notable speech "Great Society." After the ceremonies, Maddy pursued Johnson and engaged him by relating the NMC story. Johnson, impressed, dispatched his daughter Luci to the 1964 camp, where she narrated Prokofiev's *Peter and the Wolf* with the camp orchestra. To commemorate this occasion, Maddy convinced Van Cliburn to conduct Luci Baines Johnson's performance. Though this was one of Cliburn's first experiences in conducting an orchestra, RCA Victor Records produced a professional recording with Cliburn conducting the Interlochen orchestra later that summer. The recording, unfortunately, did not include the Prokofiev composition.

Because of the very favorable publicity for the camp orchestra in 1964, Maddy decided to change the name of the top NHSO. First, for Cliburn's recording, he called it the Interlochen Youth Orchestra. Then he settled on the name World Youth Symphony Orchestra (WYSO), its current name.[34]

The summer of 1964 marked the first appearance of a full professional symphony orchestra on the Interlochen campus. When the Philadelphia Orchestra performed that summer, Maddy included the concert in what he called an Interlochen Arts Festival, a name that would be resurrected in 1980 to promote Interlochen's series of professional and student concerts. Eugene Ormandy conducted the 1964 concert, which featured principal trombonist Henry Charles Smith, a former camper and later the resident conductor of WYSO. Maddy and the Interlochen community were proud of securing Ormandy's orchestra, and an Interlochen campus street was named Ormandy Drive to commemorate the concert.[35]

Because of his sudden death in the spring of 1966, Joe Maddy's last *Les preludes* concert was at the end of the 1965 summer season. He was active during that summer, preparing for a 1966 meeting of the International Society of Music Educators (ISME), to be held at Interlochen and to feature musical luminaries from both America and Europe. Zoltán Kodály, Karl Ernst, and Egon Kraus formed the international committee that visited the camp in 1965. Following Maddy's death in April, Interlochen coordinator Lyman Starr carried out Maddy's plans, and in the summer of 1966, Interlochen held the seventh world conference of ISME, attended by renowned composers Zoltán Kodály of Hungary, Dmitry Kabalevsky of Russia, and Norman Dello Joio of the United States. Though he did not live to enjoy it, Maddy had produced this Interlochen play for the world's musical stage.[36]

Clement Stone and the Interlochen Arts Academy

In 1948 Maddy had told Giddings about his dream for a winter school, but in 1957 Maddy was still having trouble getting his colleagues' support for the projected school. In that year, while still assuring the skeptical Tremaine that a National Arts Academy could not open until a sufficient number of camp buildings had been winterized, Maddy put the NMC plumbing systems, originally built for summer use, underground.[37]

Since Maddy could not convince most board members to support the winter school, he proposed that board members be limited to one, three-year term, so that he could rotate opponents off the board and add members who would help him.[38] He suggested that Tremaine, as the longest-serving trustee, should be the first to retire, and Tremaine obligingly became a trustee emeritus. Then, after securing Howard Hanson's allegiance on the issue of the winter school, Maddy advocated Hanson's return to the board. But other board members resisted the term limitations. Prominent board member Roscoe Bonisteel, who at first opposed Maddy's plans for the winter school, refused to consider the three-year limitation, and Maddy was forced to abandon this scheme.[39]

As several board members resigned, Maddy proposed the addition of new trustees who favored his winter school. In 1960, at Maddy's suggestion, the board elected Donald Gonzales, promotion director of the Williamsburg, Virginia, Restoration Project and former head of the United Press in Washington, D.C. Treasurer Mark Osterlin died that same year, so Maddy asked the board to replace him with Charles Attwood, president of Unistrut Corporation of Wayne, Michigan. Attwood, Maddy promised, was a millionaire who would contribute twenty-two thousand dollars for a new camp store.[40] The board also added Mark Osterlin's wife, Helen, who worked tirelessly for Joe Maddy and the Interlochen board until her death in 1996. In 1959 Maddy appointed John Merrill secretary and director of personnel, replacing Roger Jacobi, who had been appointed an assistant professor at the University of Michigan School of Music. Merrill, choral director in the Ann Arbor school system and formerly an army personnel director, had worked at NMC the previous three summers.

Even before Maddy had secured board approval, he asked both Merrill and Don Gillis, Interlochen's recently hired vice president of development (fund-raising), to prepare for a winter school. With his reconstituted board, Maddy persuaded the trustees, in a meeting of July 18, 1960, to approve a separate charter creating the Interlochen Arts Academy (IAA). Those opposed to the winter school were formidable. They included many longtime staff members, such as Vice President George Wilson and Maddy's secretary, Margaret Stace. Other NMC faculty and staff members did not oppose Joe, for they conceded that if he wanted the winter school, he would probably find a way to make it work.[41] Maddy, then almost seventy, retired from the University of Michigan in the spring of 1961, and in the fall, over the staff's objection, he moved the year-round NMC office from Ann Arbor to Interlochen. Though a strong academy supporter, Gillis resigned.

Still with no money in hand for buildings for the winter school, Maddy contracted to have the basement dug for a large winterized dormitory. Shocked staff members, seeing the large hole that had suddenly appeared, whispered that Joe was now "digging his own holes."[42] He believed that he would soon have the funds to open his winter school.

Maddy's new optimism stemmed from the fact that in the fall of 1961, Chicago writer Norma Lee Browning had introduced Joe to Clement Stone, president of the Combined Insurance Company of America and a well-known Chicago philanthropist. Stone recalls that he and his wife, Jessie, committed themselves to Joe at their first meeting, and the Maddys and Stones became close friends who shared similar goals.[43] Stone examined Maddy's academy plans carefully and suggested that the curriculum should include moral training. He asked Maddy to outline his principal objectives and forecast a total cost for the academy project, including an operating budget for the first years.[44]

Stone was pleased with Maddy's detailed responses to his inquiry, and in November 1961, the W. Clement and Jessie V. Stone Foundation gave Interlochen $350,000 to start the winter school.[45] Stunned by this large gift, Maddy's remaining detractors on the board reluctantly changed their votes and agreed to build the necessary buildings for IAA. Clement Stone soon joined the Interlochen board, where he was a vital force for more than three decades, including twenty years as chairman. Stone paid the academy's debts for its first ten years, and after becoming chairman of the Interlochen board in 1972, he contributed additional millions of dollars and convinced other benefactors to donate funds to Interlochen. With Stone's initial gift assured, Maddy approached famous Michigan architect Alden Dow to plan and build distinctive buildings for the academy. When trustee Franklin Dunham died in 1961, Maddy persuaded Dow to join the board, and Maddy gained still another advocate for his academy.

In 1961 Maddy made overtures to several NMC colleagues to head the academy. When Maddy solicited conductor Clyde Roller, then on the Eastman School of Music faculty, Roller replied that he would not administer the academy, but he agreed to join the Interlochen board as academy vice president from 1962 until 1965. Roller supported Maddy's plans for the academy, and he later sent his daughter to study there.[46] Finally, after other rejections from musician friends, Maddy chose Mearl Culver, formerly president of a church college, to direct IAA. Culver planned the curriculum, purchased equipment, and, with Maddy and Merrill, gathered a faculty for the academy opening. James Reed, director of adult education at Ecorse School in Detroit, became assistant academy head, and Richard Maddy, Joe's son, was registrar.

Since Maddy had instructed John Merrill to hire academy faculty and staff before enrollments or operating funds were secure, Maddy borrowed money from the NMC account to get started, an action that provoked outspoken complaints from board members and staff who opposed the academy.[47] The many details involved in starting the academy were daunting for the new administration. According to veteran teacher Robert Murphy, in a meeting held as late as July 1962, opening plans still lacked good preparation. But Maddy's ebullience and Culver's experience drove them successfully to opening day. Directing the academy, however, proved a great burden for the courtly and soft-spoken Culver, and he left Interlochen before the completion of the first academic year.[48]

Early in 1962, Charles Eilber, a mathematics teacher in Royal Oak, Michigan, read a Detroit newspaper account about the proposed arts academy. In March, Maddy and Culver interviewed Eilber, who was greatly impressed with Maddy's vision and energy. Maddy hired Eilber—who had studied forestry—both to teach mathematics at the academy and to work with NMC museum director Walter Hastings during the camp season.

In the academy's beginning years, Maddy instituted few management policies, and his administrators sometimes regretted the hasty decision making that resulted.[49] For instance, Maddy promised to house the Eilber family beginning in June 1962, but the housing was incomplete, so the Eilbers were placed in the Van Cliburn scholarship lodge. A year later, administrators surprised Eilber, then working for NMC, by asking him to vacate the Cliburn lodge for the summer so that NMC could gain additional rental income. A startled Eilber renegotiated his contract so that he could remain in the lodge.

The academy began with thirty-four faculty members, most with broad interests. John Runge, for example, head of physics, also played guitar, sang, and performed in many faculty and student events. Sadly, according to Eilber, Runge was outspoken in his criticism of Maddy and did not return for a third year.[50] Several married couples worked at the academy. Eilber's wife, Carol, taught English classes, and journalist Norma Lee Browning initiated a creative writing department, while her husband Russell Ogg engaged in promotional photography and taught the camera workshop. Browning's widely distributed personal reminiscence, *Joe Maddy of Interlochen*, was published in the summer of 1963.

Besides music, Maddy inaugurated several art studies at the academy, including creative writing, photography, theater, dance, and visual arts. William Hug headed dance and physical education. Jean Parsons, a graduate of Cranbrook Academy of Art and a Fulbright fellow in Denmark, headed the visual arts department for both the camp and the academy from 1962 until 1974.[51]

But music was Maddy's primary interest. He hired Joseph Knitzer, NMC teacher and former concertmaster of the Cleveland Orchestra, to teach violin, and he hired Doy Baker to teach music theory, composition, and double bass. Barre Hill, veteran opera director for NMC's University Division, produced the academy's radio and television programs, headed the voice department, and originated an opera workshop. Robert Murphy, who, with Parsons, continued to teach at the academy into the 1990s, was director of the chorus. Lyman Starr, instructor of low brass instruments, was also executive vice president of the Interlochen Press, which printed the academy's programs.[52]

Using borrowed, camp-generated funds to recruit students, admissions officer George Worden secured a sufficient number of students for the academy's first year, though, according to Eilber, Worden sometimes promised parents and students conditions that academy administrators could not fulfill. Eilber recalled admitting the thirteen-year-old nephew of an internationally prominent composer and dance band leader. The boy had grown up in a household where he stayed up late at night and slept until noon the following day. But his academy life was regimented in both music studies and living conditions and included James Reed's early morning calls. The boy did not adjust to the rigors, so he left the academy at Christmas break.[53]

IAA opened with 132 students and several new campus buildings. New buildings included the first of architect Dow's stunning rotunda classroom buildings and Orchestra Hall, a space that housed weekly concerts and was later converted to visual arts studios. In that first year, many classroom spaces were inadequate. Among other arrangements, the dance building was pressed into service for drawing classes, causing some faculty members to complain that Maddy was uninterested in visual arts. But according to art teacher Jean Parsons, Maddy did give spiritual support to her art classes, probably because Maddy's mother had been an amateur painter.

During the IAA's first nine-month school year, students produced, participated in, or listened to 121 concerts, recitals, television productions, plays, and ballet performances. Renowned pianist Claudette Sorel played a solo concert and taught a master class, inaugurating the tradition of artists that would troop to the academy over the years. IAA students grew to be close friends, and in May 1963, the academy sponsored a school prom that included each student and highlighted a dance band led by student Henry Young, who later became a well-known arts administrator.[54]

In 1963, the second year of the academy, Maddy enrolled eighth graders, and the student numbers approached three hundred. Traverse City guidance counselor Vernon Hawes was hired to live in the dormitory, with his family, to improve student living conditions. Donald Phillips, a former superintendent, became the new head of the academy. According to faculty members, Phillips and Maddy disagreed openly in faculty meetings, so Phillips left in midyear, with James Reed replacing him as acting head. The administration also hired a separate principal for academic subjects in 1963, but this arrangement failed because of personnel conflicts.[55]

IAA faculty in the second year included University of Michigan cellist and head of postcamp chamber music Oliver Edel, clarinetist Frank Ell, pianist Jon Peterson, and biologist John Hood, who would later head the academy. Former camper and oboist Donald Jaeger conducted the band, and his wife, Ann, taught writing. Among the students, Jean Baxstresser, later the principal flutist of the New York Philharmonic, won the competition to play a concerto with the academy orchestra.[56]

On October 17, 1963, the IAA orchestra, dressed in new red blazers, traveled to the Eastman School of Music Theatre in Rochester for a concert directed by Eastman conductors Clyde Roller and Howard Hanson. The tour concluded on the next day, with an American music program played for the New York State Teachers Association. In March 1964, the academy orchestra and dancers performed for MENC in Philadelphia and at New York City's Lincoln Center, with a program that included an academy-commissioned premiere of Alan Hovhaness's Variation and Fugue for Orchestra.[57]

At first Maddy wanted IAA to replicate the structured social regulations of NMC, but he and his administration were unprepared to supervise the students' personal lives so strictly for nine months. Dean of boys Robert Murphy and dean of girls Marcia Palmer lived in the dormitories, but they lacked a counseling staff, so faculty members took on aspects of parenting the students. In the first years, faculty members participated fully in the students' extracurricular activities, but as the young faculty matured and developed outside personal interests, the IAA administration needed to add a counseling staff to live in the large dormitories and guide the students.

Maddy also had planned to replicate the camp's artistic competitiveness at the academy. And while he assumed the academy would establish high artistic standards, he was surprised that the faculty and students would also strive for high academic attainment. IAA parents pressed for a strong curriculum in science and literature, and the energetic and competitive students, aided by a devoted faculty, set lofty standards in all classrooms. Students were excelling in every course, not only in the arts, and the academy promotional materials soon promised that IAA emphasized artistic and academic subjects equally. Though conceived as an arts school, the academy broadened its scope, even offering students science workshops in addition to those in music, acting, and visual arts.[58]

During its first thirty years, Interlochen's campus planning had been incremental but piecemeal. By 1960 NMC buildings, expanding out from the lakes by accretion, had formed a charming summer colony that subsequent campus planners would dub "Camp Chaos." In July 1962, the Michigan Historical Commission, recognizing these unique stone and wooden cabins, honored Interlochen with a marker ceremony.[59] Then, between 1960, when the Greenleaf Organ Building was completed, and 1966, when Kresge Hall was enlarged, Joe Maddy and architect Alden Dow altered the look of the Interlochen campus more than at any other time in its history. Dow's campus plan dominated Interlochen's appearance for many years. Even the construction of the Grand Traverse Performing Arts Center in 1976 and the Dendrinos Chapel in 1981 were first proposed in the early 1960s.

In the academy's first half decade, ten major buildings were built or renovated. Reorganizing the center of the camp, Dow moved buildings outward from the core and extended the fabric of the campus farther from the lakeshores into the woodland. To give students a sense of campus orientation and character, he retained much of the NMC campus, including common buildings lining the streets and cabins arranged in parallel rows and semicircles. But Dow expanded on NMC's stone-and-wood themes and created colonies of rotundas along an interior street. In the summer of 1964, Maddy dedicated this interior walkway as the Giddings Concourse, since it was built with stone from the razed Giddings Hall.[60]

To comply with the state of Michigan's requirements for a secondary school, Maddy had to build a gymnasium. The Stone Foundation donated the funds for building construction, and Maddy dedicated the Jessie V. Stone Building (JVS) in 1963. But Maddy was reluctant to spend money on such a large sports building, so he insisted that this gymnasium would also serve as an additional auditorium, complete with a stage across from the bleachers. In equipping the room, an Interlochen administrator had ordered two scoreboards, one for each end of the gymnasium. Scoreboards were expensive, so Maddy, reasoning that one scoreboard was sufficient, became furious on discovering the purchases. He quickly canceled the order on the second scoreboard. On May 24, 1963, to dedicate the gymnasium, the academy orchestra inaugurated the first Michigan Youth Arts Festival with a performance in JVS.[61]

A campus retail store was built in 1965, funded by a grant of $1,100,000, one of the final Stone Foundation grants during Maddy's lifetime. The foundation pledged another $350,000 to be paid in June 1966, to match a gift from the Charles Stewart Mott Foundation for a language-arts rotunda.[62] In 1966, just before his death, Stanley Kresge gave the funds to enlarge and roof over Kresge Hall, now called Kresge Auditorium. The newly covered four-thousand-seat pavilion greeted participants at NMC's 1966 International Music Educators Conference and continues to shelter academy graduations and camp concerts.[63]

As Interlochen constructed larger buildings next to the original, smaller buildings, the campus acquired a new ambience. During the winter, clusters of vacant cabins slumbered during the academy's bustle. Old camp roads were interrupted and new ones created, and growing student populations changed the traditional pedestrian patterns.

The founding of IAA enabled Maddy to attract an array of new luminaries to Interlochen, including operatic soprano Rose Bampton and record producer Walter Toscanini. Maddy also attracted Marten ten Hoor, who was dean emeritus of the University of Alabama's College of Arts and Sciences, Maddy's mentor on the high school curriculum, and principal speaker at IAA's opening ceremony.[64]

Trustee Charles Attwood resigned as Interlochen treasurer in 1962, and in 1963 Maddy hired Clare Burns to be the treasurer, a staff post Burns held until his 1990 retirement. In 1964, after Donald Phillips resigned as head of the academy, Maddy again asked Clyde Roller, trustee vice president of the academy, to move to Interlochen and replace Phillips. Roller declined and supported Thor Johnson's candidacy. Johnson, a former camper who had become an internationally known conductor, agreed to leave his Northwestern University position to head IAA, conduct the academy orchestra, and replace Roller as a vice president and Interlochen trustee.[65]

Johnson's arrival brought increased prestige to Maddy's new academy. In 1947, at age thirty-four, Johnson had burst on the national scene as conductor of the Cincinnati Symphony Orchestra. An early camper, his NMC roots were deep, and his conducting had unfolded at the University of Michigan, where he arrived as a graduate student in 1934. By 1938 he had founded the University Little Symphony, a music school group of approximately twenty select musicians. He soon established a strong and long-lasting professional tie with University Musical Society head Charles Sink. Promoted by Sink, Johnson made his national conducting debut with the Philadelphia Orchestra during the University Musical Society's 1940 May Festival. He returned yearly to conduct the May Festival until 1973, two years before his death.[66] After the 1940 festival, Johnson's career blossomed, and by the time of his 1963 Interlochen appointment, he had spent eleven years conducting the Cincinnati Symphony Orchestra and six years as head of Northwestern University's orchestral studies.

Johnson's academy orchestra played a concert every week, and all IAA teachers attended. Faculty members, predominantly young and vigorous, bonded into a strong community of support. Besides his worldly musical demeanor, Johnson was broadly cultured, so he promoted arts studies other than music. Sometimes he expected more sophistication from the Interlochen community than he thought he received. For instance, he arranged a Japanese art exhibition at the academy, but few students attended, much to his consternation.[67]

Academic class scheduling had been very traditional before Johnson's tenure. But English teacher Carol Eilber suggested that the academy reorganize the classes into an open curriculum. Johnson was very receptive to this idea and encouraged the faculty to experiment with newer methods to challenge the students.

Though most arts faculty members found him imaginative and creative,

Johnson became a controversial figure at Interlochen. Maddy's staff thought he was a difficult person and considered him a weak administrator. To remedy Johnson's administrative shortcomings while maintaining his artistic contributions, Maddy hired first Reginald Eldred, then Charles Eilber, to supervise the academic programs. Johnson was a frightening yet respected father figure to the students. His orchestral concerts were brilliantly executed, but many academy students resented his brutal orchestra rehearsals, which began at 3:00 P.M. and lasted until the dinner hour.[68]

In 1965 Maddy hired former camper Byron Hanson for an academy curriculum project. Byron, a recent Eastman School of Music graduate, soon assisted Johnson with the IAA orchestra. In future years, Byron served other academy conductors, then secured the conductorship himself. In the 1990s, he became Interlochen's music director, supervising music instruction in both the camp and the academy. Byron, an academy leader during the entire last third of the twentieth century, brought continuity to IAA's orchestral program and a legacy from the Thor Johnson era.[69]

WIAA

After April 1959, when new AFM president Herman Kenin removed NMC from the National Unfair List, Joe Maddy immediately launched efforts to return Interlochen broadcasts to NBC. In 1961, with AFM's approval, NBC distributed a recorded series of NMC programs called *Best from Interlochen,* programs similar to the *Music from Interlochen* series that the National Association of Educational Broadcasters had distributed during the previous decade. Few NBC affiliates carried the new series, so the network dropped the programs the following year and ended its longtime association with Interlochen.[70]

The timing of Interlochen's return to NBC was unfortunate, because commercial network radio was fading by 1960. National radio advertisers had shifted their interests and budgets to television. Network noncommercial programs, such as *Best from Interlochen,* disappeared. NBC, CBS, and ABC radio would no longer pay their affiliates to carry network programs, so to sustain themselves, individual stations sold commercials locally. Soap operas disappeared from radio, and newscasts became the primary network programming. Among the major national programs, only ABC's *Breakfast Club* and CBS's *Arthur Godfrey Show* survived for several more years.

Maddy was not truly surprised by the changes in noncommercial radio. Twenty years earlier, in 1939, following NBC's cancellation of his *Music and American Youth* instructional radio series, he had urged educators to create an educational network to broadcast classical music. College stations and networks had emerged in response. Then, in the 1950s, as radio and recording technology evolved, Maddy resonated to the emerging FM radio sound, which was superb for music. He began scheming to own and operate his own FM radio station at Interlochen.

In 1957 he persuaded the *Owosso (Michigan) Argus-Press* newspaper to donate an FM radio transmitter to NMC, and he pressed camp broadcasting director Robert Elson to start an NMC radio station by the summer of 1959. Maddy postulated that once his new camp station had become operational, the University of Michigan would contribute funds toward its maintenance and winter operation, and NMC could fund the nominal station expenses in the summer. However, Maddy soon realized that NMC lacked the basic resources to sustain a full-time radio station, even with University of Michigan help. To launch a station, NMC would need to operate with a full-time staff, and Maddy could not afford to add required space to the radio building or to pay ten thousand dollars for a radio antenna.[71]

His solution was to dovetail his dream for an FM station at Interlochen with his concurrent dream to open a year-round school. As plans for the winter school began to crystallize in 1960, he simultaneously planned his new Interlochen radio station with camp broadcasting director Harvey Herbst and chief radio engineer John Reiser. The projected year-round establishment would enable him to hire a twelve-month staff and invest in expensive recording and broadcasting equipment.[72]

On July 22, 1963, nine months after IAA opened, FM radio station WIAA went on the air from Interlochen. Radio station WUOM in Ann Arbor, which had begun broadcasting more than a decade before, was Maddy's model. Radio engineer L. D. Greilick, who would work intermittently at the station for many years, put WIAA on the air, and Dick Goerz was the first general manager. Broadcasting with 150,000 watts, the station could be heard over most of northern lower Michigan, the largest coverage area the FCC would permit. WIAA's listening audience was small, because at that time most people listened primarily to AM radio stations. Even by 1965, when WIAA was among fourteen hundred FM radio stations in the United States, more than four thousand AM stations dominated the American airways. The smaller audiences for FM did not seem to trouble Maddy, because he felt that WIAA was broadcasting to a discerning audience. He installed the most advanced technical equipment Interlochen could afford, and in 1966, the year of his death, WIAA began broadcasting with a new, stereo signal.

At first, in 1962, WIAA was on the air from 2:00 P.M. until 10:00 P.M. daily, airing recorded classical music, syndicated music services, and plays, such as the British Broadcasting Corporation's Shakespeare series. Gradually WIAA increased its hours, until the station broadcast for twenty-four hours a day in the 1980s.

Maddy could now air Interlochen performances in real time and produce, on the Interlochen grounds, nationally distributed music series, such as *Music from Interlochen*. Because of WIAA and its radio productions, NMC began to receive national and international recognition comparable to the reputation it garnered with its NBC series during the 1930s. Radio studies returned to the camp curriculum, and in 1966 Harold Boxer, director of music at Voice of America in Washington, D.C., began regular summer visits to Interlochen to tape interviews and concerts for his worldwide audience.[73]

By 1965 many American radio stations were specializing in music format styles, such as popular, country, or classical, while others emphasized news programming. As a nonprofit station, WIAA became an educational, public radio station, and in 1970 the station banded with other educational stations to form National Public Radio (NPR). Maddy did not live long enough to witness NPR's beginnings, but WIAA was a charter member of this noncommercial radio network, first envisaged by Maddy, radio engineer Jerome Wiesner, and Ohio State University's head of educational and radio research W. W. Charters at their 1939 conference on educational radio.

Television, though nationally more dominant than radio since 1952, has played a minor role at NMC. Of course, the expense of producing television has been prohibitive, but Maddy also preferred radio's dependence on sound over pictures, a view he shared with many musical colleagues. In television's early days, the sound was inferior to the FM radio sound, so Maddy's primary interest in television was its capacity to promote Interlochen more widely than radio could. Defending radio programming, he observed, "Camp programs should present fine music and continue to present it until the public has learned to understand and appreciate it."[74]

NMC's first television programs featured students performing locally over WWTV from its studios in Cadillac, Michigan, in 1954. Eight fifteen-minute programs were aired live on Thursday afternoons. In the following year, the camp hired Richard Fiegel as NMC's first full-time television producer and director, and the broadcasts shifted to WPBN television in Traverse City. Over subsequent years, students and faculty performed on both half-hour and one-hour programs. With television productions, NMC could spotlight the theater and dance departments. Though pleased with these television experiences for his campers, Maddy regretted that the productions suffered from too little rehearsal time for the camp television directors and the camera operators.[75]

In 1962, after telecasting several years of NMC's programs, television station WPBN in Traverse City began broadcasting live Sunday programs that highlighted students from the newly opened IAA. Then, in the summer of 1963, Maddy arranged Interlochen's first network television broadcast. Hugh Downs, whose children were campers, and Barbara Walters hosted NBC's *Today* show from Kresge Hall. Maddy thought he reaped great publicity from the *Today* broadcast, but he never again secured a network television broadcast from Interlochen.[76]

Part 6

One Institution: The Interlochen Center for the Arts

The faculty expressed their resentment at the separate charter for the Interlochen Arts Academy, which seemed hung out to dry.

—Roger Jacobi

Passing the Baton

On April 18, 1966, John Merrill and Margaret Stace were summoned to the hospital at 3:00 A.M. and told by the attending physician that Joe Maddy had died of a heart attack. Also present were Fay Maddy and Helen Osterlin. The funeral, held in the Jessie V. Stone Building and arranged by Lyman Starr, was attended by a large crowd of students, employees, and townspeople.

This abrupt end to Maddy's life was difficult for the Interlochen board and administration, especially since the president had left no instructions for his succession. Maddy had not believed he would go on forever: Tremaine had hounded him about the need to prepare for an Interlochen without him. But Maddy's only response had been to tell many of his associates, including Clyde Roller, Don Gillis, Lyman Starr, Maynard Klein, and Richard Maddy, that they were in line to become his successor.[1]

On April 21, 1966, the trustees met before the funeral to establish an administrative committee, including camp and academy officers, to run Interlochen until they could appoint a new president. They elected Ann Arbor attorney Roscoe Bonisteel to the new office of chairman of the board of trustees. Bonisteel had headed the board's executive committee since Mark Osterlin died in 1960, but Maddy himself had always chaired the board meetings before his death. Bonisteel now took charge, and he guided the board to appoint John Merrill as the administrative committee chair and secretary. Others on the administrative committee included George

Wilson, camp vice president; Thor Johnson, academy vice president; Clare Burns, treasurer; and Margaret Stace, assistant to the president.[2]

The enormous burden of managing an institution as complex as Interlochen without Maddy's presence struck Merrill on the Monday following the funeral. The building trades union had sent him a letter demanding to represent Interlochen's maintenance workers. Though Merrill eventually defeated the union through the workers' votes, his administrative problems continued during the following year and a half, until a new president took over. Merrill felt that the board was not sympathetic or supportive of him, and in retrospect, he thought that the board should have selected an interim president rather than the administrative committee for that period.[3] But despite administrative difficulties, camp and academy administrators made progress and initiated new classes during the presidential search period.

Soon after Maddy's death, board members discovered that he had shielded them from crucial operating data about the academy finances.[4] Chair Roscoe Bonisteel and Vice Chair Clement Stone soon presided over a split board membership, as factions opposed to the continuation of the academy became highly vocal. Adding further to contentious issues, Maddy had planned to start a college of creative arts on the Interlochen campus, an idea originally conceived by Don Gillis but opposed by most University of Michigan supporters. Though the membership was divided on the issue, the board leadership, to attract the best presidential candidates, promoted a continuation of both the academy and the college plan.[5]

With Maddy's fund-raising capabilities absent, Clement Stone paid for additional professional help and pressed Merrill to undertake a capital campaign, designated "to insure Joe Maddy's dreams." Merrill had gained experience by staffing Joe Maddy's fund-raising activities in the 1960s, when he carried Maddy's briefcase on New York trips to foundations. Maddy taught him frugality and opportunism. On one occasion, Maddy and Merrill, coupling a fund-raising journey with a Steinway Hall reception for Van Cliburn, took a cab to the East Side Terminal to check baggage, then walked some distance to Steinway Hall on Fifty-seventh Street. On the money-saving walk, Maddy met three former students, two of whom made financial contributions to the camp. On another occasion, as Merrill and Maddy walked past the Chase Manhattan Bank, Maddy stopped in midstep and said that he was going in to see David Rockefeller. Maddy succeeded in meeting Rockefeller, who agreed to attend the first academy orchestra concert in New York City and to send his daughters to NMC.[6]

Karl Haas

In the 1960s, government support for the arts increased massively, and Maddy and Merrill secured both federal and state grants for Interlochen. In 1963 Governor George Romney of Michigan appointed broadcaster Karl Haas as the second chair of the expanded Michigan Council for the Arts (MCA), a post he held for five years. Haas had worked closely with the governor's wife, Lenore, on activities for the Metropolitan Opera in New York and had gained political skills with Michigan legislators. With Governor Romney's concurrence, Haas invited members of the Michigan House and Senate Finance committees to a luncheon promoting arts in Michigan. Fourteen members attended, including one skeptical representative from Michigan's Upper Peninsula, who said he would allow Haas twenty minutes to state his case. At the luncheon's conclusion, the representative said that though he understood nothing of Haas's presentation, he liked the way Haas spoke, so he would vote for one of the first bills to fund the arts in Michigan.[7]

Maddy and Haas worked together both in Michigan and on committees to create a national arts council. In 1963 Senator Claiborne Pell of Rhode Island, with guidance from his assistant, Livingston Biddle, campaigned to create the National Endowment for the Arts. Pell's work was not the first attempt to gain U.S. government aid for the arts, since Senator Jacob Javits of New York, while in the 1948 House of Representatives, had proposed a national arts advisory committee. In the next decade, President Dwight D. Eisenhower had considered a federal advisory commission on the arts. And President John F. Kennedy had issued an executive order proposing a president's advisory council on the arts, just months before his assassination in 1963.

Support for a National Endowment for the Arts became bipartisan, with Republican senator Jacob Javits of New York being joined by Republican senator John Sherman Cooper of Kentucky and Democratic senators Joseph Clark of Pennsylvania and Hubert Humphrey of Minnesota. Even such adversaries as Democratic senator Edward Kennedy of Massachusetts and Republican senator Barry Goldwater of Arizona voted to create the National Endowment for the Arts, which finally began in 1965.

Opposition to government support for the arts rose from persons worried about creeping socialism and artistic mediocrity, although, from the beginning, the Endowment had amassed an impressively successful record of artistic achievements in music, theater, dance, and visual arts. An Endowment controversy in 1965 mirrored the unionization battles between Petrillo and Maddy. Maddy's position prevailed that time, and though the government required the Endowment to pay prevailing union wages to professional musicians, the professionals could also perform with unpaid students in government-funded concerts.

In the Michigan legislative delegation, Democratic senator Philip Hart voted to create the Endowment, but Robert Griffin, Interlochen's representative and later a Michigan senator, feared that the U.S. government would interfere in the arts, and he opposed the Endowment at first, instead supporting an advisory council on the arts. Republican representative Gerald R. Ford from Grand Rapids ultimately supported funding for the arts. During his terms as House minority leader and president of the United States, Ford voted for government arts funding, and during a 1975 presidential visit to Interlochen, he lauded NMC's positive impact on American arts.

President Lyndon B. Johnson first appointed the National Council for the Arts, then signed the law creating the National Endowment for the Arts on September 29, 1965, six months before Joe Maddy's death. Roger Stevens, later a member of Interlochen's advisory board, became the first chairman of the Endowment, and Herman Kenin, the AFM president who had removed Interlochen from the union's National Unfair List, was appointed to the National Council on the Arts.[8]

Karl Haas's work for the Endowment and MCA assured him of a spot on the candidacy list for the Interlochen presidency following Maddy's death. Mindful of differing opinions in the board and staff, James Wallace of the University of Michigan led the search committee to settle on final candidates that included Haas and the University of Michigan's Allen Britton and Eugene Troth.[9]

The search committee was drawn to Haas, who had achieved international recognition not only as a broadcaster but also as the head of fine arts programming for the Ford Foundation in Berlin and as a delegate to the International Music Congress in Rotterdam. Haas was born in Speyer, Germany, on December 6, 1913. He attended the Mannheim Conservatory and the University of Heidelberg, and he studied piano with Rudolf Fetsch and Artur Schnabel. He emigrated to Detroit in 1936, teaching piano at the Bendetson Netzorg School and later, in 1947, in his own piano studios. In 1954, Haas started his radio career as piano recitalist and commentator for the Canadian Broadcasting Corporation. Then, in 1959, he became director of fine arts for radio station WJR in Detroit, where he inaugurated a daily nationally distributed classical music program called *Adventures in Good Music.* In 1963 he was accorded a George Peabody Radio Award for *Adventures,* and over the following two years, he was granted honorary doctorates from Michigan's Albion College, Ohio's Findlay College (now the University of Findlay), and Bowling Green State College in Ohio (now Bowling Green State University).[10]

Haas had admired Maddy's descriptions of the camp and the academy when they had labored jointly on state arts groups, educational projects, and radio productions. As an academy advisory board member since 1963, Haas had come to hold Maddy in high regard. Haas thought Maddy was a remarkable man, a seer ahead of his time, and Haas believed his own ideas were in tune with Maddy's vision. Though he thought that Maddy was not always easy to get along with, Haas recognized Maddy's ability to change his mind when he saw fit, or when someone convinced him to alter directions.[11]

The possibilities for Interlochen's growth, especially the establishment of a fine arts college, intrigued Haas. He was confident that Interlochen's board would support the college, because John Merrill, with Clement Stone's help, had already begun the planning phase of this expansion. The board members, for their part, were impressed with Haas's engaging personality. Many Interlochen community members wanted the next president to emulate Maddy in a master-and-student relationship where the president was master and the staff members were students. Haas was just such a master teacher, and though not conservative enough to suit many Interlochen supporters, he was in harmony with Maddy's venturesome nature.[12]

The search committee offered him the presidency, and on April 1, 1967, a year after Maddy's death, the Interlochen board appointed Karl Haas the second president of Interlochen. In June, after dissolving the administrative committee, the board elected him to trusteeship. His formal inauguration, with an address by University of Michigan president Harlan Hatcher, took place at Interlochen on November 5, 1967. Haas quickly settled into the presidency, producing his hour-long *Adventures in Good Music* radio program at the WIAA campus studios at 8:00 A.M. each day so that he could arrive and begin work at his office at 9:00 A.M. Haas relished his association with Interlochen, and to please certain board members, he mentioned Interlochen periodically over his radio program, which by then was gaining a large and loyal listenership.[13]

When he arrived in the spring of 1967, Haas observed that Interlochen was sequestered from the cosmopolitan art world. He worried that the institution, which he thought deserved improved national and international recognition, was hidden in a Michigan forest. Haas determined to stretch Maddy's dream to combine the worldliness of Interlochen's ideas with the woodsy setting. He envisaged a world-renowned institution comparable to other great arts schools, and to plant Interlochen's flag in the world's premier cultural city, he opened a telephone office in New York.

Soon Haas found it difficult to promote both the camp and the academy as one entity. He found that a major problem lay in labeling the combined institution. A solution in 1967 was to call it the Interlochen Complex.[14] Haas, though echoing Maddy's quest to establish Interlochen as one institution, faced strong opposition. When most people spoke about Interlochen, recalls Haas, they meant the camp.[15] Haas thought that Interlochen needed to establish a broader base than either the camp or the academy in people's minds. Interlochen was not just a summer camp, important though that was. The institution needed a symbolic name for the future, a new perspective for the time following the AFM ban. Many faculty and staff believed that Haas favored the academy over the camp, but Haas maintained that his apparent favoritism resulted from his necessary support of the politically weaker academy. Throughout the Haas years, the academy faculty worried about the school's continuation from year to year. Because he was clearly a supporter of the academy, camp supporters accused him of exercising Maddy's practice of appropriating money from the camp for use in the academy, though no evidence supports that assertion.

Haas was persistent in changing the institutional name, and with the board's approval, the camp and academy were brought together as the Interlochen Center for the Arts (ICA). Though the board did not legally change the name until December 12, 1977, John Merrill mounted a 1969 fund-raising campaign called "Interlochen Center for the Arts, the Golden Decade." In the campaign's publication, Merrill listed three components of ICA, including a new college of creative arts, NMC, and IAA.

This publication contained Interlochen's first public reference to a college, though the trustees had approved a charter for such a college in November 1965, before Maddy's death. Neither Haas nor his successors opened such a college, but the board has voted yearly to retain the charter in case future plans should include such an institution. Haas's "Golden Decade" campaign proposed new programs and buildings costing twenty-five million dollars. The goal proved too ambitious, and the campaign failed.[16]

Haas differed from Maddy over certain promotional and fund-raising approaches. For instance, Haas thought that the president's office should create an aura of its important place in the world of art. So in one of his first actions, he remodeled his office, which Maddy had outfitted with rustic maple furniture. Such celebrities as Pablo Picasso's wife, who visited at Haas's invitation, could become worldwide preachers of Interlochen's message if they received positive impressions of all artistic aspects of the center, thought Haas. Haas's office remodeling became such a contentious issue with the Interlochen board that the president's office was not redesigned again for thirty years.

High on Haas's agenda was adding prominent new members to the rapidly aging Interlochen board. Howard Hanson had retired as the Eastman School of Music director in 1964, and in 1968 he became an Interlochen trustee emeritus. In that same year, Eugene Ormandy's term expired, and Haas appointed him to the newly formed President's International Advisory Board.[17]

Besides Eugene Ormandy and Van Cliburn, the listed members of the President's International Advisory Board included many other great musicians and leaders of the 1960s. Appointed were Leonard Bernstein, then the conductor of the New York Philharmonic and a successor of Walter Damrosch; Pablo Casals, the great Spanish cellist; American composer Aaron Copland; Harlan Hatcher, president of the University of Michigan; French composer Darius Milhaud; Alexander Schneider, violinist in the Budapest String Quartet; Rudolf Serkin, pianist and head of the Curtis Institute; Isaac Stern, violinist and member of the National Council on the Arts; and Roger Stevens, the first chairman of the National Endowment for the Arts and later the first head of Washington's Kennedy Center.[18]

Maddy had invited former students to return to campus and had planned to form an alumni association. Haas followed by mobilizing the Interlochen alumni. In July 1967, the Interlochen Alumni Council was organized as the official camp alumni organization, and in November of the same year, the IAA Alumni Association began. In 1969 camp alumnus David Klein, the first alumni president, attended Interlochen board meetings as an ex officio member without vote.[19]

Haas made other major appointments, though at first he embraced Joe Maddy's staff. He promoted John Merrill to vice president for administrative affairs and development, and Margaret Stace, Maddy's longtime secretary and assistant, was elected secretary to the Interlochen board, replacing Merrill. Haas then brought in a new director of personnel, Donald Stiles.[20]

In May 1967, one month after Haas's presidential designation, Thor Johnson resigned as academy director and orchestra conductor to become artistic director and conductor of the Nashville Symphony Orchestra. In June, Haas appointed assistant director Charles Eilber to succeed Johnson as academy director. Eilber, a scholar, gained wide respect from the academy faculty, who found him a clear and forceful visionary. Eilber remembers that Haas championed all the arts and increased the budgets for non-music programs. Favoring an open curriculum, Eilber started a program called Flexible Thursdays, when regular classes were canceled and special, cross-disciplinary programs were substituted.[21]

Eilber once declared a special school holiday because of good weather. On a Flexible Thursday, following a particularly long period of grim northern Michigan weather, he surprised students and faculty with special events, a trip to the Gwen Frostic Prints factory and showroom and a picnic at the Sleeping Bear Dunes on Lake Michigan. Even now, former students remember that day fondly, in part because Eilber had successfully negotiated the holiday with the academy's new orchestra conductor, an unprecedented move because of the usual prominence of orchestral rehearsals on Thursdays.

Haas was internationally minded, starstruck, and erudite. Many faculty members thought he brought a constant brightness to Interlochen and kept creativity going. With Thor Johnson's departure, Haas hired Nicholas Harsanyi to be the academy orchestra conductor. Harsanyi and his wife, Janice, who taught voice, became central musical figures at Interlochen during the Haas era. As in Maddy's days, Haas wove famous musicians, to whom he paid small stipends, into the teaching fabric, where they became new Interlochen associates. Mischa Mischakoff, concertmaster of the Detroit Symphony Orchestra, and Adele Marcus, pianist from the Juilliard School, taught master classes. Students and faculty were dazzled by Marcus, remembering her as she carried her tin tray through the cafeteria while wearing her mink coat. Aspiring musicians were thrilled to meet and work one-on-one with composer Aaron Copland. And to the delight of dancers and the community, Haas brought the famed Martha Graham Dance Company to campus.[22]

During the Haas era, the appearance of pianist Dave Brubeck, whose sons Christopher and Daniel and daughter, Catherine, attended the academy, elevated jazz to a respected level. David Sporny founded the Studio Orchestra and the Interlochen Jazz Quintet, the first jazz programs at Interlochen.[23]

Haas also persuaded acclaimed violinist Isaac Stern to perform at the academy. Stern, who charged no fee other than expenses, was sensational, and his association with Interlochen became crucial. As an outspoken board member for the new National Endowment for the Arts, Stern had been proposing to Chairman Roger Stevens that the Endowment create a master chamber orchestra under Budapest violinist Alexander Schneider.[24] Schneider's orchestra did not materialize, but Haas grasped the idea and suggested the creation of a professional Interlochen chamber orchestra, peopled by academy faculty members. Stern, impressed with the academy's potential to train talented string players, supported this idea. Unfortunately, Haas did not anticipate the potential conflicts in teaching schedules, disruption of student performances, and general resistance from conservative staff members, so the faculty split in their support for the chamber orchestra. Board members also split over creating a professional orchestra, saying that such a group was not part of Interlochen's mission. Several key board members, according to Haas, supported the orchestra, but Haas found the divisiveness unbearable.[25]

During Haas's tenure, Interlochen experienced the same student rebelliousness suffered by many colleges during the 1960s. Often the most gifted students were the nonconformists who broke with traditional Interlochen discipline. Once, when academy students were caught skiing off the Kresge Auditorium roof, Haas felt that "kids would be kids." Trustees, though, were distressed that he did not punish the students severely.[26]

Haas worried that the academy was too isolated from the affairs of the world. Academy students traveled on buses everywhere, and he observed that they could not buy a soda, because Interlochen had no corner drugstore. The camp, however, was long established, and its eight-week duration was short, so he thought the campers understood better what was going on in the world. The camp prospered in Haas's years, and in 1968 the 145 faculty members taught 1,521 campers, who presented 363 programs.[27]

Haas thought some Interlochen customs were provincial, and he believed that the traditional Interlochen uniforms repelled many celebrities. One trustee asked Haas's wife when he was going to begin wearing the corduroy pants. Karl replied that he would never wear the uniform and that he would wear his rural-looking navy blue pants on all appropriate occasions. To staff members, the uniform was symbolic, both historically and psychologically, and Haas's attitude led to clashes with the staff.

The academy uniform issue heated up as students demanded more freedom from rules. Eilber and Haas relented somewhat, proclaiming that students could change into personal clothing after four o'clock in the afternoon. But staff members, with Fay Maddy's backing, complained that the uniform was central to Interlochen. Eilber soon agreed that the students' clothing choices were inappropriate, and he modified the dress code to include the uniform and more tasteful wardrobe selections.[28]

Another Interlochen controversy became harsh when Haas grew weary of Howard Hanson's "Interlochen Theme" being played at the end of each concert. For Haas, the theme served one purpose, a signal for excited students to return quietly to their lodgings. He believed the theme was inappropriate on many occasions, and for certain concerts, especially away from the campus, he banned its performance. Once, when the academy orchestra played in Orchestra Hall in Chicago, he decreed that the orchestra should not play the theme following the final symphony, and those in the audience who knew Interlochen's tradition fumed about its absence. Another time, when Haas booked Detroit Symphony Orchestra conductor Sixten Ehrling, the concert concluded with the Sibelius second symphony, and after many curtain calls, the students dutifully played the theme. Haas had forgotten to tell Ehrling about the theme, and its insertion shocked Ehrling, who said that the students ruined the climax of the concert.[29]

After interviewing members of the Traverse City community, Haas believed that the residents resented Interlochen's distant attitude toward them. Maddy had had similar observations, but he had patched their relationships by performing in local festivals and by joining service organizations, such as the Rotary Club. Haas, in his first year, determined that Interlochen should be a greater participant in the Traverse City community. He joined the board of the local hospital and became a member of the Chamber of Commerce. As a result, when he planned to build a new performance

Fay and Joseph Maddy relax in the Interlochen Bowl in about 1960. (Interlochen Center for the Arts Archives, Interlochen, Michigan, IA 60.)

John Merrill in his office, 1968. (Interlochen Center for the Arts Archives, Interlochen, Michigan, IA 68.)

Karl Haas and a student enjoy the breeze off Green Lake in 1968. (Interlochen Center for the Arts Archives, Interlochen, Michigan, IA 68.)

Aaron Copland rehearses the World Youth Symphony Orchestra in 1970. (Interlochen Center for the Arts Archives, Interlochen, Michigan, IA 70.)

Nicholas Harsanyi and Isaac Stern prepare academy students for a concert in the Jessie V. Stone Building, 1969. (Interlochen Center for the Arts Archives, Interlochen, Michigan, IA 69.)

University Division camper Jessye Norman rehearses for an Opera Theatre production in the Opera Tent, 1968. (Interlochen Center for the Arts Archives, Interlochen, Michigan, IA 68.)

Betty Ford visits a dance class in 1975. (Interlochen Center for the Arts Archives, Interlochen, Michigan, IA 75.)

Bruce Galbraith in his academy office, 1978. (Interlochen Center for the Arts Archives, Interlochen, Michigan, IA 78.)

The Canadian Brass perform on the Kresge Auditorium stage in 1982. (Interlochen Center for the Arts Archives, Interlochen, Michigan, IA 82.)

Edward Downing, Henry Charles Smith, Mstislav Rostropovich, and Roger Jacobi prepare for a rehearsal with the World Youth Symphony Orchestra in 1982. (Interlochen Center for the Arts Archives, Interlochen, Michigan, IA 82.)

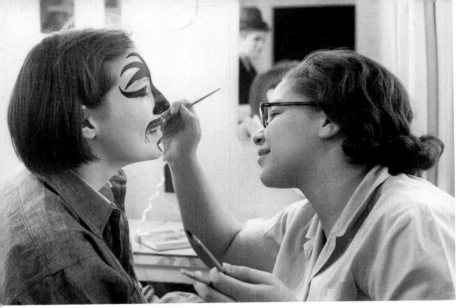

Students apply theater makeup for a 1968–69 production. (Interlochen Center for the Arts Archives, Interlochen, Michigan, IA 69.)

William Milliken and Thom Paulson at WIAA broadcast studios in 1980. (Interlochen Center for the Arts Archives, Interlochen, Michigan, IA 80.)

Roger Jacobi presents William Revelli the Interlochen Medal of Honor in the summer of 1988. (Interlochen Center for the Arts Archives, Interlochen, Michigan, IA 88.)

Dean Boal and Joseph Polisi congratulate the academy orchestra and winners of the General Motors and *Seventeen* Magazine National Concerto Competition in Corson Auditorium, 1993. (Interlochen Center for the Arts Archives, Interlochen, Michigan, IA 93.)

André Watts rehearses with the World Youth Symphony Orchestra in 1990. (Interlochen Center for the Arts Archives, Interlochen, Michigan, IA 90.)

Neeme Järvi and the World Youth Symphony Orchestra take a bow after their Kresge Auditorium concert in 1994. (Interlochen Center for the Arts Archives, Interlochen, Michigan, IA 94.)

Richard Odell chats with academy students in the Stone Student Center, 1996. (Interlochen Center for the Arts Archives, Interlochen, Michigan, IA 96.)

auditorium, later called the Grand Traverse Performing Arts Center, he proposed that the auditorium serve not only Interlochen but also the Traverse City schools, for commencement and other activities. Haas achieved some fund-raising success in Traverse City, where he garnered almost five hundred thousand dollars in commitments from businesses that had never contributed to Interlochen previously. Though not completed during Haas's tenure, the performing arts center was finally built by his successor Roger Jacobi, who similarly courted Traverse City businesses.

In another business plan, Haas proposed that Interlochen should build a conference center—to be called Three Interlochen Corners—at a vacant location in Interlochen village. Business conferences, suggested Haas, would bring in people who could also attend Interlochen activities, thus generating revenue for ICA. Though seriously considered by the trustees, the board rejected Haas's conference center idea. The trustees had usually opposed owning property, even when Maddy sought new land.[30] Moreover, some trustees and staff members felt that Haas did not consult sufficiently with involved parties before moving ahead with his plans. Eilber remembers trustee and architect Alden Dow's surprise that an outside architectural firm was making a presentation to the board. Dow was very polite about the presentation, but the event undermined much of the support that Haas needed for his presidency.[31]

As debts rose and fund-raising became more crucial, tension mounted between Haas and the trustees. At one point, Haas personally pledged a large donation to Interlochen's "Golden Decade" campaign. One trustee, a member of the search committee that chose Haas, expressed his displeasure with the success of the fund-raising campaign. Haas asked the trustee about his personal campaign contribution, and the trustee replied that he had purchased a large birdhouse for Fay Maddy. Haas berated him for his small gift. The trustee was incensed and scolded Haas for speaking discourteously to a trustee. Not recoiling, Haas reminded the trustee that Haas was not only president but also a fellow trustee and that trustees had every right to speak bluntly to one another.

Haas increasingly faced sharp criticism from his staff and board members as Interlochen entered the 1970s. Though Interlochen's admirers continued to praise its artistic and academic programs, Haas's antagonists proclaimed that he did not honor Maddy's dream.[32]

Haas later reflected that he gave Interlochen three years of honest blood, sweat, and tears but suffered terrible experiences. He thought his efforts for

Interlochen students had fallen on the biased ears of a reactionary board. Joe Maddy's wife at the time of his death, Fay, elected an honorary trustee before Haas's appointment, became his first adversary. From her point of view, Haas's rejection of uniforms and the "Interlochen Theme" reflected his insensitivity to her husband's dream for Interlochen. From Haas's point of view, Fay Maddy was impossible to work with, since she opposed most of his changes and wanted Interlochen's programs left the way they were at the time of Joe's death. Since Fay was very powerful among board members, Haas countered her resistance to new plans with care.[33]

Though both Maddy and Haas agreed that the youth symphony orchestra was Interlochen's top priority, their approaches to music education differed in many respects, and Haas's detractors faulted him for his apparent educational differences with the founder. Haas's point of view reflected his European education, with an emphasis on excellent individual teaching, while Maddy, influenced by Giddings, had built his reputation through group and ensemble instruction. Maddy had courted public school music educators to secure Interlochen students, but Haas solicited private teachers to send their outstanding students to Interlochen.[34]

In 1968 and 1969, in the midst of these music education battles, several administrative changes occurred and altered Interlochen's future. At the University of Michigan, Eugene Troth departed, and Roger Jacobi became assistant dean of the School of Music and director of Interlochen's University Division in 1968. Interlochen trustee James Wallace, also at the university, resigned as dean of the School of Music and began teaching at the Residential College. In the fall of 1969, Allen Britton replaced Wallace as dean, and, fortunately for Interlochen, he continued Wallace's policy of paying University of Michigan faculty salaries to serve as the camp's University Division instructors.[35]

That same fall, John Merrill resigned from Interlochen to take a position at Northwestern University. Haas missed Merrill's knowledge and experience. Merrill had enjoyed a dozen years at Interlochen, including almost a decade with Maddy, and he had become a staunch supporter of Haas's Interlochen vision. His strong relationships with veteran board and staff members had been invaluable for Haas. To fill the void, Haas appointed Vernon Hawes, then assistant director of the academy, to Merrill's administrative position, but he did not fill the fund-raising portion of Merrill's job.[36]

As his support from staff and board members declined over the following months, Haas found the presidency ever more unbearable. Just before the Detroit board meeting on March 7, 1970, Clement Stone asked Haas to join him for breakfast. Stone acknowledged Haas's contributions to Interlochen, citing his new ideas and the successful visits of famous musicians, but, shocking Haas, Stone advised him that his adversaries wanted him to resign. Continuing, Stone stated that he had understood and supported Haas's aspirations, and he expressed regret that their plans had not worked out. Stone concluded by observing that Haas's vision had probably been ahead of its time. Before going into the board meeting, Haas assured Stone that he intended to resign but that he would conclude with a statement to the board, warning them about the errors of their conservative attitudes. Following the meeting, Haas met with members of his staff, who expressed their astonishment at his resignation. According to Haas, he countered that they ought not be surprised, since they were the perpetrators of his resignation.[37] Haas left Interlochen immediately and expanded his career in broadcasting. His radio program *Adventures in Good Music* was a great success, continuing daily on classical music radio stations for many years.

George Wilson

With Haas's resignation, the board immediately appointed camp vice president George Wilson to be vice president of the academy and acting executive head of Interlochen. Then, on September 15, 1970, the board promoted Wilson to interim president, pending a formal presidential search. Wilson was a disciplinarian, a fine musician, and the product of a very conventional tradition. He did not favor expansion of the academy programs, and according to Eilber, he represented a very conservative backlash in respect to the academy programs constructed in the first eight years. The majority of the board and staff supported Wilson, hoping that he would return Interlochen and the academy to its Maddy roots. And most of Wilson's continuing staff members supported Fay Maddy's interpretation of Joe's legacy.[38]

Under Wilson's presidency, Charles Eilber and Vernon Hawes exchanged jobs. Eilber resigned as director of the academy to become dean of faculty, and Vernon Hawes became director of the academy, reporting directly to Wilson. Haas's fall and Eilber's demotion alarmed some academy parents. Jazz pianist Dave Brubeck, the father of a 1969 graduate and two undergraduates enrolled in the academy, wrote of his concern that drastic changes might take place at the academy. He reaffirmed his support of the academy under Eilber and the faculty and lamented that it would be a great loss if the academy should become another noble but failed experiment.[39]

The schism between proponents of the academy and proponents of the camp deepened as the academy found it hard to prove itself to the Wilson administration, either financially or educationally. In 1970, seeking to ease the academy's crisis, the board set up a study commission headed by Robert Hill, a consultant sponsored by Clement Stone. The commission included academy faculty members, such as John Hood, and staff members, such as commission secretary Edward Banghart. The board charged the commission with studying Interlochen's management practices and determining future policies.[40]

Roger Jacobi

In 1970 George Wilson declared he did not wish to be a long-term president of Interlochen. According to Roger Jacobi, the board then offered the presidency to trustee David Marvel, former vice president of Olin Corporation and an Interlochen trustee since 1965. Marvel declined, but before hiring the next president, the board persuaded Marvel to become Interlochen's vice president of development and public relations, for a salary of one dollar a year. Marvel's first wife, Elizabeth, died during their initial year at Interlochen, but he and his second wife, Marcia, became faithful boosters of Interlochen, even after he left the fund-raising position in 1975.[41]

Wilson proposed Roger Jacobi's name to the presidential search committee. The committee interviewed Jacobi and two other candidates, then, on August 13, 1971, while Jacobi was attending an Interlochen student concert, they notified him of his selection. His salary was to be eighteen thousand dollars, the same amount paid Karl Haas.[42]

Jacobi, born in Saginaw, Michigan, on April 7, 1924, began his association with Interlochen in 1948, just after he graduated from the University of Michigan School of Music. Otto Haisley, the Ann Arbor superintendent who had fired Maddy in 1927, hired Jacobi to teach at Tappan Junior High School in Ann Arbor in 1948. At the end of the summer, Jacobi and his Tappan supervisor Clarence Roth attended an Interlochen postcamp band program. Jacobi was accompanied there by his new bride, Mary Jane Stephans, a Birmingham, Michigan, pianist who would later be a strong partner in his Interlochen presidency. From that time on, Jacobi entwined a string of interlocking jobs at Interlochen and the University of Michigan, where, in 1951, he completed his formal music education with a master's degree in music.[43]

In 1953 Raymond Williams, program director at the camp, was promoted from this part-time position to personnel director of NMC, a new year-round Ann Arbor job supervised by presidential assistant Margaret Stace. At the time, Jacobi played trumpet in an Ann Arbor dance band with Richard Maddy, who recommended Jacobi to be Williams's replacement. Jacobi, in his first camp position, assembled a yearly publication that listed every music composition performed on each camp concert. Over the years, these program books became NMC's historical record of performance and an invaluable study source for the conductors' concert planning.

In 1955 Williams was appointed associate dean of education at the University of Illinois and resigned as Interlochen's personnel director. In August, just before public schools reopened, Jacobi was offered the personnel job. Jacobi was interested, but he wanted to report directly to Maddy, not to Stace. Maddy agreed to that condition, but Jacobi still hesitated, because he would have to resign at Tappan, where his supervisor insisted that Jacobi find his own replacement. Now anxious to work full-time with Maddy, Jacobi scrambled to persuade violinist Richard Massman to accept the Tappan position. Jacobi began his new job as Interlochen's personnel director and secretary to the board of trustees in February 1956. Besides helping Maddy hire the camp faculty and staff members, Jacobi supervised about twenty-five full-time maintenance and housekeeping workers who lived year-round at Interlochen.

In 1957, with Maddy's encouragement, Jacobi succeeded Allen Britton as organizer of the University of Michigan's Midwestern Conference on School Vocal and Instrumental Music, a yearly convention featuring regional high school music ensembles. This two-day-a-week appointment enabled Jacobi to court music teachers and recruit potential campers.

Jacobi remained camp personnel director until 1959, when David Mattern's death vacated a position that Maddy had once held. Mattern had been employed part-time in the university's music education department and part-time as coordinator of music education in the Ann Arbor public schools. Marguerite Hood, director of music education at the university and Jacobi's mentor, backed him for Mattern's position, and after Jacobi resigned from Interlochen in 1959, the university's School of Music selected him and appointed him an assistant professor. His career centered around Ann Arbor's music education programs over the next decade, though he continued to teach and conduct at Interlochen each summer. Jacobi became an associate professor in 1963 and professor in 1966. These positions gave Jacobi valuable executive experiences, such as planning the equipment for a new music school building at the University of Michigan.

In 1968 Jacobi accepted a job as assistant dean at the School of Music and director of Interlochen's University Division. Jacobi finished his University of Michigan tenure under James Wallace's successor, Allen Britton, who was dean of the School of Music from 1969 to 1979.

Jacobi brought stability to Interlochen. Drawing on his years as personnel director, he adopted a management philosophy that he described as hiring people smarter than he was and working to their strengths. From his acquaintance with Clement Stone, he added the discipline of "inspecting what he expected" from his workers.[44] When he arrived in 1971, he found that employees' work was not being evaluated, no hiring system remained, and no academy faculty evaluation procedures existed. He was immediately pressed with the need to compile a final compensation package for a recently fired employee. He further discovered that, because of a debt of three hundred thousand dollars, he needed to release staff members through attrition.

Two months after his appointment as president, Jacobi released Interlochen's personnel director and replaced him with Richard Fiegel, a graduate of the University of Michigan School of Music and a former NMC camper. Fiegel, who had produced some of the camp's first television programs in 1955, became a versatile problem solver for Jacobi. In his eventual position as director of operations, Fiegel supervised Interlochen's facilities until his retirement in 1992.[45]

Because of his past association with Maddy and the camp, Jacobi felt prepared to further Maddy's dream when he assumed the presidency of Interlochen in the fall of 1971. According to many who worked under him, he was a hands-on, roll-up-your-sleeves-and-work-hard person, an inspiration to others to finish tasks.[46] The camp enrollment in 1971, just before Jacobi's appointment, had been 1,372, including 225 in the University Division, 698 in the High School Division, 324 in the Intermediate Division, and 125 in the Junior Division. In 1972, Jacobi's first year, camp enrollment grew to 1,419, including thirty-two international students.[47]

Though many outstanding trustees from Haas's era continued to serve, the board of trustees changed dramatically as Jacobi started his tenure. Clement Stone opened the trustees' meetings to more outside participants, inviting representatives of alumni and parents' groups as observers. In the spring of 1971, Fay Maddy had moved to Prescott, Arizona, where she died in January 1986. Donald Currie, chair of the board in the early 1990s, became a trustee, and Kenneth Fischer, later the UMS's president, served a term as the alumni council's delegate to the board.[48]

Roscoe Bonisteel died in 1972, and Clement Stone was elected chair of the board, a post he held until he became honorary chair on December 1, 1989. Federal judge Damon Keith of Detroit joined the board, where, with long tenure, he extended Interlochen's influence to many predominantly African-American schools in Detroit.[49]

Jacobi persuaded the board to continue with one of Karl Haas's major building initiatives, known as the Grand Traverse Performing Arts Center. Unlike Maddy, Jacobi did not "dig a hole" for the building but, instead, went through appropriate procedures with the Interlochen board. In 1971 the board formed a campaign committee to raise $2.1 million, with donations to come from Traverse City contributors and board friends, such as Clement Stone. Jacobi broke ground for the new building in 1972, following a grant of three hundred thousand dollars from Thomas Corson, a builder of recreational vehicles in Elkhart, Indiana. The auditorium in the arts center was named after Corson, and after he contributed the naming grant, he committed himself to help Interlochen by joining the board, chairing the buildings and grounds committee for many years, and giving additional building project grants to Interlochen.[50]

However, Jacobi faced several obstacles before the arts center was completed. Several board members, having opposed the building when Haas proposed it, were now opposing Jacobi's building campaign, and at least one trustee resigned over its construction. Moreover, many potential Traverse City contributors were skeptical of Haas's, and now Jacobi's, declarations that the Grand Traverse Performing Arts Center would enhance Traverse City. But Jacobi finally amassed the building funds and finished the construction under budget. The Grand Traverse Performing Arts Center opened in 1975.[51]

Jacobi completed one other major building project in his tenure when, in 1981, he built a 250-seat auditorium named the Michael Dendrinos Chapel/Recital Hall with funds primarily contributed by food executive and trustee Peter Dendrinos. Two years later, on August 14, 1983, increasingly pressed with fund-raising, Jacobi dedicated the Gwen Frostic Garden, arranged and planted in honor of the local artist. Seen through a glass wall behind the stage of the chapel, the garden was stunning, and Jacobi wrote patron Frostic with a touching account of the students who had raised some of the money to pay for the garden area.[52]

In 1973 camp enrollment rose to 1,483. There were 1,491 campers in 1974: 207 in the University Division, 760 in the High School Division, 395 in the Intermediate Division, and 129 juniors. In 1975 the enrollment peaked at 1,513, and the major event was a visit by President and Mrs. Gerald R. Ford. NMC was reaching a maximum enrollment because of limited cabin capacity and beds for students, faculty, and staff. In 1976 the enrollment, for a variety of reasons related to limited living conditions, fell to 1,413 campers. Jacobi, sensing that camp life had become very complex, asked the staff, for the first time, to arrive early and meet as a group before the opening of the 1976 camp season.[53]

On September 1, 1973, Maddy's longtime assistant Margaret Stace retired as Jacobi's assistant and board secretary, though she worked part-time until 1979, assembling Interlochen archival materials for deposit in the Bentley Historical Library at the University of Michigan.[54]

When David Marvel resigned as vice president of development in 1975, he remained on the board. Jacobi elevated George Worden, IAA's first admissions officer and later Interlochen's director of public relations, to the position of vice president of development in December 1978. Worden, a persuasive speaker, continued at Interlochen until 1981, when he became development director at Traverse City's Northern Michigan College.[55]

Both Interlochen and the University of Michigan School of Music experienced major leadership changes in 1979. Allen Britton retired as the university's music dean but remained on the Interlochen board. Paul Boylan, who had taught at Interlochen and replaced Jacobi as head of the University Division, succeeded Britton as dean in July and continued the strong relationship between the two institutions for many more years, ultimately joining Interlochen's board in 1996.

Interlochen had been receiving University Division funds from the School of Music budget since 1960. But the 1980s were times of retrenchment at the University of Michigan as student enrollments decreased, and Boylan decided to cut funds targeted for Interlochen and return the University Division activities to the Ann Arbor campus.[56] The last University Division session at Interlochen was during the summer of 1987, forty-six seasons after Maddy first established this association between the University of Michigan and Interlochen. With the loss of more than two hundred University Division students, camp enrollment plummeted to 1,254 students in 1988.

In another leadership change in 1979, George Wilson retired as vice president and director of NMC. Nineteen seventy-nine was the year of another difficult task for Jacobi, as he fought off proposals to establish a prison near Interlochen. In the previous summer, to ensure a smooth transition in camp leadership, Jacobi hired University of Michigan music graduate Edward Downing as Wilson's successor.[57] When he arrived, Downing was impressed that Interlochen was frugal but not poor and that Jacobi was not financially frivolous. The camp mission was clear, focused on an eight-week program unfolding in a competent, efficient manner. The programming, though it ventured and retreated, was not artistically or compositionally in the forefront.

Downing marveled at the long tenures among the staff, faculty, and administration. Some employees were veterans of thirty or forty years, and their experience propelled a quick and flawless beginning to each new season. He concluded that much of Interlochen's strength had accrued from the consistency and predictability of the loyal workers who returned yearly, so he and Jacobi continued Interlochen's practice of hiring known and reliable camp veterans.

As had others before him, Downing observed that the camp and the academy often divided into opposing constituencies and that despite the academy's existence for more than fifteen years and Haas's and Jacobi's support of the winter school, many returning camp workers either slighted or disparaged the academy. The camp office operated separately from the academy, supervising itself, hiring the staff, recruiting the students, and scheduling the classes and building usage.

Until its end in 1987, Downing supported the University Division and considered the division's orchestra outstanding and a model for the younger camp performers. But the college-age students had also brought many social challenges to camp. Some University Division students smoked, and the college women wore skirts instead of knickers, which troubled the younger girls. With the demise of the University Division in 1987, the All-State Program remained as Interlochen's only University of Michigan curricular association. The university's School of Music continued to fund the All-State Program, and according to Downing, that program became musically stronger than in previous years. Social problems that had arisen among University Division students subsided, for administrators could better restrict smoking and enforce uniform policies with high school students.

Downing inherited a strong and dedicated staff from Wilson. His assistant, Mary Frances James, not only operated the camp office but also admitted the junior, intermediate, and high school students. She alone listened to the potential campers' audition tapes to decide who would be accepted, and Downing asserts that she raised Interlochen's performance standards through her choices. Wilson also left Austin Harding's magnificent music library system, first set up by Wilson for Interlochen in 1929. Because of the library, Downing could challenge librarian Del Weliver to provide almost any music score for the growing number of Interlochen concerts.[58]

In 1983, two years after fund-raising director George Worden moved to Northern Michigan College, Jacobi hired Paul Morris, the first Interlochen employee with professional fund-raising experience, to be vice president of development.[59] With Morris's support, Jacobi expanded the number of professional positions in his administration with the addition of a special events office.

In 1987, coincident with a U.S. governors' conference in Traverse City, Jacobi organized an Interlochen celebration to commemorate the camp's sixtieth and the academy's twenty-fifth anniversaries. The enlarged special events office arranged tours and promoted the event.[60] Trustee Charles McWhorter proposed that Interlochen hold a symposium on arts education as part of the 1987 celebration. Jacobi scheduled the event for November 8, 1987, and prominent national artists and educators participated in impressive panel discussions throughout the day. The American Council for the Arts (ACA) distributed critically appraised meeting reports to libraries and arts organizations throughout the United States. This major symposium drew further praise from ACA's Milton Rhodes and the Endowment's chairman Frank Hodsell.[61]

Sustaining the Dream

After receiving Robert Hill's 1971 study commission report on IAA, the board filed it without acting on its suggestions. The study revealed that the board had chartered the academy separately from the camp, so that if the academy failed financially, the camp would survive. For each of several years, the academy teachers had concluded their classes in May unsure if the school would reopen in September. Academy faculty and staff members had become so restive and cynical that new president Jacobi, to gain their trust, asked the board to distribute copies of the study to employees. Then Jacobi began to change the academy leadership to salvage Maddy's winter school.[62]

Charles Eilber had set the tone for the academy during the Haas years, but when Jacobi first became president, Vernon Hawes was the director, and Eilber was dean of the faculty. In 1972, at the conclusion of Jacobi's first year, Hawes resigned and moved to North Carolina.[63]

Jacobi appointed veteran faculty member Donald Jaeger to replace Hawes. Jaeger, a camp alumnus, had been creative with the band and woodwind ensembles. By placing a musician at the head of the academy, Jacobi hoped to renew Maddy's vision from the time when conductor Thor Johnson was director. But Jaeger was not suited to the academy directorship, so he resigned in the spring of 1973. Eilber, disagreeing with Jacobi's policies and saying that the academy had retrogressed ten years, also resigned, later to attain prominence as the founding head of the North Carolina School of Science and Mathematics.[64]

No academy director was chosen until August 1973, when Jacobi finally selected John Hood, the academy's ecology and biology teacher. Hood, whose wife, Mary Lou, had been a camper in 1944, had been on the academy faculty for eleven years, where he had been a favorite of both faculty members and students. Over succeeding years, he cultivated friendships of both camp and academy alumni, mitigating some of the schism between camp and academy. Hood served for four years, longer than any previous academy director, then became assistant to Jacobi for special projects until July 1, 1980, when he became the headmaster of the White Mountain School in New Hampshire.[65]

Hood encouraged curricular experimentation. Students investigated exotic instruments and literature. They participated in a film festival that introduced student filmmakers to abstract animation, and in an exciting theater project, they acted alongside faculty members in a company called the Janus Players. According to students, choral conductor Kenneth Jewell, who was grandfatherly in his prime, demanded high standards of discipline and artistry.[66]

IAA staff members began to send students to choice colleges systematically. At this time, the academy enrolled about three hundred students, but because Interlochen provided little personal counseling, they needed to be socially mature. Student activities, both artistic and social, were often inspired by students. However, the drug culture of the 1970s engendered problems. The academy expelled approximately 50 students in 1979 and sent 160 students home in 1983 because of drug use.[67]

In September 1977, when Jacobi made Hood his assistant for special projects, he recruited Bruce Galbraith to be director of the academy. Galbraith had graduated in music from the University of Michigan, where Jacobi had supervised his student teaching in band. Though he had not taught or administered in a private school before, Galbraith had gained a master's degree in school administration and had been the full-time executive secretary of the Michigan School Band and Orchestra Association for eight years before his academy appointment.[68]

Galbraith was not a camp alumnus, but after the academy appointment, he taught at the camp and conducted the high school concert band each year. He, Downing, and Jacobi worked well together. Galbraith gained the confidence of faculty members and, according to Jacobi, became the most influential of the academy's many directors, bringing state and national recognition to Interlochen. He became active with the National Foundation for Advancement in the Arts, the organization that administers the Presidential Scholars in the Arts awards. Galbraith was appointed to the Michigan Council for the Arts by Republican governor William Milliken and was the only member retained by Democratic governor James Blanchard.[69]

In his first year, 1977, Galbraith's administration expelled twenty-six students for various reasons, including academic failure and drug use. An earlier report from an outside consultant had urged tighter enforcement of student conduct, and Galbraith set goals to improve student artistic presentations, academic achievement, and social behavior. He stimulated Interlochen's student participation in competition for the yearly Presidential Scholars in the Arts awards, first in creative writing, then in music and visual arts. By 1979 Galbraith's academy enrolled 393 students, and excepting a 1982 dip, it maintained that size until leaping to 425 students in 1985.[70]

The academy, like other boarding schools across the country, maintained student discipline with difficulty from the late 1960s until the 1980s. The academy had begun with harsh black-and-white rules, inherited from the eight-week camp. But beginning in the Eilber years and continuing into the middle of the Galbraith years, high school students everywhere sought more independence from supervision and more opportunities to experiment in their studies and social life. By 1980, while recognizing generational changes in students, Galbraith was establishing stricter guidelines for student events and enforcing nonsmoking policies, aided by a stronger counseling staff. When his assistant, Carl Scheffler, left in 1980, Galbraith hired Raymond Rideout, later an academy director, to create a committed and compassionate environment for the students. Students began to receive more adult counseling.

In 1983, in a far-reaching innovation, the academy offered its first classes in English as a second language, to aid international students. Rideout observed the relaxation of student tension at this time. Before the middle 1980s, said Rideout, students in both the camp and the academy reacted to harsh, but unevenly implemented, rules by painting graffiti in dormitory rooms and cabins. As Interlochen improved its counseling and support services, students became happier and more responsible for their actions and the appearance of the campus.[71]

Jacobi and Galbraith became very active in a network of the nation's high schools devoted to the performing and visual arts. In April 1981, the Los Angeles Unified School District and the Los Angeles County Music Center invited a dozen of "the leading high schools of the arts" to an organizational meeting. IAA was the only private school in the organization. Others included the Cincinnati School for Creative and Performing Arts; Washington, D.C.'s, Duke Ellington School of the Arts; Houston's High School for Performing and Visual Arts; New York City's LaGuardia High School of Music and Art; the New Orleans Center for Creative Arts; and the North Carolina School of the Arts.[72] This network of high schools for the arts matured and met again at Interlochen in April 1982.[73] Galbraith became president of the group, thereby strengthening Interlochen's influence on arts education throughout the United States.

In 1984 the American Council for Private Education and the U.S. Office of Education cited IAA as an exemplary school. As Galbraith participated in more national arts and boarding school associations, he became widely respected and a prime candidate for headmaster positions elsewhere, positions that promised greater financial resources than Interlochen's. Late in 1986, after ten years at IAA, he accepted the headmaster position at the Park Tudor School in Indianapolis, Indiana. Jacobi appointed a faculty search committee that chose Martha McClure of Cincinnati to succeed Galbraith. Students thrived during 1987 and 1988, but at the end of her second year, McClure resigned to return to Cincinnati.

In September 1989, two months before his retirement, Jacobi appointed IAA assistant director Ray Rideout to be vice president and director of the academy. In response to a society intensely concerned with addictions, Rideout and assistant academy director Timothy Wade made an important contribution to the academy's stability by establishing a program for student substance-user identification and counseling, a program that lasted until 1994.[74]

During the camp sessions, Jacobi continued Van Cliburn's yearly concert appearances with NMC's World Youth Symphony Orchestra (WYSO). He also expanded on Maddy's and Haas's practices of honoring American composers with ceremonial awards and with commissions and performances of their music. In the 1970s Phi Mu Alpha music fraternity held periodic national conventions at Interlochen, where the fraternity gave composer Aaron Copland an award for *The Tender Land,* and where Gunther Schuller conducted one of his new compositions with WYSO.

In 1977 the camp alumni commissioned Howard Hanson to compose his seventh symphony, called *A Sea Symphony* and dedicated to NMC on its fiftieth anniversary in memory of Joseph Maddy. On August 7, Hanson conducted NMC High School Choir and WYSO in the symphony's premier performance at Interlochen. This performance capped Hanson's fifty-year association with Interlochen, where he had conducted, composed, taught students, and served various terms as a trustee. Since Howard Hanson's death in 1981, Seattle Symphony Orchestra conductor Gerard Schwarz has memorialized Hanson's symphonic writings with award-winning recordings. Schwarz attributes his inspiration to having conducted Hanson's "Interlochen Theme" at camp while a teenage camper in 1962.[75]

The camp's fiftieth anniversary celebration spawned several other commissions from American composers. Five years after Jacobi had introduced jazz studies into the camp curriculum, the student jazz band premiered a composition by Martin Mailman, commissioned by Phi Mu Alpha, and a work by Tommy Newsom of television's *Tonight Show,* commissioned by W. T. Armstrong. The C. G. Conn instrument company, which had funded some of Maddy's start-up costs in 1928, commissioned Alan Hovhaness to write a euphonium concerto performed by Henry Charles Smith, Philadelphia Orchestra member and NMC alumnus.[76]

In 1973, by inaugurating celebrity jazz concerts, Jacobi changed Interlochen's performance series in two ways. In that year, Duke Ellington's band spiked the jazz program by presenting the first jazz concert at the camp since Paul Whiteman's 1941 concert. Moreover, in a departure from most earlier seasons, campers did not participate in most of the professional performances. In the following year, Jacobi booked Count Basie's jazz band at the camp, and jazz clarinetist Benny Goodman and his band played in 1975; both concerts were presented without wide camper participation. Also in 1975 Clement Stone persuaded comedian Bob Hope to headline the appearance of the camp's stage band.[77]

By 1978, when Downing arrived, the camp was giving 336 programs, not as many as Haas's then record 363 programs in 1968, but concerts with greater variety in style and type. Downing would later venture into computer music programming in 1986 and concerts by minimalist composers in 1989, but his program philosophy under Jacobi was traditional at its core. Downing and Jacobi began to consider presentations by professional musicians without student participation as legitimate Interlochen fare. In 1980 they booked the Canadian Brass to inaugurate a concert series they called the Interlochen Arts Festival, a name first used by Maddy when the Philadelphia Orchestra played at Interlochen in 1964. Both the Philadelphia Orchestra concert and the Canadian Brass concert occurred without the participation of students in the performance and were thus uncommon occasions in Interlochen's history but forerunners of future Interlochen presentations. Downing said that he and Jacobi engaged in great soul-searching when they first engaged the Canadian Brass in 1980, so in later seasons, members of the performing groups began to teach master classes and invite students to perform with them.[78] Jacobi soon contracted the Chicago Symphony Orchestra for its first appearance at Interlochen, to be followed later by another departure, country music concerts of the Oak

Ridge Boys. In 1980, because of a need to schedule this expanding concert and event series, the camp hired academy English teacher Howard Hintze to organize a camp program office.[79]

A major change in compensating celebrity performers arose after Interlochen's 1959 reinstatement by AFM. Though Maddy could lure John Philip Sousa and Paul Whiteman to donate their services before the union's NMC ban, most major artists now charged small stipends or full fees to appear at Interlochen. Van Cliburn and Isaac Stern were notable exceptions in donating their services to NMC and the academy. In 1964, though Eugene Ormandy donated his services, Maddy did pay the union members of the Philadelphia Orchestra for their performance. By 1982, when Jacobi was able to book Mstislav Rostropovich for a performance with WYSO, Interlochen paid the celebrated cellist his fee of twenty-five thousand dollars plus travel costs and expenses. In the 1990s, Interlochen could engage and pay expensive major artists, such as André Watts and Itzhak Perlman, because these artists could attract large crowds to the four-thousand-seat Kresge Auditorium at premium prices.[80]

For the camp session of 1983, Jacobi and Downing instituted a chamber music residency under the leadership of pianist André-Michel Schub. The residency included four concerts, open rehearsals, and ensemble classes for the most gifted students. Artist teachers besides Schub were violist Walter Trampler, cellist Nathaniel Rosen, IAA graduates David Shifrin (clarinet) and Ida Kavafian (violin and viola), and camp alumna Ani Kavafian (violin and viola).[81]

Following the success of the summer arts festival, Jacobi added a winter season of six or seven professional concerts during the academy year, some combined with music, theater, or dance workshops. But Jacobi still amassed the largest variety of concerts for the camp season, and by 1988 the camp offered more than 450 programs over the eight weeks. In contrast to the 1980 campers, the busy 1988 students experienced scheduling conflicts and could no longer attend all events. When he retired in 1989, Jacobi had transformed the camp experience from a fixed-menu artistic dinner into a cultural cafeteria.

Unlike his predecessors, Jacobi was not a broadcaster. Maddy and Haas, as professionals, prized radio station WIAA. But in 1970, following Haas's resignation, no senior Interlochen officer endorsed the station. Interlochen was then in debt, so the trustees seriously considered closing the station. Two factors prevented the shut down. First, in 1970 WIAA had become a charter member of National Public Radio (NPR), a national system of more than eighty noncommercial radio stations. The Corporation for Public Broadcasting (CPB), launched by the federal Public Broadcasting Act of 1967, both established NPR and provided grants to public stations, such as WIAA, to air educational and cultural programs. In return for funding, CPB required the stations to maintain a core professional staff, operate with sufficient power to reach a broad community base, and broadcast a full, regular schedule.[82] Maddy had been pushing for such a network since he and his assistant Jerome Wiesner organized the 1938 Michigan Conference on Educational Radio. Haas had wanted WIAA to join NPR because member stations would then broadcast *Music from Interlochen.* If WIAA continued on the air, rather than closing, CPB grants would be available to reduce WIAA's expenses.

Second, Traverse City trustee Helen Osterlin proclaimed that WIAA's programming attracted the Traverse City public to Interlochen and that the station ought to be preserved. In 1971 she enlisted the aid of local civic leaders Peter Dendrinos, Wilbur Munnecke, and Frank Stulen to launch a fund-raising campaign to save WIAA. She was successful, and the Interlochen board voted to retain the radio station.

To ensure that the station would not be threatened with closure again, the trustees, under Osterlin's leadership, then organized a citizen's advisory board for WIAA. This advisory board believed that its role was to protect the station from threatening forces, even from Interlochen administrators or trustees who might meddle in programming or business decisions. Both the advisory board and CPB demanded that WIAA maintain its professional staff, so in 1972, to give campers appropriate broadcasting experiences, the Interlochen administration opened the low-powered student station WIRD.

Program director and announcer Edward Catton shaped the sound of WIAA from the early years until his 1997 retirement. At first the programming was a mixture of plays, book readings, record programs, and syndicated music programs, with a heavy infusion of live-on-tape concerts featuring major world orchestras. In 1981 Catton stopped using syndicated book readings and began reading from books himself. Later, when book-reading programs fell out of fashion, music and news programs dominated the schedule.

In 1975 commercial radio networks were waning, but WIAA increased its broadcast schedule to eighteen hours a day. Though NBC's modestly successful program *Monitor* ceased broadcasting that year, WIAA and other public radio stations were attracting larger audiences and devoted volunteers for their advisory boards. WIAA offered NPR's afternoon news magazine *All Things Considered,* and in 1979 the station hired Bob Allen to present local news. WIAA was becoming a station that had not been in Maddy's mind, yet the station continued to broadcast and distribute Interlochen programs to a growing listenership.

In 1980 the public radio system began to broadcast over America's first satellite distribution system. NPR could then transmit high-fidelity stereo music programs directly to its stations instead of bicycling audiotapes from station to station. With this improved capability, WIAA distributed *Music from Interlochen* by satellite from 1983 until 1988, when NPR station managers lost interest in such programs.[83]

In January 1981, Jacobi appointed Thom Paulson to be manager of WIAA, where in 1976, at age twenty-one, he had dawned as host of the early-morning classical music show. In 1979 Haas-appointed general manager Angus Forrester had persuaded Paulson to work as fund-raiser for WIAA, a better-paying position than hosting a radio program. Noncommercial radio stations were beginning to secure sponsorships called underwriting, which were announcements similar in tone to commercials on 1920s radio stations. Paulson succeeded quickly, securing the station's first underwriting from Traverse City's Old Kent Bank and Milliken's Department Store. In 1980, following the lead of most public stations, Paulson instigated WIAA's first over-the-air fund-raising campaign. His amiable fund-raising style propelled him into the station's managership in the following year.[84] Paulson, according to Jacobi, charmed the advisory board and honed his management skills to become one of Jacobi's most significant Interlochen appointments. In 1984 Paulson scheduled American Public Radio's overnight classical music service, enabling WIAA to broadcast twenty-four hours a day.

WIAA became an important local news source in northern Michigan, and the station needed to develop editorial policies to prevent biased reporting. In 1987 a local resort wanted to build a golf course that a regional environmental organization opposed. WIAA's newsman, later revealed to be on the board of the environmental organization, sometimes reported on the resort's affairs. The owner of the resort, a major financial contributor to Interlochen, became irate at some of the reporter's features, so Paulson had the reporter broadcast an apology for his apparent conflict of interest. Because of this incident, Paulson wrote editorial policies that both guided the station's supervision of its reporters and established the station's independence from financial contributors.[85]

In 1986, three years before Jacobi's retirement, the board wrote a mission statement for ICA. Veteran trustee Donald Currie, a retired Michigan education executive, led a special committee of board and staff members to craft a declaration that, with modest exceptions, remains intact.

> The mission of Interlochen Center for the Arts is to offer gifted and talented young people the opportunity to develop their creative abilities in a wholesome community under the guidance of an exemplary faculty of artists and educators. Undergirding this mission is an accelerated curriculum which emphasizes uncompromising standards, character and leadership development, and individual initiative practiced within a framework of healthy competition and frequent public performances. These serve as the foundation for Interlochen's two major educational programs: Interlochen Arts Academy and National Music Camp. Through its mission, Interlochen is committed to serve as an advocate of all the arts, a model and innovative teaching center, and presenter of outstanding artistic achievement in service to a diverse regional, national and international constituency.[86]

In 1991 National Music Camp was renamed Interlochen Arts Camp (IAC), and the word *presentations* replaced *performances* in the mission statement, to acknowledge visual arts and creative writing exhibits. In 1994, to recognize WIAA's prominence and expansion, the trustees added Interlochen Public Radio (IPR) as Interlochen's third program, next to IAA and IAC.

Jacobi retired on December 1, 1989, after eighteen years as president. He had saved the academy and WIAA from financial collapse, but he had also vaulted over a narrower classical music pit to add jazz and country music to the Interlochen Arts Festival. By most accounts, he extended Maddy's philosophy, but in hiring Edward Downing for the camp, Bruce Galbraith for the academy, and Thom Paulson for WIAA, Jacobi fulfilled his very personal interpretation of the Interlochen dream.[87]

Epilogue

When Roger Jacobi told the board he wished to retire as president of Interlochen in 1989, the board appointed a trustee search committee, chaired by Donald Currie, that chose the present writer, Dean Boal. On December 3, 1989, I became president, Jacobi became president emeritus, and the board elected eighty-seven-year-old Clement Stone honorary chair and Currie board chair.[1] Stone remained active on the board, and in 1991 he gave Interlochen one hundred thousand dollars as a challenge grant to replace lost funding from the Michigan Council for the Arts.[2]

The Currie board and the Boal administration reaffirmed the 1986 mission statement, strongly aided by trustee Charlotte Roe. Then, in the first months of the administration, three staff teams developed goals for Interlochen's educational and performance programs, business systems, and outreach. The result, a paper called "A Vision for the Future," was approved by the board in March 1990.[3] The vision paper affirmed Interlochen's aspirations to be a superior arts education center that would become increasingly attuned to world, national, state, and local trends in the arts. The board also charged management to bring an increased number of world-class artists to Interlochen, thus augmenting ICA's national reputation as an arts presenter for students and the general public.

In December 1991, after two years in office, Currie stepped down as board chair, and the trustees elected James Tolley, a retired Chrysler executive, in his place.[4] Following Tolley's election as board chair, the trustees added many new members, until the board numbered more than forty.

Clare Burns, the treasurer appointed by Maddy, retired in March 1990, to be replaced by David Stave, a Traverse City management consultant, who assumed broader business responsibilities as vice president for finance. In the fall of 1990, Paul Morris retired as vice president for development, and Timothy Ambrose, a symphony orchestra fund raiser, became vice president for institutional advancement. After several Interlochen offices were combined, Ambrose supervised fund-raising, public relations, special events, and alumni activities. In July 1992, Thom Paulson, ICA's general manager of radio, was promoted to vice president of Interlochen Public Radio, a newly named position that reflected WIAA's expansion and centrality to the ICA mission.[5]

A major team project of the 1990s was the development of a campus master plan. Alden Dow had prepared the previous master plan in the early 1960s, when the first academy buildings were built. Dow's plan satisfied the space requirements for the academic and support functions of the new winter school, but it included no buildings for music, theater, or visual arts.[6] In addition, many of the outdoor summer buildings were deteriorating and becoming inadequate for the increasing number of students and student programs.

In December 1990, after an offer from former trustee Herbert Dow and trustee Barbara Dow to fund a campus master plan, the staff and board chose architects Sasaki and Associates to conduct the study. Sasaki consulted with staff members, academy and camp faculty, and trustees, then, on July 25, 1991, presented its plan to the Interlochen board, which voted overwhelmingly for its acceptance.[7]

All of Sasaki's proposed construction was within the central core of the campus. Though the Interlochen campus consists of twelve hundred acres, less than 25 percent of the property has been developed, because the balance of the land is not suitable for construction. Moreover, the Interlochen community prefers to preserve those natural lands for teaching purposes and to reaffirm Interlochen's isolation from the world.[8] Besides siting the buildings, the Sasaki plan spurred the administration to erect building signs, reroute traffic patterns, and plant appropriate shrubbery. In addition, with the board's encouragement, the administration launched a multiyear fund-raising campaign to renovate deteriorating summer cabins.[9]

In the midst of the Sasaki planning, patron James Harvey approached the administration to build a box theater with versatile staging. The resultant Phoenix Hall was opened in the summer of 1993 and winterized the following year. With its computerized lighting and adaptable staging, Phoenix Hall replaced the aging Grunow Hall as Interlochen's primary theater.[10]

During the first months of 1993, Sasaki drew plans for three new buildings identified in the master plan: a music building complex, a theater, and a campus center. The Interlochen board accepted these plans at its July

1993 meeting, and fund-raising for these buildings commenced immediately.[11] At WIAA, with the aid of an anonymous donor, Paulson initiated and supervised the construction of a new state-of-the-art broadcast building, which was occupied in 1995.

To advance the integration of all aspects of the center, Interlochen's division names were revised between 1990 and 1995. The National Music Camp (NMC) became the Interlochen Arts Camp (IAC); the camp and academy alumni organizations became one Interlochen Alumni Organization (IAO); and WIAA, its relay stations, and the recording department merged as Interlochen Public Radio (IPR). The names of the Interlochen Arts Academy (IAA) and Interlochen Arts Festival (IAF) were unchanged. Several ICA offices consolidated. The admissions offices of the camp and the academy combined in 1990, and, thus strengthened, the new director of admissions, Thomas Bewley, reversed diminishing enrollments of the late 1980s, particularly in the academy, which has maintained capacity enrollments of 430 to 450 students.[12] In another step to join functions, the camp and academy music offices came together under Byron Hanson in 1994.[13]

In its first break from the eight-week summer tradition, the camp initiated two four-week programs for juniors in 1991.[14] The intermediate program followed with two four-week sessions in 1995. Enrollments in these divisions soared, and in July 1997, because of Interlochen's need for more facilities, the University of Michigan and Interlochen announced that in 1998 the university would move the Intermediate All-State Program to the Ann Arbor campus, while the Interlochen Intermediate Division would expand into the former campus of the All-State Program. With this change, the University of Michigan reduced its yearly presence on the Interlochen campus to the four weeks of the High School All-State Program. The shorter Interlochen sessions responded to parents' wishes for more curricular choices for their children. Year-round schooling in the public schools prevented some children from attending the full eight weeks, but they could attend one or more of Interlochen's shortened sessions.[15]

Continuing Interlochen's touring history, the IAA orchestra performed for the Ronald McDonald Foundation in Chicago in 1991 and 1993.[16] To mark the two-year Mozart Bicentennial Celebration, the IAA orchestra and chorus, under Margaret Hillis, toured to Detroit and then to New York City's Lincoln Center in February 1992.[17] On campus, the General Motors and *Seventeen* Magazine National Concerto Competition for high school students was held in the spring of 1993 and again in the spring of 1994.[18]

A new WIAA relay station was added in Harbor Springs, Michigan, in December 1989. In 1991 Interlochen's recording services produced and sold their first compact-disc recording, honoring Joe Maddy and featuring music from Interlochen recordings produced in the years since 1937. By 1996 Interlochen recording services produced compact discs with the latest digital technology, allowing students, campers, parents, and the public to purchase their favorite and memorable programs at the academy or camp. Concerts and excerpts from programs were broadcast nationally over American Public Radio and over National Public Radio's daily arts program, *Performance Today.*

André Watts first visited Interlochen in the summer of 1990, when he played Johannes Brahms's Piano Concerto no. 2 with WYSO and gave student master classes. In 1991 Interlochen expanded the summer IAF beyond the eight-week camp period to include a shoulder season, extending the concert series to more than ten weeks and providing additional program options for area patrons.[19] With these added weeks and the vigorous pursuit of key international artists, the budget for professional concerts rose from six hundred thousand dollars to two million between 1990 and 1995. In 1991 the Detroit Symphony Orchestra (DSO), under Neeme Järvi, came for the first of its continuing yearly residencies. Orchestra members gave student workshops and chamber recitals, then played in a concert with WYSO, sitting side by side with campers. Many members of DSO had been campers themselves ten to thirty years before, and they enjoyed their return each year.[20] Violinist Itzhak Perlman came back for six seasons, and cellist Yo-Yo Ma, the Boston Pops Orchestra, and the Chicago Symphony Orchestra became major additions to the summer IAF.

Interlochen has always displayed a "drive for glamour."[21] The leaders have sought uniqueness in the contributions of visitors, from Sousa to Perlman, Ma, and opera singer Cheryl Studer, an IAA alumna. By 1995 Edward Downing could say that Interlochen was known throughout the country as a major presenter of celebrity concerts. The IAF, held in both summer and winter, now has a broader base than ever before, because it presents more varied styles of music, including folk and country. The expanded fare has included the Beach Boys and Motown's Four Tops.[22]

On August 1, 1991, the Interlochen Arts Academy Alumni Association, originally created in November 1967, and NMC's Interlochen Alumni Council, originally organized in July 1967, merged into the Interlochen Alumni Organization.[23] The director of alumni relations, Gayle Shaw, and the first IAO president, Karla Herbold, spearheaded the reorganization. Also in that summer, the first of yearly Interlochen Arts Awards was given to violinist Itzhak Perlman in appreciation of his Interlochen service. On each visit when he performed with WYSO, Perlman also hosted question-and-answer sessions for over two hundred campers, teachers, and visitors. Awards in following years have gone to NMC alumnus Peter Yarrow of Peter, Paul, and Mary; the Canadian Brass; and conductor Neeme Järvi.[24]

I retired from the Interlochen presidency on February 1, 1995, and the board selected Richard F. Odell of Chicago to be the fifth president of Interlochen.[25] Lawrence Clarkson, president of Boeing Enterprises, became the chair of the Interlochen board in 1996.[26] They reaffirmed the mission of Interlochen, broadened the programs of ICA, and embarked on a massive fund-raising campaign to construct several buildings mapped out in the campus master plan.

Continuing Interlochen's traditions of broadcasting, on March 7, 1996, the academy orchestra was featured on a live television program of the Public Broadcasting Service on behalf of MENC. The program, called "The World's Largest Concert," highlighted school choruses from many parts of the United States singing "live" while the IAA orchestra played from Interlochen. In the summer of 1996, WYSO toured to Atlanta to perform at the Cultural Olympiad, an important feature of the 1996 Summer Olympic Games.[27]

Interlochen has had a great impact on the arts and arts education in America and the world. Some of this impact can be attributed to its sheer size and longevity, but its major innovations have changed lives and reshaped our arts institutions. Even before the camp opened, its founders exerted strong influences on the arts nationally. Both Joseph Maddy and T. P. Giddings espoused ideas that shaped American politics and the arts: the rejection of aristocracy, the celebration of entrepreneurship and invention, and the fervent devotion to religions and causes. They championed American arts education and spurned the European ways of teaching music, which they believed were geared toward the wealthy and privileged. Maddy, in particular, devoted his adult life to democratizing the arts in America by making fine music and other arts available to a general public. He sensed that most Americans love the arts and support arts education as a part of general education, and he was among the first to promote art music through the new media of radio and motion pictures.[28]

Giddings and Maddy were influential in acquainting the public with art music, but they followed in the footsteps of the pioneers in public school music, such as Lowell Mason. In the 1830s, at the time when President Andrew Jackson was suggesting that all American citizens ought to enjoy the privileges of the wealthy, Mason, the first teacher of music in public schools, proposed that all students should enjoy the singing classes previously available only to private school students. Mason's public school program in Boston was so successful that it was expanded and copied in many cities. Giddings and Maddy, coming of age at the end of the century, were students in such programs, Giddings in Minnesota and Maddy in Kansas. After World War I, as professional educators, they became national leaders in fostering performance ensembles in the public schools, including bands, orchestras, and choirs.

Under the auspices of MSNC, Maddy led an effort, joined by Director Howard Hanson of the Eastman School of Music and other educators, to write the first standards for instrumental music performance in the nation's high schools. After these standards were acclaimed and accepted, the MSNC educators tackled a larger problem. Maddy and Giddings, with the help of music administrators from colleges and conservatories, including Earl Moore of the University of Michigan, convinced principals and superintendents in many school systems to grant high school credit to students for general music classes, choruses, and instrumental ensembles, just as for English or mathematics classes.

Maddy, flush with these victories, then turned his attention to teaching gifted music students, who, he reasoned, in this democracy ought to have opportunities to realize the full potential of their talents. He discovered that talented young people responded to the challenges of public performance at the NHSO presentations in Detroit and Chicago. So he based his camp's educational approach on the new idea of unifying instruction and performance. Many schools throughout the United States incorporated this idea into their music programs.

Maddy and Giddings created Interlochen to be an American camp, incorporating Western music's European heritage but expanding in new egalitarian ways. Maddy immediately began programming American compositions in his concerts, and Interlochen has always presented newly composed American music as part of its performances. In fact, as America's population becomes less European in its heritage, American art absorbs and embraces more and more influences from all parts of the world. A challenge for Interlochen and other major arts institutions entering the twenty-first century is to include a wider variety of arts from around the globe.

Interlochen made art music available to the general public through its concerts and broadcasts. For Maddy, art music included music composed by Europeans; music composed by Americans writing in European forms, such as symphonies and tone poems; and certain light classics. Determining whether compositions were art music was sometimes difficult in the past, just as it is today. In the 1920s, salon music was considered art music, but jazz was not. Students and faculty, including Maddy, played jazz for recreation, but jazz was not considered appropriate for formal programs. Paul Whiteman's visit in 1941 marked the first appearance of a professional jazz orchestra in the Interlochen schedule, thereby extending the concept of art music to include symphonic jazz. Jazz gained even greater respectability as art music in the 1960s, when the academy added jazz to the curriculum during Karl Haas's presidency. In recent years, concerts by Peter, Paul, and Mary, the Oak Ridge Boys, and contemporary artists, such as Garrison Keillor, were added to the more traditional concerts, thus extending the definition of art concerts still further. Interlochen's concerts and exhibitions now number more than 750 and attract audiences of more than one hundred thousand people each year. The audiences include students and their parents, residents of Traverse City, and tourists and summer residents of northern Michigan. Students may choose from a variety of symphony orchestra concerts, plays, art exhibitions, and dance recitals, where they form lifelong habits of making choices about attending arts events.

Maddy's adoption of radio as an important educational medium enabled him to broaden the audience for good music. He developed radio programs to instruct students on musical instruments, to teach music appreciation classes, and to broadcast classical music for the general public. He consulted with colleges and universities in Michigan, training them in ways to establish public radio stations and bring the arts to Michigan audiences. Finally, in 1962, he was able to launch WIAA, Interlochen's public radio station, a powerful tool for edifying the public who lived in the Interlochen area. Besides live and recorded programs from public radio networks, WIAA broadcasts major student and faculty concerts. With the station's wide coverage, listeners in northern Michigan can experience the spirit of Interlochen over radio, though they may rarely attend events on the campus.

In his years of searching for support for the camp, Maddy became an advocate for government funding of the arts and radio. The first of many Interlochen grants from the state of Michigan, obtained in 1938, provided funds for advertising Interlochen as a tourist site in northern Michigan. For the rest of his life, Maddy assiduously sought government funding for Interlochen, educational radio, and other arts groups, in his efforts to democratize good music. He argued that the high arts were in the mainstream of the American democracy and that they belonged to the whole fabric of our society.

In 1963, two years before the National Endowment for the Arts was established, Governor George Romney of Michigan had already shown his support of the arts by reconstituting the Michigan Cultural Commission as the Michigan Council for the Arts. He asked Karl Haas, then a host and producer of a classical music radio program in Detroit, to chair the council, and he asked Joseph Maddy of Interlochen to be a council member. Maddy and Haas worked closely together on the council until Maddy's death, helping to define the role of state arts funding in Michigan. Over the next twenty-five years, Michigan elected a series of governors, both Republican and Democratic, who were sympathetic to the arts.[29]

Presidents Maddy, Haas, and Jacobi all cultivated strong personal relationships with Michigan governors and legislators during the years when Michigan contributed generously to the arts. In the 1960s and 1970s, they lobbied vigorously for the National Endowment for the Arts and the Michigan Council for the Arts. Because of their efforts, Interlochen received sizable yearly grants from the Michigan council. In 1991, when Michigan's funding for the arts fell precipitously, Interlochen's grant was cut in half. But at that time, Interlochen still commanded strong support among government officials, who included the grant as a line item in the state budget. When Michigan experienced severe budget deficits, state senator George McManus, representing Interlochen's district, rallied the legislators to continue funding the arts at a reduced level, even as leaders in his Republican party wanted to end all state arts grants.

Though they advocated government support, Giddings, Tremaine, and Maddy were proud of creating Interlochen as an independent institution that could survive without the government grants it received. Interlochen has endured times of adversity because the organization is large enough to weather an occasional setback. Large organizations, such as Interlochen, are more successful in business negotiations than smaller institutions. For example, when the camp was on the verge of bankruptcy in the 1930s and when it needed more land in the 1940s, Tremaine and Maddy exercised the power of negotiation to survive the Great Depression and double the size of the campus. Also, because Interlochen is a comprehensive school—embracing a camp, an academy, radio station WIAA, and the arts festival—the center can mount a professional staff and create exceptional offices of admissions, public relations, and fund-raising.

Size and survivability allow Interlochen to innovate and give it an edge in leading other institutions. Interlochen can take occasional artistic and financial risks without fear that the presentation of a particular program will prove disastrous. Interlochen can experiment with new musical compositions or theatrical productions, risking an occasional error of judgment. Imagining Interlochen today without jazz or folk music is hard, yet the inclusion of these musical forms first came about after they were included experimentally. Maddy often introduced new artistic ideas, but some, such as accordion bands and roller-skating ballet, attracted neither serious consideration nor loyal audiences, and such programs were discarded. Ultimately, Interlochen's programs have excelled because the best of the experimental classes or concerts have been duplicated and folded into the more traditional programs.

Maddy and Giddings charted other new directions by adding classes in arts other than music, making Interlochen a comprehensive institution. The original camp for orchestral students eventually evolved into a camp and academy including classes in theater, dance, visual arts, and creative writing. Many colleges and universities followed Interlochen's lead and combined several art forms to create fine arts departments.

Maddy aspired to create an institution that would be a powerful model for music education. Interlochen's success grew over the years, to a point where organizations elsewhere in the country and in other parts of the world traveled to Interlochen to learn how to establish an arts camp or arts high school. In the early 1930s, the Eastern Music Camp was modeled after Interlochen, and a decade later, Tanglewood began in Massachusetts after a study of Interlochen's operations. The North Carolina School of the Arts, opening a year later than IAA, accomplished what had been Maddy's dream of incorporating a collegiate program along with a high school for the arts. In the 1960s, representatives from Israel and Japan visited with George Wilson, director of NMC, to learn how to create arts camps. And the Idyllwild Arts Academy in California opened in 1986 to replicate IAA on the West Coast. Interlochen's success undoubtedly inspired the explosion of major summer music festivals like Aspen's and Tanglewood's, and in a turn of events, the newer festivals now compete with Interlochen's camp for the most talented high school students.

Interlochen's individual students are its chief beneficiaries. They have reaped the benefits of educational ideas introduced by Giddings, Maddy, and succeeding generations of teachers. Early camp innovations included the introduction of reading music at sight, weekly performances of major compositions, study of a large repertoire of pieces, and students' taking responsibility for conducting as well as playing in performances. Later years saw the inclusion of similar attention to repertoire in drama and dance, as well as the addition of creative composition in music, visual arts, and writing. The academy has evolved to offer students excellent comprehensive education along with concentrated study and performance in the arts. New and international art forms unlock yet wider experiences for recent student generations.

Of the many stellar accomplishments achieved by Interlochen and its students, a few are especially exemplary in American education: The academy holds the national school record for the number of Presidential Scholars in the Arts, with twenty-nine awards from 1980, the first year of the program, through 1997. It is not unusual for a major conservatory or music school to have ten to twenty Interlochen graduates in its first-year class, and the academy sends more students on to study at Oberlin Conservatory of Music and Eastman School of Music than does any other high school in the United States. A tally in 1993 found eighteen alumni of either IAA or IAC in the Detroit Symphony Orchestra, twelve in the Boston Symphony Orchestra, twelve in the National Symphony Orchestra, ten in the Chicago Symphony Orchestra, and eight in the Saint Louis Symphony Orchestra.[30]

Some students, stimulated by excellent programs and the presence of world-class talent, go on to attain great artistic careers. For them, Interlochen provides the opportunity to study in their artistic fields before they go to college. Since dance students often begin their careers immediately after high school, they may enroll at the academy to study in a rigorous curriculum that still allows them to concentrate on dance. Many Interlochen students become teachers in the public schools, while others perform in professional organizations, such as symphony orchestras, opera companies, theaters, and television. Some alumni have become executives in the arts.

However, most campers and academy students choose careers other than the arts. Each summer's sifting process of campers propels several highly talented youth toward professional arts careers, a larger number toward arts education in the schools, and most toward amateur endeavors that stimulate them to promote musical culture in their business and professional lives. After enduring the competition for positions in orchestra or ballet, many students rethink their interests and change their career goals. Some students, gifted in several fields, elect to make their careers outside the arts. Others perform in amateur orchestras or volunteer as members of arts organizations. Even those who abandon artistic careers preserve their devotion to Interlochen and applaud it for having enriched their lives. Study of the arts has enhanced their education by encouraging creativity, rewarding diligence, and ennobling cooperation.

As in other institutions, one challenge to the Interlochen management in the 1990s was to translate Interlochen's traditions and values into computer-age services. Interlochen now participates in the world of computer networks as well as in that of radio, television, newspapers, and magazines. Interlochen's faculty, students, and workers correspond by E-mail, and they purchase supplies, sell concert tickets, and create enrollment and financial databases by computer.

But the Interlochen traditions live. At camp, WYSO still gives eight performances in eight weeks, with each performance followed by the "Interlochen Theme." The uniform continues to be an important part of the culture, though the corduroy may vanish to accommodate changes in fashion and to take advantage of new fabrics.[31] Interlochen, said camp alumnus Peter Yarrow, "has a certain immutable continuity." [32] Alumni still burst onto the national scene. In 1997 Jewel Kilcher, a 1992 IAA graduate, was named the nation's best new popular entertainer of the year and became the first graduate to appear on the cover of *Time* magazine.[33] Her classmate Jonathan Holland has already garnered performances of his compositions with the symphony orchestras in Cleveland, Atlanta, Baltimore, and Detroit.[34]

The image of Interlochen is spiritual, formative, and built on shared experiences. Its participants have a passion and love for its unique mission. People who work at Interlochen care about the institution much more than a job. The students of the 1990s continue to be disciplined, while displaying friendliness and comradeship.[35] They elect to attend, and they talk their parents into letting them leave home. Though, as conductor Clyde Roller remembers, "there have always been stars" in every class at IAA or IAC, the 1990s classes are more evenly balanced, with excellent students in all ensemble sections and in all the arts disciplines.[36]

Interlochen's successes seem detached from the throes of arts education in the United States. Many school systems are dropping music programs from the curriculum, because the programs are unsupported by their school boards. A fundamental consensus on the importance of the arts, a consensus built by Lowell Mason in the 1830s, by Joe Maddy, and by his successors since the 1920s, may be disappearing. Many gains made by Mason and Maddy may vanish, including the granting of high school credit for music classes and the popularization of the classical arts among the masses. But Interlochen's stories show how similar challenges were overcome, whether by proposing new solutions, as Tremaine did in dealings with camp creditors and as Maddy did in turning to school and university teachers during the AFM ban, or by amassing key supporters, as Maddy did in his confrontations with academy foes. Schools, symphonies, and dance companies can take courage from an institution that might have closed many times but did not.

Interlochen will survive in the twenty-first century, because it has achieved its reputation and stability. Ups and downs are always possible, though the size of Interlochen, its historical longevity, and the fierce devotion of its alumni, faculty, staff members, students, and board members will keep the dream alive. Interlochen's administrators may continue to disagree among themselves and with board members, but as the institution and its supporters become more international, more mature, and wiser, these disputes will be settled without acrimony.

Alumni will be nostalgic for the way things were when they attended the camp or the academy, but today's boards and administrators know that to attract the best students, teachers, supporters, and patrons, Interlochen needs to compare favorably with national and international expectations in the arts and education, not with a sometimes fuzzily remembered "Brigadoon." Maddy's Interlochen would not have survived if it really had been a Brigadoon: Maddy changed what needed to be changed, invented when he needed to invent, and "dug holes" when he needed to dig. May Interlochen prosper and the dream live.

Notes

Part 1

Epigraph from Levon E. Horton, "Noted Virtuosi See Bright Future for U.S. Music as Children Swell Ranks of Nation's Orchestras," *Mount Vernon (N.Y.) Daily Argus,* 7 March 1934, in Interlochen Center for the Arts Collection, box 66, Bentley Historical Library, University of Michigan (hereafter cited as B with box number).

1. C. M. Tremaine to Joseph E. Maddy, 6 May 1958, B 12.
2. Roger Jacobi, interview by the author, tape recording, Fife Lake, Mich., 24 July 1995.
3. Byron Hanson, interview by the author, tape recording, Interlochen, Mich., 13 January 1995.
4. Papers from Joseph E. Maddy's early years may be found in B 1.
5. Raymond Rideout, interview by the author, tape recording, Interlochen, Mich., 19 January 1995.
6. Timothy Ambrose, interview by the author, tape recording, Interlochen, Mich., 16 January 1995.
7. Edward Banghart, interview by the author, tape recording, Interlochen, Mich., 24 January 1995.

Part 2

Epigraph from Tremaine to Maddy, 6 May 1958.

1. Edward Bailey Birge, *History of Public School Music in the United States* (Washington, D.C.: Music Supervisors National Conference, 1928), 25.
2. Birge 1928, 55, 99, 112, 118.
3. State-Wide Committee in Esteem of Thaddeus P. Giddings to members of Minnesota music organizations, 7 February 1939, B 5.
4. T. P. Giddings, *Giddings' Public School Class Method for Piano* (Boston: Oliver Ditson Company, 1919), 7.
5. Giddings 1919, 7.
6. Birge 1928, 127–28.

7. Giddings 1919, 7.

8. Clyde Roller, interview by the author, by telephone, San Antonio, Tex., 5 March 1996.

9. Paul Boylan, interview by the author, tape recording, Ann Arbor, Mich., 1 February 1995; Karl Haas, interview by the author, tape recording, by telephone, New York, N.Y., 23 January 1996. For Maddy's career, see George N. Heller, "Maddy, Joseph Edgar," in *The New Grove Dictionary of American Music,* ed. H. Wiley Hitchcock and Stanley Sadie (New York: Macmillan Press, 1986), 159; Joseph E. Maddy Papers, B 1.

10. Maddy Papers, B 1.

11. Birge 1928, 162, 248.

12. Maddy Papers, B 1.

13. Will Earhart to Joseph E. Maddy, ca. April 1951, B 13; Joseph E. Maddy to Will Earhart, 28 March 1951, B 13.

14. Joseph E. Maddy, personal and employment history submitted to University of Michigan Personnel Record, 18 October 1945, TS, B 1.

15. Maddy Papers, B 2.

16. Maddy Papers, B 1; Maddy, personal and employment history, 18 October 1945, B 1.

17. Allen Britton, interview by the author, tape recording, Ann Arbor, Mich., 2 February 1995.

18. Banghart interview; Tremaine to Maddy, 6 May 1958.

19. Jacobi interview.

20. Harriet Payne, conversation with the author, Interlochen, Mich., 5 August 1996.

21. Frederick Huber, conversation with the author, Interlochen, Mich., 4 August 1990.

22. Britton interview.

23. Norma Lee Browning, *Joe Maddy of Interlochen: Profile of a Legend* (Chicago: Contemporary Books, 1992), 69, 71; Banghart interview.

24. Tremaine to Maddy, 6 May 1958; Roller interview.

25. Banghart interview; Britton interview; Boylan interview.

26. Banghart interview; Haas interview.

27. Banghart interview; Jacobi interview; Haas interview; Frederick Fennell, interview by the author, tape recording, Interlochen, Mich., 5 August 1996.

28. Jacobi interview.

29. Britton interview; Haas interview.

30. Birge 1928, 229.

31. Birge 1928, 243.

32. Birge 1928, 248.

33. Birge 1928, 194–96.

34. Birge 1928, 194–96.

35. Henry Root Austin, "History of Broadcasting at the National Music Camp, Interlochen, Michigan, 1928–1958," Ed.D. diss., University of Michigan, 1959, 2; Joseph E. Maddy, "Music Takes to the Woods," *Saturday Evening Post,* 31 August 1940, 16–17, 46–47, 49, 51; Joseph E. Maddy, "Statement to a Senate Hearing into American Federation of Musicians' Ban on Network Broadcasts of Student Musical Organizations in Washington, D.C.," *Music Educators Journal* 30, no. 5 (April 1944): 14–17.

36. *Interlochen Bowl Program* 1928, 11, 21, in Interlochen Center for the Arts Publications, 1928, Interlochen Center for the Arts, Interlochen, Mich. (hereafter cited as IP with year [28 = 1928, etc.]); Birge 1928, 283.

37. Maddy to Tremaine, 12 November 1940, B 1.

38. Richard Crawford, *100 Years of Music at Michigan* (Ann Arbor: Edwards Brothers, 1979), 23.

39. Editorial, "Summer Music Schools," *Etude Music Magazine,* April 1929, 263.

40. For historical information, see Colorado Chautauqua Association, "Chautauqua History," 1998. <http://www.chautauqua.com/chauhist.com> (1998).

41. Burnet Tuthill, "Orchestra Camp Colony: History," 1968, TS, B 2.

42. Harriet Payne conversation; Maddy to Tremaine, 12 November 1940; Norma Lee Browning, *Joe Maddy of Interlochen* (Chicago: Henry Regnery Company, 1963), 187.

43. Maddy to Tremaine, 12 November 1940.

44. See Dorothy Marden, "Eastern Music Camp Association," *Music Supervisors Journal* 17, no. 6 (February 1931): 54.

45. Maddy to Tremaine, 12 November 1940.

46. Austin 1959, 8.

47. Russell McLauchlin, "Unique Music Idea Promoted," *Detroit News,* 1 September 1927; Maddy to Tremaine, 12 November 1940.

48. Maddy, *Saturday Evening Post,* 31 August 1940; Austin 1959, 10; Tremaine to Maddy, 6 May 1958.

49. Austin 1959, 10; Tremaine to Maddy, 6 May 1958.

50. "Tremaine, Charles Milton," *International Cyclopedia of Music and Musicians,* 10th edition, ed. Bruce Bohle and Oscar Thompson (New York: Dodd, Mead, and Company, [ca. 1975]), 2305; C. M. Tremaine, *History of National Music Week* (New York: National Bureau for the Advancement of Music, [ca. 1925]), 11, 73; Birge 1928, 224.

51. Banghart interview.

52. Tremaine to Maddy, 6 May 1958.

53. Britton interview; Maddy to Tremaine, 12 November 1940.

54. Gail W. Rector, *The University Musical Society of the University of Michigan Celebrates One Hundred Years, 1879–1979* (Ann Arbor: University of Michigan, 1979), 160, 165.

55. Maddy Papers, B 1.

56. McLauchlin, *Detroit News,* 1 September 1927.

57. McLauchlin, *Detroit News,* 1 September 1927.

58. Camp records, Interlochen Center for the Arts Archives, records for 1928, Interlochen Center for the Arts, Interlochen, Mich. (hereafter cited as IA with year [28 = 1928, etc.]).

59. *Interlochen Bowl Program* 1928, 19, 30, IP 28; Joseph E. Maddy, "National Orchestra Summer Camp News," *Music Supervisors Journal* 14, no. 3 (February 1928): 53; Joseph E. Maddy, "Another $10,000 for Orchestra Camp," *Music Supervisors Journal* 14, no. 4 (March 1928): 73.

60. Louis Green, "Mecca of American Musical Youth," *Christian Science Monitor,* 3 September 1929, B 71.

61. Austin 1959, 9, 14.

62. Camp records, IA 28.

63. National High School Orchestra and Band Camp, *The Overture, 1928: Yearbook* ([Interlochen, Mich.]: National High School Orchestra and Band Camp, 1928), 16, IP 28.

64. Camp records, IA 28; Marguarite S. Kerns, "The National High School Orchestra Camp," *Grand Rapids Sunday Herald,* 28 July 1928.

65. *Interlochen Bowl Program* 1928, 10, IP 28.

66. Chester Belstrom Papers, IA 29; "Bulletin," 29 July 1929, B 2.

67. 1930 National High School Orchestra Rules, B 2; Camp records, IA 30.

68. Editorial, *Etude Music Magazine,* April 1929, 263–64; Green, *Christian Science Monitor,* 3 September 1929, B 71.

69. Editorial, *Etude Music Magazine,* April 1929, 264.

70. Austin 1959, 12.

71. Maddy to Tremaine, 12 November 1940.

72. Joseph E. Maddy, "Instrumental Music Department," *Music Supervisors Journal* 15, no. 5 (June 1929): 61; "The National High School Orchestra Camp," *Music Trade News,* September 1929, 14, B 71.

73. Austin 1959, 12.

74. Board of Supervisors of Grand Traverse County, proclamation, 1929, B 2.

75. Paul E. Bierley, *John Philip Sousa, American Phenomenon* (New York: Appelton-Century-Crofts, 1973), 198; Frederick Fennell, "Bands at Interlochen," *BDG* (March–April 1992): 2–3.

76. "Symphony of Young America," *Southwestern Musician,* March–April 1942, 10–11, B 71; Boylan interview; Fennell interview.

77. Louis Nicholas, *Thor Johnson: American Conductor* ([Ephraim, Wis.]: Peninsula Arts Association, 1982), 14.

78. George Wilson, interview by the author, by telephone, St. Louis, Mo., 14 June 1997.

79. Fennell interview.

80. National High School Orchestra and Band Camp, *The Overture, 1929: Year Book Op. 2* ([Interlochen, Mich.]: National High School Orchestra and Band Camp, 1929), 22, 34, IP 29.

81. John Erskine, *My Life in Music* (New York: William Morrow and Company, 1950), 272.

Part 3

Epigraph from "Why is Sousa?" *Musical Courier,* 10 August 1911, quoted in Bierley 1973, 142.

1. Bierley 1973, 9, 10.

2. From the 1925 Sousa Band press book, quoted in Bierley 1973, 143.

3. Bierley 1973, 139.

4. Bierley 1973, 139.

5. *National Music Camp: The First Twenty-five Years* (Ann Arbor: National Music Camp Publications, 1952), s.v. "1931," IP 52.

6. *Scherzo,* 3 August 1930, 1, quoted in Austin 1959, 18.

7. Bierley 1973, 86.

8. *The First Fifty Years* (Interlochen, Mich.: Interlochen Center for the Arts, [1978]), s.v. "1932," IP 78.

9. Maddy, *MEJ,* April 1944, 16, 17.

10. Austin 1959, 42.

11. National High School Orchestra tour program, 1930, B 2.

12. *National Music Camp: The First Twenty-five Years,* 1952, s.v. "1930," IP 52.

13. Browning 1963, 221; Karl Detzer, "Youth and Music Join in a Great Experiment," *Musical America,* 25 May 1933, 13.

14. Austin 1959, 24; *New York Times,* 23 August 1939, Rotogravure section.

15. *Overture,* 1928, IP 28; *First Fifty Years,* [1978], s.v. "1932," IP 78; Interlochen board of trustees minutes, 1991, IA 91.

16. Marden, *MSJ,* February 1931, 54; Joseph E. Maddy, "The National Camp," *Music Supervisors Journal* 17, no. 4 (March 1931): 37; Music Supervisors National Conference, *Supervisors Service Bulletin* (March–April 1931), B 1; George Oscar Bowen, "Eastern Music Camp," *Music Supervisors Journal* 18, no. 1 (October 1931): 61.

17. Tremaine to Marie Maddy, 4 December 1935, B 3; Joseph E. Maddy to Ruth Mathews, editor of *Band World,* 9 May 1938, B 2.

18. Browning 1963, 156; Britton interview; Banghart interview.

19. Crawford 1979, 26; Maddy Papers, B 1; Maddy, personal and employment history, 18 October 1945, B 1.

20. Karl Detzer, "Axes and Fiddlesticks," *American Magazine*, December 1932, 46, 47.

21. C. V. Buttelman, "Important Announcement," *Music Supervisors Journal* 20, no. 5 (May 1934): 5.

22. Britton interview.

23. Austin 1959, 17; Green, *Christian Science Monitor*, 3 September 1929, B 71; Maddy, *MSJ*, June 1929, 59.

24. Maddy, *Saturday Evening Post*, 31 August 1940, 51; Camp records, IA 31.

25. Erskine 1950, 133.

26. Austin 1959, 22.

27. Emma Knudson to Helen Hollingsworth, 22 May 1939, B 5.

28. Joseph E. Maddy to John W. Beattie, 25 January 1939, B 5; Giddings to Maddy, 23 February 1939, B 5.

29. Maddy to Giddings, 16 January 1939, B 5; Giddings to Maddy, 24 January 1939, B 5.

30. NMC summer brochure ([Ann Arbor, Mich.]: [National Music Camp], 1941), IP 41.

31. Contrary to Norma Lee Browning's point that the depression first forced advertising in 1933 (Browning 1963, 219). See also E. B. Knauft, Renee A. Berger, and Sandra T. Gray, *Profiles of Excellence* (San Francisco: Jossey-Bass, 1991), 78; *Interlochen Bowl Program* 1928, IP 28.

32. Jacobi interview.

33. Maddy, *Saturday Evening Post*, 31 August 1940, 47; Austin 1959, 14; *First Twenty-five Years*, 1952, s.v. "1930," IP 52.

34. Maddy, *Saturday Evening Post*, 31 August 1940, 49; Fennell interview; Browning 1992, 180.

35. James Larson contract, B 2.

36. Maddy, *Saturday Evening Post*, 31 August 1940, 47.

37. Maddy to Tremaine, 12 November 1940.

38. Maddy to "Dear Friend," 11 January 1932, B 2.

39. Tremaine to Maddy, 6 May 1958.

40. Tremaine to Maddy, 6 May 1958.

41. *Scherzo*, 21 July 1935, 3, 6, IP 35.

42. C. H. Beukema, [*Ann Arbor News?*], 1 August 1934, B 71.

43. A. F. Rebhine, "History of the Fire of Cottage Number One," 31 January 1935, TS, B 2; Tremaine to members of the board of control, 16 January 1935, B 56.

44. Frederick Fennell, "The Rudiments of Drum Majoring and the Art of Twirling," 1935, syllabus, B 2.

45. Tremaine to members of the board of control, 19 July 1935, B 2; Tremaine to Maddy, 21 December 1935, B 2.

46. Jane Priscilla Sousa to Joseph E. Maddy, 29 January 1935, B 2.

47. Browning 1963, 228; "History of the New York Philharmonic," 1995. <http://www.nyphilharmon.org> (1998).

48. *School Musician,* September 1936, 23, B 71; Joseph E. Maddy, "The Accordion as an Orchestral Instrument," *Accordion World,* November 1940, 10, B 71.

49. Browning 1963, 228; *Crescendo,* summer 1993, 1, IP 93.

50. F. J. Cochran of Cochran and Crandell, Attorneys, Northville, Mich., to Maddy, 31 August 1937, B 5.

51. Burnet C. Tuthill, "A Typical Day at the National Music Camp," *New York Times,* 15 August 1937; Austin 1959, 22; Browning 1963, 229, 272.

52. Maddy, personal and employment history, 18 October 1945, B 1.

53. Joseph E. Maddy to Ernest Hutcheson, 19 January 1939, B 5.

54. Grainger as quoted in an interview by Edna Horton, *Musical Courier,* 1 October 1939, 10, B 66.

55. *Detroit News,* Pictorial section, 23 July 1939, 13, B 71.

56. Giddings to Maddy, 27 January 1939, B 5.

57. Tremaine to Giddings, 24 November 1939, B 57.

58. Fake page on Giddings, *Minneapolis Journal,* 19 February 1939, B 5.

59. Maddy to Tremaine, 12 November 1940.

60. Maddy to Indiana University, ca. 1938, B5; Maddy to Michigan State College, ca. 1939, B 6.

61. Tremaine to Maddy, 6 May 1958, 2, B 12.

62. Tremaine to the board of control, [1939], B 56; Maddy to Tremaine, 12 November 1940.

63. Frederick A. Stock to Joseph E. Maddy, 27 September 1940, B 66; Browning 1963, 230.

64. Dateline Interlochen, *Grand Rapids Herald,* 10 June 1940, B 71.

65. Maddy to Tremaine, 12 November 1940; Jacobi interview.

66. C. M. Tremaine, fund-raising flyer, 1941, B 71.

67. Maddy to Tremaine, 12 November 1940.

68. *Southwestern Musician,* March-April 1942, 10–11.

69. John Tasker Howard and George Kent Bellows, *A Short History of Music in America* (New York: Thomas Y. Crowell Company, 1957), 190, 244.

70. Howard and Bellows 1957, 200; Birge 1928, 210.

71. *International Cyclopedia of Music* [ca. 1975], 2305; Birge 1928, 224.

72. "Record Record," *Time,* 3 July 1939, 26; National Committee for Music Appreciation advertisement, *Traverse City Record Eagle,* 25 June 1940.

73. National Committee for Music Appreciation advertisement, *Traverse City Record Eagle*, 25 June 1940.

74. Edward T. Ingle, *Report of the National Committee for Music Appreciation (1940–1941)* (Washington, D.C.: National Committee for Music Appreciation, 1940), 400, B 71.

75. Erskine 1950, 209.

76. Administration records, IA 40; B index.

77. Austin 1959, 35; Howard and Bellows 1957, 235. WWJ of Detroit, licensed in October 1921, is one of the first four continuously licensed stations in the United States.

78. Maddy, *MSJ*, February 1928, 53; Maddy, *MSJ*, March 1928, 71; Austin 1959, 37, 50.

79. Austin 1959, 35.

80. Austin 1959, 37.

81. Austin 1959, 39.

82. *Scherzo*, 20 July 1930, 4, quoted in Austin 1959, 44.

83. Grigsby-Grunow Co., Chicago, *Voice of the Air* 2, no. 7 (1930): 4, B 66; Austin 1959, 44.

84. Jean N. Hillman to the author, 5 June 1997.

85. Grigsby-Grunow Co., Chicago, *Voice of the Air* 2, no. 7 (1930): 4, B 66; Austin 1959, 58; Mike Wallace, narrator, *Joe Maddy's Interlochen*, Interlochen Center for the Arts compact disc DIDX 010543.

86. Austin 1959, 47.

87. *Program and Scherzo*, 19 July 1931, 21, quoted in Austin 1959, 52.

88. James Perone, *Howard Hanson* (Westport, Conn.: Greenwood Press, 1993), 1.

89. Perone 1993, 49; Carolyn Bert, liner notes to sound recording, National Music Camp, Fiftieth Anniversary, *World Youth Symphony Orchestra No. 1*, NMC 1977–20; Emily Boyd, E-mail to the author, 6 March 1997.

90. William Kephart to Roger Jacobi, 30 September 1976, B 54.

91. Maddy, personal and employment history, 18 October 1945, B 1.

92. *NBC Educational Bulletin*, 12 August 1938, 1, B 16.

93. Austin 1959, 24, 58; "National Music Camp," *Violins*, July 1938, 154; *NBC Educational Bulletin*, 12 August 1938, 1, B 16.

94. Maddy to W. W. Charters, 22 October 1938, B 17; Maddy to Governor Frank J. Murphy, 23 November 1938, B 17; Maddy, personal and employment history, 18 October 1945, B 1; *Wellington (Kans.) Daily News*, 5 May 1941, 2.

95. Austin 1959, 58.

96. The Internet Movie Database Ltd., "Awards Information," 1990–98. <http://us.imdb.com> (1998).

97. Catherine Conrad Edwards, "Not What they Used to be! [*sic*]," *Parents Magazine*, October 1940, 27, B 71.

98. *Wellington (Kans.) Daily News,* 5 May 1941; *There's Magic in Music* (Hollywood, Calif.: Paramount Pictures, 1941), movie.

99. *Wellington (Kans.) Daily News,* 5 May 1941.

100. *There's Magic in Music* 1941.

101. *Wellington (Kans.) Daily News* 5 May 1941.

102. Edwards, *Parents Magazine,* October 1940, 27.

103. Joseph Rezits, E-mail to the author, 29 September 1996.

104. Advertising flyer for *The Hard-Boiled Canary* (Hollywood, Calif.: Paramount Pictures, 1941), B 71.

105. *Wellington (Kans.) Daily News,* 5 May 1941.

106. "The Hard-Boiled Canary," *High School Thespian* 12, no. 8 (May 1941), 20–21.

107. *Wellington (Kans.) Daily News,* 5 May 1941; Joseph Rezits, conversation with the author, Interlochen, Mich., 5 August 1996.

Part 4

Epigraphs from James C. Petrillo to James L. Fly of the Federal Communications Commission, 10 July 1942, *International Musician,* August 1942, 1; Maddy to Giddings, 1 October 1947, B 12.

1. George Seltzer, *Music Matters* (Metuchen, N.J.: Scarecrow Press, 1989), 8.

2. Maddy, *MEJ,* April 1944, 14–17.

3. Austin 1959, 37.

4. Austin 1959, 40.

5. Robert D. Leiter, *The Musicians and Petrillo* (New York: Bookman Associates, 1953), 150.

6. Browning 1963, 223.

7. Austin 1959, 66.

8. Petrillo to Fly, *International Musician,* August 1942, 1; Seltzer 1989, 33.

9. Seltzer 1989, 46–47.

10. "The Boston Symphony Orchestra Unionized," *International Musician,* December 1942, 1.

11. Willis Pennington to Joseph E. Maddy, 4 June 1941, B 2.

12. Maddy, *MEJ,* April 1944, 16.

13. Leiter 1953, 151.

14. *Traverse City Record Eagle,* 22 July 1941.

15. Leiter 1953, 151; Seltzer 1989, 47.

16. Joseph E. Maddy, "The Interlochen-Petrillo Controversy," 1947–48, TS, B 38; Austin 1959, 63; Marvin Arrowsmith, "Camp Promotes American Music," *Saginaw (Mich.) News,* 10 August 1942, B 66.

17. Maddy, *MEJ,* April 1944, 17.

18. Maddy, *MEJ,* April 1944, 16–17; Leiter 1953, 151.

19. "No Records," *New York Times,* 12 July 1942.

20. Seltzer 1989, 47; Leiter 1953, 153.

21. Maddy, *MEJ,* April 1944, 16.

22. Petrillo to Fly, *International Musician,* August 1942, 1.

23. Maddy, *MEJ,* April 1944, 16.

24. "Synopsis of Entire Recording Controversy," *International Musician,* December 1944, 1.

25. Petrillo to Fly, *International Musician,* August 1942, 1.

26. Maddy, *MEJ,* April 1944, 16.

27. Maddy, *MEJ,* April 1944, 14–17.

28. Leiter 1953, 151.

29. Leiter 1953, 152.

30. Margaret A. Stace, "Interlochen Officers and Administration," n.d., TS, B 57.

31. Joseph E. Maddy, "President's Report," 30 September 1961, TS, B 59.

32. Petrillo to Fly, *International Musician,* August 1942, 1.

33. Seltzer 1989, 48.

34. Maddy, *MEJ,* April 1944, 16.

35. Joseph A. Padway, "Judge Barnes Decides the A. F. of M. in the Right," *International Musician,* November 1942, 1, 19, 20.

36. Padway, *International Musician,* November 1942, 20.

37. Undated, untitled paper, B 66; Maddy, *MEJ,* April 1944, 14–17.

38. Maddy, *MEJ,* April 1944, 14–17.

39. James C. Petrillo, "Third Installment of President Petrillo's Report," *International Musician,* January 1944, 10.

40. Austin 1959, 66.

41. Maddy, *MEJ,* April 1944, 14–17.

42. *International Musician,* December 1944, 1.

43. *International Musician,* February 1945, 1.

44. Burnet C. Tuthill to Joseph Maddy, 4 July 1945, B 12.

45. Austin 1959, 66.

46. Leiter 1953, 158.

47. Maddy to Giddings, 7 February 1947, B 12.

48. Leiter 1953, 160, 161; Jay Walz, "High Court Curbs Petrillo Powers," *New York Times,* 24 June 1947.

49. Walter W. Ruch, "Kearns Congress Investigator," *New York Times,* 10 June 1947.

50. Maddy, "Interlochen-Petrillo Controversy," 1947–48, B 38.

51. C. V. Buttelman, "Hunt, Richman, Petrillo Sign the Code," *Music Educators Journal* 34, no. 1 (September–October 1947): 23.

52. Maddy, "Interlochen-Petrillo Controversy," 1947–48, B 38.

53. Maddy, "Interlochen-Petrillo Controversy," 1947–48, B 38.

54. Maddy, "Interlochen-Petrillo Controversy," 1947–48, B 38.

55. Maddy, "Interlochen-Petrillo Controversy," 1947–48, B 38.

56. Austin 1959, 112.

57. Maddy to Giddings, 1 October 1947, B 12.

58. Buttelman, *MEJ,* September–October 1947, 24–25.

59. Maddy to Giddings, 1 October 1947.

60. Joseph E. Maddy, "How I Beat Petrillo," *Coronet,* March 1948, 151.

61. Maddy to Douglas Ingells, 11 November 1947, B 38; Douglas Ingells to Maddy, [1948], B 38; R. R. Jalbert to Maddy, 22 January 1948, B 38.

62. Phillips Carlin to Maddy, 18 May 1948, quoted in "Mutual Cancels Music Camp Series," *New York Times,* 28 May 1948.

63. "Interlochen," *Detroit Educational News,* 6 May 1942, 2; Austin 1959, 148.

64. Austin 1959, 116.

65. Austin 1959, 29, 116, 133, 134, 144, 149, 191.

66. House Committee on Education and Labor, *Hearings before the Committee on Education and Labor, House of Representatives, 83rd Congress, First Session, Pursuant to House Resolution 115 on Matters Relating to the Labor-Management Relations Act of 1947, Washington, D.C., 17, 20, 21, and 22 April 1953* (Washington, D.C.: U.S. Government Printing Office, 1953), 2661, 2668, B 38.

67. Maddy to Tremaine, 10 May 1958, B 12 ; William Kulsea, "Interlochen Cancels Concerts at Bridge," *Ann Arbor News,* 30 April 1958.

68. John Merrill, interview by the author, by telephone, Fort Myers, Fla., 27 February 1996.

69. Maddy to Herman Kenin, 6 April 1959, B 38; Stanley Ballard to Don Gillis, 11 February 1960, B 38; Maddy to Herman Kenin, 22 April 1960, B 38.

70. Henry Zaccardi to Donald Gillis, 22 December 1960, B 38.

71. Seltzer 1989, 50.

72. Leiter 1953, 163.

73. Ned Guthrie, "How We Won the Lea Act Repeal," *International Musician,* January 1981, 1; Seltzer 1989, 50.

74. Crawford 1979, 27.

75. Rector 1979, 165.

76. Banghart and Jacobi interviews; Austin 1959, 29.

77. Willis Pennington to Maddy, 8 March 1941 and 4 June 1941, B 2; Austin 1959, 25.

78. "National Music Camp Enlarges Its Facilities," *Ann Arbor News,* 29 October 1943, B 71.

79. Maddy to Giddings, 7 March 1946, B 12; Jacobi interview.

80. Maddy to Willis Pennington, 25 August 1941, B 2.

81. Marvin Arrowsmith, "Camp Promotes American Music," *Saginaw (Michigan)*

News, 10 August 1942, B 66; NMC advertisement, *Music Educators Journal* 29, no. 4 (February–March, 1943): 41, 42.

82. Britton interview; Austin 1959, 25; *Ann Arbor News,* 29 October 1943.
83. NMC flyer, B 66; Nicholas 1982, 102.
84. Austin 1959, 25; "William D. Revelli," *Music at Michigan* 28, no. 1 (fall 1994): 1–3; Boylan interview.
85. Maddy to Frank Campbell-Watson, Music Publishers Holding Corporation, RCA Building, New York City, 28 August 1944, B 11.
86. Austin 1959, 26; Britton interview.
87. Maddy, *MEJ,* April 1944, 14; Austin 1959, 24.
88. Austin 1959, 132.
89. Jacobi interview; Howard Hintze, interview by the author, tape recording, Interlochen, Mich., 30 January 1995; Roller interview.
90. Camp records, IA 45; Austin 1959, 28.
91. Camp records, IA 45–60; Crawford 1979, 27, 28, 35.
92. Browning 1963, 278.
93. Maddy to T. P. Giddings, 25 May 1948, B 12; Maddy to Tremaine, 3 June 1948, B 12; Kenneth Bassett, ed., *Interlochen Center for the Arts: A Master Plan for the Campus* (Watertown, Mass.: Sasaki Associates, 1991), 5; Austin 1959, 29.
94. Eleanor Nangle, "Youth on the Campus," *Chicago Sunday Tribune,* 4 August 1946; Banghart interview; Roller interview; Robert Murphy, interview by the author, tape recording, Interlochen, Mich., 25 January 1995.
95. Maddy to Betty Cass, 24 March 1948, B 41.
96. Britton interview.
97. Tremaine to Maddy, 22 September 1948, B 12.
98. Jacobi interview; Maddy to Tremaine, 24 September 1948, B 12.
99. *First Fifty Years,* [1978], s.v. "1950," IP 78.
100. Edward Downing, interview by the author, tape recording, Interlochen, Mich., 11 January 1995.
101. Murphy interview.

Part 5

Epigraph from Maddy to Tremaine, 17 January 1957, B 12.

1. M. Dallman to Joseph E. Maddy, 7 June 1953, B 12; Maddy to Doctor Spierzem, 12 June 1953, B 12.
2. "Barre Hill Reengaged for Seventh Season as Director of Opera Workshop at Interlochen, Michigan," *Musical Leader,* June 1953, 11, B 71.
3. John F. Cherry, fax to Joseph E. Maddy, 7 March 1958, B 12.
4. Browning 1963, 269; T. Ray Uhlinger, *Sound the Call* ([n.p.]: TRU Associates, 1987), 87, 61.

5. Uhlinger 1987, 76, 87, 100; Browning 1992, 189.
6. Britton interview.
7. Tremaine to Maddy, 26 November 1957, B 12.
8. Camp records, IA 57; Austin 1959, 29, 330; Browning 1992, 184; Hanson interview.
9. Giddings to Maddy, 12 February 1948, B 12.
10. Tremaine to Maddy, 10 July 1958, B 12.
11. Tremaine to Maddy, 26 November 1957, B 12; Tremaine to Maddy, 28 August 1958, B 12; Roller interview.
12. Camp records, IA 58; Austin 1959, 32, 33.
13. Britton interview.
14. Maddy to Tremaine, 26 February 1958, B 12; Margaret A. Stace to Mauricia D. Borromeo, 4 October 1972, B 12.
15. Austin 1959, 28, 143.
16. Browning 1992, 69.
17. Maddy to Giddings, 24 April 1949, B 12; Maddy to Giddings, 21 January 1951, B 12.
18. Tremaine to Maddy, 6 May 1958, B 12.
19. Tremaine to Maddy, 6 May 1958.
20. Tremaine to Maddy, 6 May 1958.
21. Tremaine to Maddy, 10 July 1958, B 12.
22. Tremaine to Maddy, 6 May 1958.
23. Maddy to Tremaine, 10 May 1958, B 12.
24. Tremaine to Maddy, 6 May 1958.
25. Tremaine to Maddy, 6 May 1958.
26. Austin 1959, 186.
27. Roller interview.
28. Perone 1993, 5.
29. Roller interview.
30. Charles Eilber, interview by the author, tape recording, Boulder, Colo., 30 September 1995.
31. Camp records, IA 60, 61.
32. Van Cliburn, conversation with the author, Fort Worth, Texas, 20 February 1990.
33. Camp records, IA 62; Hanson interview.
34. Norma Lee Browning, liner notes to sound recording, *Van Cliburn Conducts,* RCA Victor LSC-2807.
35. Boylan interview; Camp records, IA 64; Bert 1977.
36. Camp records, IA 65, 66.
37. Britton interview.
38. Merrill interview; Maddy to Tremaine, 9 November 1959, B 12.

39. Merrill interview.
40. Maddy to Tremaine, 9 November 1959.
41. Merrill interview; Clyde Roller interview.
42. Jacobi interview.
43. Clement Stone, conversation with the author, Chicago, Ill., 14 May 1990.
44. Clement Stone to Mr. and Mrs. Russell Ogg, 5 September 1961, B 12.
45. John Merrill to Tremaine, 29 November 1961, B 12.
46. Roller interview.
47. Merrill interview.
48. Eilber interview; Murphy interview.
49. Knauft, Berger, and Gray 1991, 79; Hanson interview.
50. Eilber interview.
51. Jean Parsons, interview by the author, tape recording, Interlochen, Mich., 27 January 1995.
52. Browning 1963, 293; Murphy interview.
53. Eilber interview.
54. Academy records, IA 63; Murphy interview.
55. Eilber interview; Murphy interview.
56. Academy records, IA 62.
57. Academy records, IA 63, 64.
58. Academy records, IA 62, 63; Murphy interview; Parsons interview; Hintze interview.
59. Bassett 1991, 1.
60. Bassett 1991, 6.
61. Academy records, IA 63.
62. Interlochen board of trustees, central executive committee minutes, 30 March 1965, IA 65.
63. Camp records, IA 66.
64. Academy records, IA 62.
65. Roller interview; Nicholas 1982, 239.
66. Rector 1979, 168.
67. Hintze interview; Parsons interview; Murphy interview.
68. Eilber interview; Hintze interview; Roller interview.
69. Hintze interview.
70. Austin 1959, 150, 186.
71. Maddy to Tremaine, 10 May 1958.
72. Austin 1959, 150, 185.
73. Thom Paulson, interview by the author, tape recording, Interlochen, Mich., 12 January 1995.
74. Austin 1959, 164.

75. Austin 1959, 29, 53, 167, 190.
76. Academy records, IA 62, 63.

Part 6

Epigraph from Jacobi interview.

1. Merrill interview.
2. Interlochen board of trustees minutes, 21 April 1966, IA 66; 9 February 1960, IA 60.
3. John Merrill to the author, 28 February 1996.
4. Knauft, Berger, and Gray 1991, 79.
5. Hintze interview; Merrill to the author, 28 February 1996; Haas interview.
6. Merrill to the author, 28 February 1996.
7. Haas interview.
8. Livingston Biddle, *Our Government and the Arts: A Perspective from the Inside* (New York: ACA Books, 1988), 15, 18, 42, 52, 87, 129, 144.
9. Banghart interview; Britton interview.
10. Photocopy of Biographic Data Form submitted by Karl Haas to Marquis Who's Who, Inc., Chicago, Ill., June 1968, B 48.
11. Haas interview.
12. Boylan interview; Haas interview; Merrill interview.
13. Boylan interview; Haas interview.
14. *Crescendo,* fall 1971, 1, IA 71.
15. Haas interview.
16. Interlochen Arts Academy, liner notes to sound recording, *Interlochen Arts Academy Studio Orchestra,* David D. Sporny, conductor; Silver Crest custom recording IAA-1972–1; Hintze interview; Eilber interview; Haas interview; Merrill to Harry Calcutt, 6 December 1968, B 49; Interlochen Center for the Arts, "Interlochen Center for the Arts, the Golden Decade" ([Interlochen, Mich.: Interlochen Center for the Arts], 1969), 6, IP 69; Interlochen board of trustees minutes, 23 July 1994, IA 94; Interlochen board of trustees minutes, 6 November 1965, IA 65.
17. Haas interview.
18. *Interlochen Arts Academy Catalog* ([Interlochen, Mich.]: Interlochen Arts Academy, 1968–70*),* 59, IP 69.
19. Interlochen Center for the Arts, "Interlochen Center for the Arts: 1991 Restructure of Alumni Organizations," 20 July 1991, ratification document, IA 91.
20. Jacobi interview.
21. Banghart interview; Jacobi interview; Hintze interview; Eilber interview.
22. Murphy interview; Hintze interview; Boylan interview; Eilber interview.

23. Interlochen Arts Academy, liner notes, 1972.

24. Biddle 1988, 248.

25. Haas interview; Eilber interview; Murphy interview; Hintze interview.

26. Haas interview.

27. Camp records, IA 68.

28. Haas interview; Eilber interview.

29. Haas interview.

30. Haas interview.

31. Eilber interview.

32. Boylan interview; Haas interview; Wilson interview; Jacobi interview.

33. Haas interview.

34. Merrill interview.

35. Britton interview.

36. Haas interview; Merrill interview.

37. Haas interview.

38. Eilber interview; Wilson interview; Parsons interview; Boylan interview.

39. Wilson interview; David Brubeck to Clement Stone, 17 March 1970, in the possession of Charles Eilber; Eilber interview.

40. Banghart interview; Hintze interview; Jacobi interview.

41. Wilson interview; Jacobi interview; Rideout interview.

42. Knauft, Berger, and Gray 1991, 80; Jacobi interview.

43. Jacobi interview; Browning 1992, 189–99.

44. Jacobi interview.

45. Jacobi interview.

46. Banghart interview; Paulson interview.

47. Camp records, IA 71, 72.

48. Administration records, IA 71, 72.

49. Rideout interview.

50. Roger Jacobi to Donald Gillis, 2 February 1973, B 50.

51. Jacobi interview.

52. Roger Jacobi to Gwen Frostic, 19 July 1983, B 52.

53. Roger Jacobi to John Hood, 22 June 1976, B 52.

54. Administration records, IA 85.

55. Jacobi interview.

56. Camp records, IA 87.

57. Camp records, IA 78.

58. Downing interview.

59. Camp records, IA 85–89.

60. Administration records, IA 87; Geraldine Schubert Greenspan, interview by the author, tape recording, Interlochen, Mich., 20 January 1995.

61. Charles McWhorter to Roger Jacobi, 11 February 1985, B 52; James E. Cape to file, 5 June 1986, B 52.

62. Jacobi interview; Knauft, Berger, and Gray 1991, 81.

63. Eilber interview.

64. Jacobi interview; Eilber interview.

65. Hintze interview; John Hood, interview by the author, tape recording, Interlochen, Mich., 5 August 1966; John Hood to Roger Jacobi, 12 May 1980, B 52.

66. Greenspan interview.

67. Greenspan interview; Rideout interview.

68. Bruce Galbraith, interview by the author, by telephone, Indianapolis, Ind., 23 June 1997.

69. Rideout interview; Jacobi interview; Galbraith interview.

70. Galbraith interview.

71. Rideout interview; Galbraith interview.

72. Report on the Conference of High Schools of the Arts, Los Angeles, 2–4 April 1981, B 54.

73. Jacobi to educators, 5 March 1982, B 54.

74. Rideout interview.

75. Perone 1993, 94, 95; Gerard Schwarz, conversation with the author, Seattle, Wash., 28 January 1992.

76. George Wilson, report to the Interlochen board of trustees, 5 March 1977, IA 77.

77. Interlochen Arts Festival records, IA 73–75.

78. Downing interview.

79. Downing interview; Interlochen Arts Festival records, IA 78; Hintze interview.

80. Jacobi interview.

81. Camp Chamber Music Series, letters and brochures, 1983–85, B 54.

82. Carnegie Commission on the Future of Public Broadcasting, *A Public Trust* (New York: Carnegie Corporation, 1979), 188, 189.

83. Paulson interview.

84. Jacobi interview; Paulson interview.

85. Paulson interview.

86. Interlochen board of trustees minutes, 19 July 1986, IA 86.

87. Rideout interview; Boylan interview.

Epilogue

1. Interlochen board of trustees minutes, 3 December 1989, IA 89.

2. Interlochen board of trustees minutes, 2 March 1991, IA 91.

3. Interlochen board of trustees minutes, 15 March 1990, IA 90.

4. Interlochen board of trustees minutes, 7 December 1991, IA 91.

5. Interlochen board of trustees minutes, 18 July 1992, IA 92.

6. Bassett 1991, 1.

7. Interlochen board of trustees minutes, 25 July 1991, IA 91.

8. Bassett 1991, 21.

9. ICA central administrative staff minutes, 15 August 1991, IA 91.

10. *Crescendo,* summer 1993, 1, IP 93.

11. Interlochen board of trustees minutes, 24 July 1993, IA 93.

12. ICA central administrative staff minutes, 12 September 1990, IA 90.

13. ICA central administrative staff minutes, 2 February 1993, IA 93.

14. Camp records, IA 91.

15. *Crescendo,* fall 1994, 1, IP 94.

16. *Crescendo,* fall 1991, 1, IP 91; fall 1993, 1, IP 93.

17. *Crescendo,* winter 1992, 1, IP 92.

18. *Crescendo,* summer 1993, 1, IP 93; summer 1994, 1, IP 94.

19. ICA central administrative staff minutes, 10 October 1990, IA 90.

20. *Crescendo,* summer 1991, 1, IP 91.

21. Hintze interview.

22. Downing interview.

23. Interlochen Center for the Arts, "Interlochen Center for the Arts: 1991 Restructure of Alumni Organizations," 20 July 1991, ratification document, IA 91.

24. *Crescendo,* fall 1991, 1, IP 91; fall 1992, 1, IP 92; fall 1993, 1, IP 93; fall 1994, 1, IP 94.

25. Interlochen board of trustees minutes, 3 December 1994, IA 94.

26. Interlochen board of trustees minutes, January 1996, IA 96.

27. Academy records, IA 96.

28. Tom Bradshaw, "Counting on Audiences: The State of Arts Participation Research," May 1996.
   <http://arts.endow.gov/Archive/Contents/Features2.html> (1998).

29. Jacobi interview; Haas interview.

30. Camp and academy records, IA 93–97.

31. Downing interview.

32. Peter Yarrow, comment from Kresge Auditorium stage, 23 July 1992.

33. Howard Chua-Eoan, "The Shaping of Jewel," *Time,* 21 July 1997, 67.

34. *Crescendo,* summer 1996, 13, IP 96.

35. Fennell interview.

36. Roller interview; Hanson interview.

Bibliography

Austin, Henry Root. "History of Broadcasting at the National Music Camp, Interlochen, Michigan, 1928–1958." Ed.D. diss., University of Michigan, 1959.
Copy in the library of the Interlochen Center for the Arts.

Bassett, Kenneth, ed. *Interlochen Center for the Arts: A Master Plan for the Campus.*
Watertown, Mass.: Sasaki Associates, 1991.

Bensman, Marvin R. "History of Broadcasting (1920–1960)." 1995.
<http://www.people.memphis.edu/~mbensman> (1998).

Bert, Carolyn. Liner notes to sound recording, National Music Camp, Fiftieth
Anniversary, *World Youth Symphony Orchestra No. 1.* NMC 1977–20.

Biddle, Livingston. *Our Government and the Arts: A Perspective from the Inside.* New
York: ACA Books, 1988.

Bierley, Paul E. *John Philip Sousa, American Phenomenon.* New York: Appelton-Century-Crofts, 1973.

Birge, Edward Bailey. *History of Public School Music in the United States.* Washington,
D.C.: Music Supervisors National Conference, 1928.

Bradshaw, Tom. "Counting on Audiences: The State of Arts Participation Research."
May 1996. <http://arts.endow.gov/Archive/Contents/Features2.html> (1998).

Browning, Norma Lee. *Joe Maddy of Interlochen.* Chicago: Henry Regnery Company,
1963.

———. *Joe Maddy of Interlochen: Profile of a Legend.* Chicago: Contemporary Books,
1992.

———. Liner notes to sound recording, *Van Cliburn Conducts.* RCA Victor LSC-
2807.

Carnegie Commission on the Future of Public Broadcasting. *A Public Trust.* New
York: Carnegie Corporation, 1979.

Colorado Chautauqua Association. "Chautauqua History." 1998.
<http://chautauqua.com/chauhist.com> (1998).

Crawford, Richard. *100 Years of Music at Michigan.* Ann Arbor: Edwards Brothers,
1979.

Dalley, Orien. "Dream and Realization: An Intimate Account of Interlochen." Ann
Arbor, Mich., 1988. Photocopy.

Edwards, Arthur C., and W. Thomas Marrocco. *Music in the United States*. Dubuque,
    Iowa: Wm. C. Brown, 1968.

Erskine, John. *My Life in Music*. New York: William Morrow and Company, 1950.

Giddings, T. P. *Giddings' Public School Class Method for Piano*. Boston: Oliver Ditson
    Company, 1919.

"History of the New York Philharmonic." 1995. <http://www.nyphilharmon.org>
    (1998).

Howard, John Tasker, and George Kent Bellows. *A Short History of Music in America*.
    New York: Thomas Y. Crowell Company, 1957.

Ingle, Edward T. *Report of the National Committee for Music Appreciation (1940–1941)*.
    Washington, D.C.: National Committee for Music Appreciation, 1940.

Interlochen Arts Academy. Liner notes to sound recording, *Interlochen Arts Academy
    Studio Orchestra,* David D. Sporny, conductor. Silver Crest custom recording
    IAA-1972–1.

Interlochen Center for the Arts Archives, 1928–97. Interlochen Center for the Arts,
    Interlochen, Mich.

Interlochen Center for the Arts Collection. Bentley Historical Library. University of
    Michigan.

Interlochen Center for the Arts Publications, 1928–97. Interlochen Center for the Arts,
    Interlochen, Mich.

International Cyclopedia of Music. 10th edition. Ed. Bruce Bohle and Oscar Thompson.
    New York: Dodd, Mead, and Company, [ca. 1975].

Internet Movie Database Ltd., The. "Awards Information." 1990–98.
    <http://us.imdb.com> (1998).

Knauft, E. B., Renee A. Berger, and Sandra T. Gray. *Profiles of Excellence*. San Fran-
    cisco: Jossey-Bass, 1991.

Koehler, Kathleen, Christine Weideman, and Marjorie Barritt. *The Board of Regents of
    the University of Michigan*. Ann Arbor: Bentley Historical Library of the Uni-
    versity of Michigan, 1996.

Leiter, Robert D. *The Musicians and Petrillo*. New York: Bookman Associates, 1953.

Miller, Neil Arthur. "A History of the National Music Camp." M.Mus.Ed. thesis, Uni-
    versity of Michigan, 1965.

Mishkind, Barry. "Broadcast FAQ List." 1994.
    <http://www.oldradio.com/current/bc_faq.html> (1998).

The New Grove Dictionary of American Music. Ed. H. Wiley Hitchcock and Stanley
    Sadie. New York: Macmillan Press, 1986.

Nicholas, Louis. *Thor Johnson: American Conductor*. [Ephraim, Wis.]: Peninsula Arts
    Association, 1982.

Perone, James. *Howard Hanson*. Westport, Conn.: Greenwood Press, 1993.

Pincus, Andrew. *Scenes from Tanglewood*. Boston: Northeastern University Press, 1989.

Rector, Gail W. *The University Musical Society of the University of Michigan Celebrates One Hundred Years, 1879–1979.* Ann Arbor: University of Michigan, 1979.

Reich, Howard. *Van Cliburn.* Nashville: Thomas Nelson Publishers, 1993.

Seltzer, George. *Music Matters.* Metuchen, N.J.: Scarecrow Press, 1989.

Sullivan, Edmund, ed. "History of Columbia University." 1995. <http://www.columbia.edu/cu/facets95/12.html> (1998).

There's Magic in Music. Hollywood, Calif.: Paramount Pictures, 1941. Movie.

Tremaine, C. M. *History of National Music Week.* New York: National Bureau for the Advancement of Music, [ca. 1925].

Uhlinger, T. Ray. *Sound the Call.* [U.S.]: TRU Associates, 1987.

Wallace, Mike, narrator. *Joe Maddy's Interlochen.* Interlochen Center for the Arts compact disc DIDX 919543.

White, Thomas H. "Pioneer Broadcast Stations in the United States." 1998. <http://www.ipass.net/~whitetho/pion622.htm> (1998).

"William D. Revelli." *Music at Michigan* 28, no. 1 (fall 1994): 1–3.

Index